Scheming virtuously:
the road to collaborative governance

Scheming virtuously:

the road to collaborative governance

Gilles Paquet

INVENIRE BOOKS
Ottawa, Canada
2009

© 2009 Invenire

Library and Archives Canada Cataloguing in Publication

Paquet, Gilles, 1936-
    Scheming virtuously : the road to collaborative
governance / Gilles Paquet.

ISBN 978-0-88970-131-1

    1. Public administration--Citizen participation.
2. Political participation. I. Title.

JF1525.P6P356 2009   323'.042   C2009-901906-X

Published by Invenire Books, an imprint of Invenire,
PO Box 87001
Ottawa, Canada K2P 1X0
www.invenire.ca/books

Designed and Printed in Canada by Cheriton Graphics

Distributed by:
Commoners' Publishing
631 Tubman Cr.
Ottawa, Canada K1V 8L6
(613) 523-2444
fax: (613) 260-0401
sales@commonerspublishing.com
www.commonerspublishing.com

*"... to chart its course by a compass that lacks a pole
toward which it can point ..."*

– Lon L. Fuller

"Je déteste la résignation"

– René Magritte

" I don't have a plan"

–Robert Lepage

Invenire Books, an imprint of Invenire

Other books in the series:

Invenire
Books

Robin Higham
Who do we think we are: *Canada's reasonable*
(and less reasonable) accommodation debates,

2009

Invenire
Books

Ruth Hubbard
Profession: Public Servant

2009

sample chapters and further information at www.invenire.ca/books

Invenire *is an Ottawa-based "idea factory" specializing in collaborative governance and stewardship. Invenire and its authors offer creative and practical responses to the challenges and opportunities faced by today's complex organizations.*

Contents

Foreword

... mon domaine est celui du possible ...
il faut bien que je me passe d'idéal
– **Friedrich Dürrenmatt**

I have been working on governance issues, broadly speaking, for forty years, and I have carried out a systematic program of research in this field for the last decade or so. Many books and very many articles have been produced over that period: some of them identifying and denouncing pathologies of governance; others trying to construct a new vocabulary and new approaches likely to generate a better appreciation of the sources of governance failures, and of the ways in which they might be repaired.

The intent of the present book is not to cover this territory anew, but to explain why this program of research was launched in the first place, how it has led to a focus on collaborative governance, and why it has entailed a cultural change – a move away from scientistic problem-solving toward systems thinking, concerns about problem-setting and design (rather than problem-solving of set issues), and maintaining action within the bounds of what is acceptable to the appreciative system of organizations.

Human governance concerns were triggered by the failures of economic, social, and political stewardship to live up to the expectations developed in the post-World War II era. This led to a search for better ways of understanding problems that were ever more complex and pressing.

It was fortuitous that in the decade following the war, two sets of concepts about *information* and about *systems* were set loose in the general intellectual community. They provided a new language in which to talk about the perplexing experience of the times, and a new point of view from which to regard it.

Discussions about information as a change agent distinguishable from energy had been initiated in the 1930s and 1940s by Hayek (1948), and had become used by 1960 (Hurwicz 1960) in the world of comparative economic systems. As for general systems thinking, it was already in focus by the mid-1950s (Von Bertalannfy 1956). Geoffrey Vickers (1965, 1987) began to use this new language and this new point of view to rethink human governance in the 1950s and 1960s, and Donald Schön (Schön 1971) in the late 1960s.

By the early 1970s – at a time when socio-economic and political realities had become very perplexing – these notions were not yet in good currency, but they were beginning to be a source of inspiration for those searching for new vistas and better tools.

At the time, the myth of Big G government being in charge and pursuing goals echoing the shared values of citizens appeared frankly surreal. A reality check readily showed that power, resources, and information were widely distributed, and that nobody was fully in charge; moreover, it was clear that widely diverse values were legitimately held by various groups of citizens, and that shared values were a myth. The best one could hope for was maintaining a complex and ever-changing set of activities within bounds deemed acceptable according to certain standards.

This Vickersian book tries to reconstruct some stages in the voyage from the 1970s when the paradigm in good currency (Big G centralized State government in charge) showed signs of trouble, to the 2000s when small g collaborative governance (involving private/public/civic partners, since nobody is fully in charge) is beginning to emerge as the alternative paradigm.

Reporting on this transition is perilous, and remains a work in progress. The very notion of transition is controversial. It is openly challenged by an important rearguard, claiming that any reduction in the size of the state is a tragedy, and can only entail an impoverishment of our way of governing ourselves. These persons cling to the centrality of the State (with a capital S) as the only way to allow the common will and the public interest to emerge.

This book in six steps

1.   After a short preamble that has a personal flavour, the introduction provides some explanation of the reasons why the conventional ways of thinking are not as useful as they used to be, why a different way of thinking is required, and what the foundations of this new way

of thinking are. The key notions of process, design, and reflexivity are showcased.

2.   Part I underlines two preliminary steps taken in the 1970s to use systems thinking in the analysis of the socio-economy as instituted process: (a) a shift of policy analyses from a focus on goals and control to a focus on intelligence and innovation; and (b) the probing of the socio-economy as instituted process through an analysis of sub-processes (demography, production and exchange, finance, state, distribution of income and wealth, and ecology of groups and their motives).

3.   Part II discusses critically some of the key assumptions of the old way of thinking: the omnipresence of state-centricity and the myth of shared values; the occlusion of the solidarity sector as an alternative to state and market; and the fixation on the elusive notion of leadership as a result of the assumption that someone has to be in charge.

4.   Part III provides three illustrations of how a collaborative governance approach might be used: the design of federalism as social technology, an informational approach to regulation, and the centrality of moral contracts in the redesign of the federal public service.

5.   Part IV presents in a more formal way the informational view of organizations that has been the underpinning of the new way of thinking: organizations can be identified by the nature of messages exchanged. The two chapters present Lamberton as a pioneer on this front, and then sketch a provisional formal stylization of this informational approach.

6.   The conclusion puts forward some guideposts to help in the transformation of our ways of governing: the role and burden of office of both public intellectuals and citizens, the ethical corridor to be respected in design experimentation, and the centrality of contingent moral contracts and reflexivity in all this.

This is meant to whet the reader's appetite.

If the reader accepts the argument we are presenting, there may be an urge to know more. If so, you may wish to look at some of the more specialized work undertaken in this vein under the auspices of the Centre on Governance and INVENIRE at the University of Ottawa. A list of books is presented in the appendix to this foreword.

For those interested in the practical implications for the world of public management of the new perspectives developed in this book, I would suggest a visit to www.cpsrenewal.ca where Nicholas Charney and Mike Mangulabnan have developed Scheming Virtuously – A Handbook for Public Servants as a reaction to a Summer 2008 lecture where I was inviting them to become subversive virtuous schemers.

References

L. von Bertalanffy, "General System Theory" *General Systems Yearbook*, Vol. 1, 1956.

F.A. Hayek, *Individualism and Economic Order*, Chicago : The University of Chicago Press, 1948.

L. Hurwicz "Conditions for Economic Efficiency of Centralized and Decentralized Structures" in G. Grossman (Ed.) *Value and Plan*. Berkeley: The University of California Press, 1960, 162-183.

D.A. Schön, *Beyond the Stable State*, New York : Norton, 1971.

G. Vickers, *The Art of Judgment*, London: Chapman & Hall 1965.

G. Vickers, *Policymaking, Communication, and Social Learning*, New Brunswick: Transaction 1987.

Appendix

Pathologies of governance

G. Paquet, *Oublier la Révolution tranquille*, Liber 1999.

G. Paquet, *Pathologies de gouvernance*, Liber 2004.

R. Hubbard, G. Paquet, *Gomery's Blinders and Canadian Federalism*, University of Ottawa Press 2007.

G. Paquet, *Deep Cultural Diversity: A Governance Challenge*, University of Ottawa Press 2008.

G. Paquet, *Tableau d'avancement – Petite ethnographie interprétative d'un certain Canada français*, Presses de l'Université d'Ottawa 2008

G. Paquet, *Crippling Epistemologies and Governance Failures*, University of Ottawa Press 2009.

Governance frameworks

P. Laurent, G. Paquet, *Epistémologie et économie de la relation*, Vrin 1998.

G. Paquet, *Governance though social learning*, University of Ottawa Press 1999.

G. Paquet, *Gouvernance: une invitation à la subversion*, Liber 2005.

G. Paquet, *The New Geo-Governance: A Baroque Approach*, University of Ottawa Press 2005.

G. Paquet, J.P. Wallot, *Un Québec moderne 1760-1840*, Editions Hurtubise HMH 2007.

G. Paquet, *Gouvernance: mode d'emploi*, Liber, 2008.

Preamble

The genealogy of a *manière de voir*

"Exister c'est différer"

–Gabriel Tarde

This is a report on the genealogy of a *manière de voir* that has evolved over the last few decades.

It had its origin in the practice of the social sciences of another era, when the priority concern imparted to students was a *fringale de sens* – making sense of what was going on – and when there existed a cautious optimism about the ability of social scientists to suggest repairs to existing social technologies, to help design organizations and systems better able to deal effectively with issues of concern, and to nudge these changes into existence.

This centrality of issues, à la John Dewey, and this cautious optimism inspired by the helpful if modest *bricolage* that social sciences felt they could promise, gave way to greater ambitions in the middle third of the 20th century. And those who where trained in the 1950s, as I was, could not but be swayed by the magnificent dynamics of the Keynesian era that appeared to promise the garden path of a third-way between the disasters generated by irresponsible laissez-faire and utopian central planning.

By the 1950s, armed with relatively simplistic models of the socio-economy, and bathtub-inspired theorems of stocks and flows, the conventional wisdom suggested that one could design from the center some guidance mechanisms that would fine-tune the performance of the socio-economy, and ensure the appropriate mix of efficiency, stability and equity – whatever that mix might be.

In the private, public, and social sectors, the arrogance of the managerial and technocratic class appeared to know no bounds: claiming to have the requisite arsenal necessary to deliver on these promises and to be fully in charge.

Surfing on a strong wave of productivity increase generated in post-World War II by massive urbanization and the elimination of barriers to international trade, and confident that, through the right mix of fiscal, monetary, and social policies, the business cycle had been tamed, private and public managers claimed to have discovered the winning formula of private-public collaborative governance – vitality and innovation being provided by the former, and reliability and stability by the latter – and did not hesitate to take some credit for the rapid growth in living standards in the post-World War II era.

Signs of trouble: who's in charge?

Already by the late 1950s, and most certainly by the 1970s, the seemingly winning formula of the complementary private-public sectors working hand in hand to ensure growth, efficiency, stability and equity began to show signs of strain. Globalization, the new challenges of demographic booms and of rapid urbanization, and the blatant blunders in the management of private and public organizations forced even the most enthusiastic observers to recognize that things might not be as simple as the great simplifiers of the immediate post-World War II period had suggested.

Whiffs of pathologies and incompetence revealed that trust in persons purported to be in charge in both the private and public sectors might not be warranted. At a time of turbulence on the global scene, and important demographic shuffling at the national level, it raised questions about whether one could presume that those supposedly brought to a position of authority through competition, election or meritocratic formulas could really be said to be in charge, and be capable of taking the required corrective actions when necessary.

After their grandiose sermons of the immediate post-World War II period, the opinion-molders of the 1950s could not easily come to terms with the idea of nobody being in charge. Somebody had to be in charge! And the debates, therefore, were focused on identifying the parties in charge who could be indicted for the observed slippages.

Moreover, the beliefs that more state intervention held the key to prosperity and progress, and that the state had the necessary instrumentation to ensure economic, social and political progress, remained in good currency. Indeed, there was a utopian quality to that age. The state (mostly spelled with a capital S) acquired a quasi-theological status: it was purported to be a sort of embodiment of the collective interest and the common will that transcended the legitimacy of individual claims. Not only was the state seen as the agency capable of correcting market failures, but the new credo suggested that more intrusive state intervention should be regarded as the only reasonable strategy to correct government failures – which were ascribed simply to insufficient state intrusiveness. In this delirious era, the most bizarre ideologies took root, and many of them are still in good currency.

Economic history as an eye opener

One of the great advantages of having an education imbued with economic history is that it provided an early experience with complex socio-economic-political multidimensional systems, permeated by symbolic, psychological and ideological forces and much inter-subjectivity. Economic history operates with a modicum of data, and requires imagination to fill the gaps left by the surviving archives.

Moreover, economic historians are also crucially aware, with the benefit of hindsight, of the immense degree of false consciousness of persons and groups *in situ*. Swayed by forces they do not fully understand, and armed with representations and interpretations that are imperfect and incomplete but also marred by distortion that is ascribable to more or less conscious ideological lenses, such persons and groups often pursue strategies that can only lead to their own destruction. As a result, simplistic mechanical explanations rarely impress economic historians.

Additionally, economic historians are daily confronted in their research by the fact that, despite the rhetoric of those claiming to be in charge, the dynamic of change is a process of creative destruction that, in most instances, no one person or group can be said to control. Planned outcomes go unrealized, and very minor surprising events often trigger crucial path-dependent drifts.

As a result, there exists in the soul of every economic historian a profound skepticism about all forms of inevitability or providentialism – be it via the invisible hand of the market, or the visible hand of the state.

Finally, economic history is quite conscious that it must maintain a healthy disrespect vis-à-vis economics as its mother discipline, and some diffidence vis-à-vis a reified view of the economy stylized as a thing. The reconstruction of the historical process draws insights from economics, but recognizes the limitations of the disciplinary perspective as quite restrictive and blocking out many other fundamental dimensions; and the economic historian cannot easily accept a reified notion of the economy when he experiences it daily as a field of forces, a process of change as the socio-economy gets re-instituted anew from place to place and from time to time.

Distrust of a constraining ideology and of a reified notion of the socio-economy has forced economic historians to develop new vocabularies and new frames of analysis. Thereby, its modus operandi has also served as a useful template for those searching for less restrictive and constraining approaches to socio-economic political realities.

In that sense, I might say that my economic history training under the guidance of Albert Faucher has served me immensely well in legitimizing much licence vis-à-vis the strictures of the scientistic social sciences that were becoming the new gospel in the post-World War II era, and in encouraging a more imaginative and interpretative use of the social sciences as a tool to disclose alternative worlds.

Consultancy and journalism as eye sharpeners

If economic history was an invitation to epistemological eclecticism, it was to a long practice of consultancy and journalism that I must ascribe my propensity to follow John Dewey's invitation to focus on "issues".

"In the beginning is the issue" was John Dewey's exhortation. And the constant confrontation with issues of the day (on which one had to report and that one had to analyze) cannot but draw attention to the chasm between the sources of concern of the citizenry and the topics of interest in the realm of academe.

I was privileged to participate from the very beginning of my academic life in debates forced onto the agenda by the political turmoil of the late 1950s in Canada, by the massive impact of the Baby Boom and of the aging of Canadian population on the whole fabric of social policy, by the massive transformations of the urban landscape as a result of World War II, by the emergence of the information society and the multinational firm on the global scene, and by the transformative impact of science and technology on the evolution of the socio-economy.

More important I was forced by my parallel activities in journalism to analyze those issues à chaud, and to explicate them in plain language to emergent publics demanding more and more to be better informed, and to make sense of what was going on, at the very time when a significant portion of the emerging academic community was choosing to withdraw into the Ivory Tower to pursue their scientistic travails.

In earlier periods, there had been a sound mingling of academic and preceptoral work, and journalists and public intellectuals had acted as important knowledge brokers. This was certainly the case for many of my professors at Laval in the 1950s. And I was immensely fortunate that in my first full-time teaching job at Carleton University, the leading member of the Department of Economics at Carleton at the time – Scott Gordon – was a brilliant academic, a public intellectual, and a columnist in the *Financial Times*, who was instrumental (through an influential pamphlet) in the defenestration of James Coyne as Governor of the Bank of Canada.

I was, therefore, urged from the very start of my academic life to pursue a hybrid career that led me to spend much of my time commenting on public affairs and getting involved in organizational redesign. Over the last forty years, this work provided a steady diet of conundrums to be made sense of, of issues to be probed, of falsehoods to be exposed, of poseurs to be deflated, and of bad ideas to be killed.

In such endeavors, critical thinking was an asset, being a *libre penseur* was seen as being free from mental prisons, and being heretical was a permission to question the conventional wisdom. Nothing could make such questioning easier than the weekly confrontation with issues to which the conventional wisdom would appear to provide no reasonable and understandable answer.

Collaborative governance as an emergent integrative concept

Searching for a better way to make sense of what was going on, one day and one issue at a time, might not have been the optimal strategy, but it was the only one available. As a result, it was only through trial and error and experimentation that a usable conceptual framework emerged.

It would take years of fumbling with issues, of wrighting and wroughting, and of groping and questioning for the governance *problématique* to crystallize as the most flexible, useful, and illuminating way to guide inquiries.

In a world so complex and turbulent that nobody can be said to be in charge, where the economic process has drifted from energy and natural resources dominance to information and knowledge dominance, and where power, resources and information are widely distributed, the new dynamic calls for a new institutional order, based on cognition, coordination, collaboration, and social learning.

Governance is the word that captured the essence of this new institutional order, but it means much more than a family of institutional forms or processes. Governance is also a *manière de voir*, an analytical framework, a language of problem definition and problem solution, and an *outillage mental* to help in the clinical evaluation of problematic issues, and in the design of useful responses to such problems.

Why is this new perspective called for?

Disconcertation generates ever more important problems of poor coordination, and the reductive approaches and ideologies in good currency too often tend to ascribe glitches, slippages and coordination failures to specific factors (human resources, finance, etc.). This is the case even though these factors are at best symptoms of the dysfunction rather than the source or cause of it. A *nouveau regard* on an emerging institutional order that is more adaptable, evolvable, and breeds novelty, but would appear to be much less controllable by any mega-actor, is therefore necessary, particularly if one is to get a handle on the new dynamic and to develop collaborative ways to nudge erratic organizations and systems (suffering from various pathologies) in less destructive directions.

Both families of great simplifiers – believers in the perfection of the invisible hand of the market, and in the visible hand of the state – have been quite diffident about allowing governance to enter their perspectives. They have come to regard governance as an unnecessary complication in a world that their ideologies had already sanitized.

Such crippling epistemologies are endowed, like all paradigms, with a protective belt that, through the mechanisms of cognitive dissonance and sophistry, simply deflects any criticism as irrelevant. This explains the great reluctance of the professionalized academic disciplinary social sciences (anchored in the sort of knowledge generated by academic disciplines as *manières de voir* – according to codes and rules approved by professional disciplinary guilds, and enforced by union-type strictures in universities and colleges) to dare to question their very stylized, reductive and largely sterile version of professional knowledge by critically appraising their premises and their practice – as the governance *problématique* suggests is necessary (Paquet 2009).

The market for ideas being quite imperfect, and plagued with intellectual culs-de-sac, it has been a most fascinating intellectual pastime to speculate on what might have happened if some crucial intellectual differences of opinion (like the one between Emile Durkheim and Gabriel Tarde, or the one between J.M. Keynes and F. Hayek) had been resolved the other way (Latour and Lépinay 2008). Entire canons that have bamboozled generations of practitioners might have been turned on their heads.

The stonewalling of the governance approach by the action of disciplinary phalanxes has made it very difficult for the governance paradigm to get appropriately aired and critically discussed. Instead, it was summarily dismissed in academe. This is why any *mode d'emploi* for the governance approach has been so long in the making, and so slow in coming forth (Paquet 2008), although this approach was embraced by both citizens and practitioners as quite enlightening.

About the way in which this *manière de voir* evolved

As the rest of this book will show, my own experience in exploring this territory has been anything but linear: my work was pursued in four broad zones *au fil des circonstances*, with much meandering back and forth among those terrains.

First and foremost, it proceeded in a very pedestrian way, by probing (in a pragmatic and exploratory manner) some of the issue domains that were hotly debated but that remained very much terra incognita in the 1960s. This was done in an eclectic and hesitant way, and often suffered from the contamination by the zeitgeist of the day that favored centralization and state approaches. This period of probing proceeded in ways that merrily trespassed across academic disciplinary frontiers, but may probably have shown still too much deference *vis-à-vis* the conventional wisdom.

A second zone was an epistemological consequence of this sort of eclectic probing: raising questions about assumptions in good currency in the study of socio-political economies. Consequently, much time was spent appraising assumptions that were too uncritically accepted, or questioning the strictures imposed by organizing ideas in good currency. Again, this work was done somewhat unsystematically very much as a result of circumstances.

A third zone was the use of a variety of disparate laboratories in which I was allowed to try my hand at organization design. These laboratory experiences (social security, science policy, federalism, public governance, and the like) were most instructive. The three sketches presented below – on federalism, on regulation, and on the Canadian federal public service) are illustrative of this sort of work.

Finally, underlying all the work mentioned above, there has been a nagging and continuous concern about the informational fabric of organizations and socio-economic systems. Organizations are usually defined in terms of power structures and stylized roles, but one may equally well (and maybe with more ensuing illumination) analyze organizations in terms of the information flows that such structures and roles entail. In that sense, information flows are the flip side of the organizational structures. The flip side of a hierarchical organization is a flow of commands, while the flip side of a horizontal organization is more in the nature of simple anonymous messages.

Nobel economist Leonid Hurwicz spent most of his career studying informationally decentralized systems, and showing how the informational *verso* can illuminate the organizational *recto*. This is an approach to organization that has been in good currency in some limited circles since the 1960s, but has never quite managed to attract the attention it deserved in the governance world. I was always fascinated, from the 1960s on, by the profound insights such an approach was providing and returned to the question time and time again over the last decades.

The four sets of papers presented in this volume echo some of the work done in each of these four zones. While each paper is mainly anchored in one terrain, many have indulged in much extra-territoriality, and have drawn insights from other zones. Moreover, as will become obvious, some of the early papers suffer from a whiff of state-centricity – a sentiment prevalent in the zeitgeist of the time.

An emerging governance research program

Much of the work done over the last four decades in these different zones may be regarded as more or less successful efforts to provide some basis for a more realistic and therefore better approach to the governing of organizations. It has consistently raised questions about the paradigms in good currency, improvised in the face of issues not fully theorized, and generated a certain amount of rabble-rousing in debates that had been declared – maybe prematurely – permanently resolved.

The series of books on governance that have been produced recently are a testimony to the importance of the approach as a meaningful response to the problems of the day. Even though one may not find any of the existing models of governance entirely satisfactory, this is no reason for despairing. We now know a bit more about the pathologies of governance, about key mechanisms likely to improve governance, and about the principles that might guide better organizational design (Paquet 2004, 2005a, 2005b, 2008).

The next phase in the development of a more satisfactory approach to collaborative governance is the multiplication of experiments in a vast array of issue domains where mass collaboration is not only promising, but might be regarded as the only way to ensure effective governing when power, resources and information are widely distributed.

This focus on experimentalism will not be an easy sell in a world of conventional social sciences that has been plagued by scientism. The only way to persuade the skeptics is to demonstrate *la possibilité du mouvement en marchant*. It is only through the multiplication of experiments with prototyping and serious play (as I suggest later) that the academic disciplinarians will be shaken off their dogmas.

This game will have to be played very much as the game of GO is – through encirclement and attacks on all fronts: showing the promises of decentralization, mass collaboration, prototyping and experimenting, and open-sourcing, as well as the high costs of clinging to crippling epistemologies (Paquet 2009).

The introduction that follows is meant to provide the intellectual foundations to make sense of the proposed voyage in the governance world.

References

B. Latour, V.A. Lépinay, *L'économie, science des intérêts passionnés.* Paris: La Découverte, 2008.

G. Paquet, *Pathologies de gouvernance.* Montréal : Liber, 2004.

G. Paquet, *Gouvernance : une invitation à la subversion.* Montr/al : Liber, 2005a.

G. Paquet, *The New Geo-Governance: A Baroque Approach.* Ottawa: The University of Ottawa Press, 2005b. .

G. Paquet, *Gouvernance: mode d'emploi.* Montréal: Liber, 2008

G. Paquet, *Crippling Epistemologies and Governance Failures: A plea for experimentalism.* Ottawa: The University of Ottawa Press, 2009.

Introduction:
Foundations

Je déteste l'indifférence. J'ai esssayé et j'ai eu honte.

Brice Parain

This work is baroque in the sense that it strings together beads and stones of different shapes and forms that would not normally find a common jewelry box. They are drawn from different sources, and originate in different times.

This book is also fundamentally unfinished and truly a work in progress: these various pieces as a mosaic do not aim to provide a fully-worked out integrated framework that would constitute a complete alternative to the paradigm in good currency in the social sciences. Such a framework is needed, but will have to await the travails of a more creative integrator.

The unfinished nature of the work is ascribable to the fact that there is, at this time, no satisfactory theory of collaborative governance, and no template for the strategic state nested at the core of it. Under the circumstances, the best that can be hoped for is the provision of some elements of an effective response to challenges faced by the governance apparatus and the strategic state – in a world where power, resources and information are widely distributed, and where nobody is in charge.[1]

---

1 The lack of a fully satisfactory theory of governance and a suitable theory of the strategic state does not mean that we cannot work with what we have. Prototypes have been constructed and experimented with. Indeed, such prototypes are sufficient to guide preliminary work on an open-source framework, based on the development of technologies of cooperation and the provision of platforms enabling a very large number of stakeholders to become actively and practically involved as producers of governance. This approach is intent on producing an alternative to the cosmology in good currency in the social sciences – the one based on technical and instrumental rationality, command and control, state-centricity, and the like. As will become clearer as the book unfolds, this alternative cosmology is based on social learning, reflexive governance, and the centrality of knowledge and information. While it is not the mission of this book to flesh out this alternative cosmology, the road traveled here is paving the way to this new cosmology. It should also be clear that the new cosmology is a direct consequence of the *manière de voir* that is developed throughout this book, and is the result of a critical appreciation of the limitations of the cosmology in good currency.

1

Despite the baroque and the unfinished nature of the project, these papers constitute a promising basis on which to build the new synthesis *qui s'en vient*, and have helped enrich and guide my own research program in collaborative governance. This explains the meaning of the sub-title of this volume: such exploratory work in quite different terrains has allowed a certain *manière de voir* to emerge. As for the main title, it underlines the only meaningful focus of the social sciences that I have practiced: helping people to understand social processes so as to enable them to make something different happen, something that will make some better off and, in most circumstances, nobody worse off.

Collaborative governance: *manière de voir*

The broad features of this new and unconventional *manière de voir* are anchored in three basic strategic choices:

- first, following John Dewey, the choice of a philosophy of experimentalism as a mode of inquiry, as the sort of probing and "intelligence in operation" most likely to be fruitful in tackling what Dewey aptly called issues and affairs;
- second, following Albert Hirschman and Roger Caillois, the choice of trespassing freely across disciplinary boundaries to escape the tyranny of disciplines, fundamentalist ideologies, and other mental prisons, in the never-ending quest for better methods of making sense of what is going on, and deciding what one can do about it;
- and third, following Donald Schön, the choice of focusing on social science as a design profession (design of coordination and collaboration mechanisms), but with a full awareness of the limits to such designing activity (always plagued by incomplete information, imperfect rationality, and unintended consequences) and the inherently unpredictable dynamics of the social learning that underpins it.

In John Dewey's approach, inquiry and social intelligence are used to solve problems of practical interest. Practical intelligence embodies an experimental method, using diversity, deliberation and dynamic feedback to probe and to discover imagined responses to problems, while trying to anticipate whether these responses are technically feasible, socially acceptable, implementable, etc.

Practical intelligence requires abandoning dogmatism, and accepting the consequences of our experiments as the key evidence prompting us to revise views, certitudes, and beliefs. It is a process based on cooperative social experimentation (Dewey 1927, 1935; Lindblom 1990; Anderson 2006). This inquiring and probing approach aims less at disconfirming an already well-defined hypothesis than at experimenting, at generating new knowledge that goes substantially beyond the initial hypothesis, and aiming at nothing less than the disclosure and exploration of other worlds, the creation of a new reality.

Experimentalism calls for imagination, and for the use of a very eclectic tool-box. This sort of eclecticism is based on the premise that prescribing methods blocks the development of better methods.

Such an exploration has taken many forms. Two notable ones are: (a) probing remote and startling connections, à la Caillois (1960), among entirely disconnected fields in search of meta-pherein (of generative metaphors) capable of reframing perspectives in one zone with the use of patterns observable in other entirely disconnected fields; (b) making the highest and best use of singular terrains as testing grounds for experimenting with the use of structures and tools in vogue in cognate or neighboring areas. This latter sort of trespassing à la Hirschman (1970, 1981) is less draconian, and likely to encounter less resistance, and might be particularly cost-effective when nexuses of problems would appear to pose more wicked problems that call for ad hoc experiments, or the invention of new vocabularies to untangle what would appear to be unresolvable conundrums.

As for Donald Schön, he has redirected the attention of social scientists toward the design process, and toward the epistemology of practice on which the design professions are built. This view of the social scientist as reflective practitioner is rooted in the centrality of social learning, and is skeptical vis-à-vis the dominant technical rationality of positivism. It also entails quite a different mix of *savoirs*, *savoir-faire*, and *savoir-être* in the education of the reflective practitioner (Schön 1983, 1987; Paquet 2006)

Bent Flyvberg (2001) has characterized endeavors of that ilk as a phronetic approach to social science work.

This approach takes some distance from concerns with the production of knowledge that is invariable in time and space (episteme), or the application of technical know-how according to instrumental rationality (techne), and instead emphasizes practical knowledge and practical ethics that cannot be encapsulated by universal rules. Phronetic researchers do not neglect episteme and techne, but focus on the concrete, the particular, the practical, and the ethical.

Their approach may be regarded as an extension of the Dewey imperative – in the beginning is the issue – and it is underpinned by four questions: where are we going? is this desirable? what should be done? who gains and who loses? (Flyvberg 2001:60). Action follows from the answers to these questions.

Flyvberg has even suggested some cautious and provisional guidelines for such a reformed social science: reminding phronetic researchers of the centrality of values and power at the core of their analyses; of the need to remain close to reality and practices; of the need to pay close attention to little things and particular circumstances, of the core importance of the historical context as a focal point and of the dynamic question "how does one engineer the collective action that seems to be required"; of the necessity at all times to focus jointly on agency and structure; and of recognizing fully the polyphony of voices in the forum and the centrality of meaningful dialogue in context.

In the words of Flyvberg (2001:140), "the result of phronetic research is a pragmatically governed interpretation of the studied practices".

This family of approaches has Aristotelian roots; it was deployed in the work of Nietzsche and Foucault, and it blossomed in the works of Pierre Bourdieu (1972), Schön (1983), Dreyfus et al (1986, 1997) and Sabel (2001). But it is fair to say that it has not yet crystallized into a canonical form. Indeed, it may well be that it is antithetic to any canonical form.

One fundamental tenet of this family of approaches is that the process provides a *platform* for mass collaboration rather than a precise design. For practical social scientists, it entails nothing less than a conversation with the situation, reflection-in-action, and learning-by-doing – a regime where problem-setting and problem-solving are tackled jointly, new trials are based on learning from earlier ones, and where the ultimate pragmatic test is whether this sort of inquiry generates anything to help nudge the social system in preferred value-adding and welfare-generating directions (Schön 1990).

Mental toolkit / Outillage mental

The priority of the particular, and the emphasis on little things, have both had considerable influence on the development of phronetic-style social science. It explains the need not only to use whatever tool is available, but also to forge new ad hoc indicators and instrumentations, as required.

This is a lesson learned early by budding economic historians who, from time immemorial, have had to develop imaginative indicators and new organizing ideas to deal effectively with the particular configurations of values and facts they are faced with. Often the most indirect and circuitous ways of gauging key socio-economic parameters have to be invented, and even the *outillage mental* to interpret such data has to be custom-built.

For instance, the kinked oligopoly demand schedule was forged by Paul Sweezy as a custom-made tool to make sense of decision-making in the English coal trade, 1550-1850, but was then widely used as a standard model of oligopoly in modern economics (Sweezy 1938).

I learned, early on, that this lesson held even more generally than I had imagined, and far beyond the confines of economic history.

In the early 1960s, John Meisel and I (I was a graduate student, working with him on what was to become my first co-authored paper) were trying to explain the important shifts in party support on the occasion of the Canadian federal elections of 1957 and 1958. We needed to co-relate voting behavior with economic status, but the income data from the 1951 census were clearly out of whack with the realities of 1957-58. So, having observed a strong correlation between economic status and the percentage of households with lodgers at the census tract level in some urban settings in 1951, we chose to use the lodger intensity data, available in the 1956 census, as a fair proxy for economic status, and boldly built our analyses on this presumption (Meisel & Paquet 1964).

My forays in social policy in the 1960s and early 1970s conveyed the same message of invitation to boldness: the Senate Committee on Aging with Senator David Croll and his associate Richard Davis in the early 1960s; health policy work with the original *Comité de recherches sur l'assurance-santé au Québec* with Claude Castonguay and Thomas Boudreau in the mid-sixties; work with the unemployment insurance redesign team with Douglas Hartle & Co. around 1970; and work with Senator Maurice Lamontagne for the Senate Committee on Science Policy.

All this was to strengthen the conviction that perfectly adapted data do not materialize when needed, and that the tools likely to be useful often have to be invented to deal with the issue at hand, for they are most certainly not already available in some notional toolbox. Albert Hirschman has been a social scientist particularly inventive on this front (Hirschman 1967, 1970). In all those laboratories I was exposed to, to make imaginative use of whatever data and to forge new tools to do the job proved the only way, and yet these tools often subsequently acquired a life of their own, outside the particular context in which they were invented. (Paquet 2008b, 2008c).

The schizophrenic gap between the textbook theories and ideologies that attempt to force reality into their issue-machine, and practices that call for improvisation and social learning on the spot, has often meant that social scientists have become trapped in methodological and ideo-logical mental prisons perpetrated by the canonical texts. As a result, some work in the social sciences has come to look like the scrambling of the infamous drunk who had lost his watch in the dark back-alley but was searching for it under a lamppost because there was more light there.

Old style social scientists who were my mentors used to warn against the sirens of positivism and methodism, and other such mental prisons, by repeating to us students that reducing epistemology to methodology, and methodology to the protocols in good currency in the experimental sciences (or in other ideological presbyteries) was not very promising for the social sciences.

It was the advice of such elders that immunized a good portion of my generation (but not all) from the positivist pox and other such plagues that played an important reductive role in the social sciences during the 30 years that followed World War II. It would be decades before the work of Schön, or the new institutional economics in the manner of Douglass North, would prove to a broader public that this sort of advice was bang on.

Three foundational assumptions: process, design, reflexivity

The new mindset, trying to overcome those various plagues, is built on three important assumptions: first, the assumption that process has a primacy over things and substance; second, the assumption that intervening in a process creates a design problem; and third, the assumption that reflexivity is consubstantial with the social sciences. These assumptions may sound somewhat metaphysical, and indeed they are. But this does not make them less important.

Indeed, the lack of a full appreciation of the centrality of process, design, and reflexivity is important in explaining the failures of the traditional epistemologies of the social sciences, and of the governance processes these epistemologies have fostered.

Process

The process approach is a general strategy for the description and explanation of reality. It is a generalized approach, rather than a unified doctrine. It does not deny that things exist, but it suggests that material bodies (like all stable structures) are rooted in process, and constitute only temporary bundles of powers generated by a process that remains unfinished and open-ended.

The process approach and the object approach are traditions that have their roots in classical Greece, in the opposition of Heraclitus and Parmenides, and the lineage of each tradition is impressive. But the object tradition has been overwhelmingly dominant as a result of the impact of positivism. Emile Durkheim, maybe more than anyone else, has been associated with doctrine that "les faits sociaux sont des choses", and should be approached as such. While in the more recent past (more or less at the time that Hayek was denouncing scientism) Jules Monnerot (1946) wrote a most celebrated denunciation of Durkheim's stance, it did not have a determinant impact. Most mainstream social sciences remained associated with the object approach.

The vision of the world in good currency until very recently remained some version of social physics – but a pre-quantum physics – i.e., one still enamoured with atemporal equilibrium analysis as exemplified most clearly by economics.

This is not to say that heterodox movements did not exist. The Austrian school in economics challenged the economics orthodoxy à la Samuelson. The same may be said of the other social sciences. But the mainstream social sciences remained dominated by the object approach, and human agency played second fiddle.

There has been a recent shift to a focus on process, emphasizing a dynamic open-ended approach in terms of flows. (Rescher 1996, 2000). It has aptly restated the basic tenets of process philosophy, and anti-reductionist social scientists have begun to see the human world as consisting of processes, with "objects" having a derivative status.

Design

An offshoot of the process perspective is that intervening in the process is in the nature of design. The design process has often been somewhat sanitized, and reduced to problem-solving steps, fully programmable under a set of rules (Schön 1990:112). This is unduly reductive, since it assumes that the problem space (like an actual maze) has a structure that is already given.

The design process does not really start with such givens. Schön has proposed to define it as intelligent exploration of a terrain (125), as an inquiry guided by an appreciative system carried over from past experience that produces "a selective representation of an unfamiliar situation that sets values for the system's transformation. It frames the problem of the problematic situation and thereby sets directions in which solutions lie and provides a schema for exploring them" (131-2). In fact, designing is a frame experiment: a conversation with the situation that leads to inventing structures that in turn reveal conflicts and dilemmas in the appreciative system.

Since participants talk across discrepant frames, designing "is a process in which communication, political struggle, and substantive inquiry are combined... (that) may be judged appropriate ... if it leads to the creation of a design structure that directs inquiry toward progressively greater inclusion of features of the problematic situation and values for its transformation" (138-9).

Such exploration or inquiry leads designers to learn by doing, but more importantly to escape from straight deductive thinking (proving that something must be), and indulging in abductive reasoning (suggesting that something may be, and reaching out to explore it) (Martin 2004). This is fundamental in the world of design, which "involves inquiry into systems that do not yet exist" (Romme 2003:558).

This new way of thinking underlies the whole new generative governance of social systems, building on experimentation and serious play, and making the highest and best use of grappling, grasping, discerning, and sense-making as part of reflective generative learning (Chait et al 2005: ch.6).

Design as we use the word here is therefore more in the nature of a platform from which intelligent exploration is carried out. It focuses much more on the process of inquiry than on the structure or form that may result from it, temporarily, as the conversation with the situation progresses.

Reflexivity

A final assumption of the new approach is the taking into account of reflexivity: a fundamental condition for effective governance of the new sort based on social learning. Reflexivity is defined by Jessop (2003:7) as "the ability and commitment to uncover and make explicit to oneself the nature of one's intentions, projects and actions and their conditions of possibility; and, in this context, to learn about them, critique them, and act upon any lessons that have been learnt". Reflexivity means that knowledge acquired gets integrated during the process and unfolds in order to modify the outcome.

As Douglass North (2005:) clearly states, traditional social sciences have done a very poor job at factoring in human intentionality, and the human capacity for representational redescription. The belief systems underpinning these representations have an immense impact on the institutions themselves. The new mindset recognizes that the complexity and turbulence of the context are such that agents cannot fully understand and grasp it. This entails a process of inquiry with a built-in on going critical ability to think about the implications of particular choices, and an on going capacity to modify means and ends as learning evolves. It means learning how to learn reflexively: one might say double-looped learning à la Argyris and Schön (1978)

These three assumptions of the new mindset are ways to respond to three weaknesses of the old mindset. The old mindset is plagued by its assumptions about an object-world, its view of intervention as problem-solving within a maze-like world where the problem is already set, and a neglect of human intentionality and its key role in a governance process that must be reflexive. This explains the static and timeless dimensions of the traditional approaches.

Emergence of the concept of collaborative governance

This less reductive *manière de voir* was brought forth slowly and painfully, and at different stages and paces, for the different social sciences. For economists, it was the result of two sets of challenges: the first was the stagflation crisis of the 1970s that forced us to critically re-appraise the conventional *outillage mental* in use; and the second was the productivity decline that began in the 1970s. Both these experiences revealed the greater inherent complexity of the issues at hand, and the consequent need to develop a new *outillage mental* likely to be more useful. Other social sciences went through a similar catharsis on the occasion of similar crises.

The reason for the slowness and painfulness in the emergence of the new cosmology is easy to understand.

One is always deeply trapped in the zeitgeist of one's time. Economists educated in the post-Second World War period could not but be fascinated by the promises of Keynesianism, a social science apparatus that had invented modern macroeconomics, and promised to ensure, through its use, the optimal control of socio-economies.

There were some forewarnings by Hayek in 1952, but so strong were the winds of Keynesianism, and so brainwashed was the profession, that it was only with the tragic awakening of the late 1960s and 1970s that the Keynesian bubble was presumably burst. The magnificent economics meant to take us all to the promised land had led to an extensive period of imprudent policies, and to inflationary pressures that would take decades to override. This in turn meant a period of questioning of many an assumption, and to a rediscovery of the works of Hayek, with its emphasis on the centrality of knowledge.

Hayek had clearly understood that nobody has complete information, and, therefore, that nobody can be in charge in modern socio-economies, and that those pretending to be in charge were charlatans. He had also understood the fundamentally fragmented and distributed nature of knowledge, and the great importance of practical and tacit knowledge, that is widely sprinkled throughout the socio-economy, but also throughout large organizations.

The central challenge was to design ways in which one might modestly and prudently intervene in a manner that would help mobilize this distributed knowledge and nudge certain behavioral changes to avoid the worst outcomes, while keeping in mind that unintended consequences are most likely to swamp these efforts.

Fifty years of cautionary tales have had very little impact on the mindset of many social science tribes. Much of the doctrine on which management and public administration schools have built their programs is still a primitive version of organizational life: an instrumental view of organizations as control mechanisms, put in place to ensure that the vision of the "leader" is implemented and carried out through the highest and best use of physical, human, financial and symbolic resources. Weasel words, like leadership and performance management, are therefore used to brand such schools: unsuspecting students are promised that they will acquire the requisite leadership quality by osmosis, and the requisite formula for high performance by focusing on machinery and rote learning.

Both in the private and public sectors, the academic expertise purporting to lead such charges is largely bogus because of the insistence on a cartoonesque view of reality, and a criminal complaisance with evasive thinking. Fukuyama has characterized these mechanistic approaches to organizations, inspired by Frederick Taylor, as a "black hole" (Fukuyama 2004: 76ff). For despite the immense fiascos experienced over the last decades, and the enlightening work of Chester Barnard, who exploded these myths as early as 1938, the Taylorian model remains the canon in many schools of management and public administration.

One might have expected that the agonistic 1980s would trigger a change. The old ways were obviously not providing useful insights, and yet the new ways of fundamentalist neo-liberalism were no more promising.

Indeed, in the late 1980s, *collaborative governance* emerged as the new code word that appeared to synthesize the basis of a new approach, one that would replace the old Big-G-government approach (and the similar Taylorian dogmas in the cartoonesque view of large private corporations) in good currency since the late 1930s. While these questions were bubbling up in many places under many rubrics, the 1993 Nobel Prize in Economics, awarded to Douglass North, might serve more or less as a marker of a revival in institutional economics, and of the surge of governance studies in the modern sense of the term.

Not all those who have taken part in this renewal process share the same views, but in general, there has been a consensus that (a) a focus on the bigger picture of institutions and evolution, and a return to a broad political economy perspective were warranted; (b) scientism was a crippling epistemology, and experimentalism provided a much more promising alternative; (c) governance and the emphasis on the design of better prototypical mechanisms and social architecture would seem to provide the basis for a very fruitful alternative research program; and (d) the centrality of the problem of knowledge, information and cognitive economics could not be avoided.

Despite this relatively recent challenge, given the immense amount of intellectual capital invested by post-World War II social scientists in the utopian idea of the State (or the Leader) smoothly and effectively guiding the socio-economy (the organization), the credo is still with us. As the 2008 financial crisis revealed, the old Keynesian reflexes appear to be decision-makers' only reflexes in the face of the crisis: debauching the currency, mindless bail-outs, and massive unproductive public spending.

The State has become the new religion in the post-Second World War period: it has induced a level of comfort and dependency in the citizenry that is only very slowly being eroded, and it generated a *confort intellectuel* for the intelligentsia that might be even more difficult to uproot. One can read contemporary political scientists still declaring, in the first decade of the 21st century, that any reduction in the size of the State can only entail an impoverishment of governance. A similar view about "Leadership" is in good currency in schools of management today.

Given the obvious glitches that have marred an economic, political and social scene dominated by such state-centricity and fixation on leadership, it is easy to understand that this caused democracy to fall into disrepute, and to bureaucracy's developing a renewed attack on the democratic citadel to try once more to argue in favor of an hegemony of the managerial class. Yet despite the strange collusion of cohorts of bureaucrats, columnists, and adjudicators in support of such a view, distrust has reached such levels in the citizenry that it is unlikely to succeed.

Collaborative governance starts from the basic premise that nobody is in charge, and that only collaboration can generate effective coordination. This entails ensuring the right balance in two dimensions.

First, the right balance between democracy, republicanism, and liberalism will have to be invented. The only thing that is clear, and underpins the governance research program, is that there is a risk, were any one of these principles to become dominant, of triggering a tyranny of the majority, a tyranny of the elites, or a tyranny of the rich (O'Donnell 1998).

Second, good governance also requires a balance between the legal, the socio-historical and the political: any hegemony of one family of regulatory mechanisms might have crippling unintended consequences – reification, inertia, or whimsicality (Gauchet 2000; Paquet 2008a ch.9). And this is true in all sectors.

Search conference writ large: metaphor for inquiry and collaborative governance

"Search conferences" (Emery and Purser 1996) are structured participatory processes emphasizing experiential and community learning. They aim at producing an adaptive relationship between an organization and its uncertain and changing environment. Whether the "search conference" takes the canonical form of a two-day meeting, or creatively designs a venue capable of generating some such result, it brings in the views of the different stakeholders in a system in order to help them develop mutual perceptions of their existing circumstances and constraints, their different frames of reference, their desired futures, and the means to get there, by assembling their knowledge of the system and its environment, drawing on their experience, and constructing and reconstructing progressively (going with the flow) a process of deliberation about the steps necessary to initiate changes that are technically feasible, socially acceptable, implementable, and not too politically destabilizing.

The central feature of the process is the generation of new and broader perspectives, a focus on desired futures, and the recognition that conflicting views must be synthesized through blurring and blending, but also by completely reframing the issues one is confronting. The central challenge is for people to learn and plan together.

Learning must proceed on the basis of open-system thinking (any system has an open and direct relationship with its larger social environment), ecological learning (humans can extract information from their environment), democratic participation (people who do the work are responsible for the control and coordination of that work), a decision-making process that makes differences and conflicts clearer and more understandable, and an implementation process that engages the entire group.

The challenge is (1) to ensure that the search process leads to the unearthing of assumptions one may not be aware one is making, to a discussion of the extent to which such assumptions may be revisited and a blurring of perspectives may ensue; and (2) to tap into the history, experience, and prospective outlook of participants to generate new ways of addressing the issues of interest.

What is aimed at is not a consensus, but a common ground in which one may identify where the thin line between agreement and disagreement is located. Clarification is the proximate objective, while the ultimate objective is the sort of "reframing" of perspectives that is necessary. This entails some transformative and generative work: new rules of the game, new alliances, new partnerships, new networks, new processes (social architecture), but also new *manières de voir*, new blended or blurred perspectives, new beliefs, etc. Such a reframing cannot be mechanically engineered. It often depends on particular circumstances that considerably weaken the powers of cognitive dissonance and dynamic conservatism. That is why one must frame the questions in such a way as to make the highest and best use of tipping points: the loci of particular levers, triggers, and pressure points where minimal or at least less intrusive intervention may yield important if not maximum impact.

Collaboration, common knowledge, and absurd results

One of the most important blockages in the development of effective coordination when power, resources, and information are widely distributed is (1) the strong reluctance of rational actors to accept the seemingly incomprehensible (and quasi-magical, in their view) emergence of some order from seemingly chaotic environments, and (2) their effective use of episodic monumental failures of this process as persuasive determining evidence that one cannot rely on self-organization and self-steering, but rather that one must ensure that someone is in charge.

This is not the place to develop a full counter-argument to this skeptical stance, but one cannot ask the reader to suffer through a whole book arguing that this is the most promising way out of the present quandary without at least providing a sketchy plausible counter-argument.

This counter-argument builds first on a better understanding of the way in which collaboration materializes in large groups. Collaboration is dependent upon communication generating social negotiation and creative output. Such mass collaboration was first observed and studied in animal societies, where it has been shown that explicit and conscious social negotiation was not necessary for mass collaboration to materialize. It is in this context that Pierre-Paul Grasse has coined the term *stigmergy* to connote a method of communication (and implicit negotiation) in which individuals communicate with one another by modifying their local environment. It helps understand "how disparate, distributed, ad hoc contributions could lead to the emergence of the largest collaborative enterprises" (Elliott 2006).

A new trans-disciplinary approach has developed to provide the new literacy needed to understand and make sense of collaboration. Its origin is in the emergence of social dilemmas in which individual rationality would appear to lead to collective irrationality. The best example is the tragedy of the commons, where common property resources are depleted by the overuse of the resource as a result of each myopic individual trying to make the highest and best use of it for himself.

A relatively simple and yet powerful avenue out of this sort of dilemma is the development of a broader perspective through generating common knowledge: partaking in rituals producing common knowledge, i.e., letting all know exactly what other audience members know. Once, other persons' views are made known, collaboration is made possible. Indeed, increasing common knowledge becomes a way to foster coordination and collaboration (Chwe 2001).

A more sophisticated perspective requires a richer literacy of key concepts derived from various disciplines to understand the process of cooperation. Saveri et al (2004) have provided a synthesis of the recent work on this front, and shown that concepts of synchrony, symbiosis, group selection, catalysis, commons, collective action, and collective intelligence provide the raw material from which one may draw a description of the dynamics that can be tuned to foster cooperation. Building on this platform, Saveri et al (2005a, b) have suggested a strategic map of cooperation-amplifying technologies, and suggested ways to leverage these technologies of collaboration.

The usefulness of these technologies has been illustrated by reference to a wide variety of successful experiences in the private, public, and social sectors, and the work of Charles Sabel has shown how the public policy process can be informed and improved using those technologies (Sabel 2001).

Nothing in such processes ensures automatic success. Indeed, poor communication, attention lapses, procedural errors, technical mistakes, and errors of comprehension or representation leading to a misapprehension of events as they are unfolding, may lead to cascades of errors leading to catastrophes. Such catastrophes have been documented and analyzed (Morel 2002). It has been shown that the process of collective validation of some aberration often plays a more important role than sheer power. But to the extent that open-source mobilizes a broader information base, and ensures that critical thinking is effectively deployed, the probability of an aberration would appear to be much less when such an open-source process is in play than when someone not totally well-informed is in charge.

While the full job of demonstrating the feasibility and effectiveness of open-source collaborative governance (based on experimentalism, prototyping, and serious play) is for another book, our criticism of the conventional reductive disciplinary methodism does not lead to an impasse. It is sufficient at this time to claim that feasibility is plausible. The full proof of its optimality (at least in the case of Canada, in domains like federalism, health, and education) will require another book intent on showing more fully the heuristic powers of the new *manière de voir*.

Structure of this book:

Part I is a prudent reflection on the philosophy of process that has informed my *manière de voir* in a fundamental way, but it also echoes a period of transition when probing to find better ways remains (in Canada but also elsewhere, as we will see in chapter 9) encumbered by concerns inspired by the conventional wisdom.

> **Chapter 1** sketches a view of the dynamics of social sciences based on social learning that has permeated almost everything I did over the last 40 years.
>
> **Chapter 2** suggests a meso-perspective best able to help in analyzing socio-economico-political realities. This partitioning of the socio-economy as instituted process into a number of stylized sub-processes was first used to provide a diagnosis of Canada of the early 1980s, but this scheme has subsequently been used to structure much of the work Jean-Pierre Wallot and I have done on 19th century Canada and Quebec.

Part II is the demolition part of the project. It dwells on many fundamental assumptions of conventional social sciences that have had to be questioned along the way.

> **Chapter 3** uses the discussion of a "model" of Canadian public administration as an occasion to critically discuss state-centricity. It underlines the ideological underpinnings of such a position that stands in the way of any effort to refurbish the governing apparatus.
>
> **Chapter 4** debunks some of conventional wisdom about the lack of usability of solidarity organizations and shows them to be a true alternative or complement to market and state organizations in the ecologies of governance of the future.
>
> **Chapter 5** raises serious questions about the weasel word *leadership*, and suggests focusing on stewardship as a substitute for leadership.

Part III illustrates through three sketches the role of professional social sciences as purveyor of design and architecture.

> **Chapter 6** offers an earlier suggestion about how one might reframe the notion of federalism as social technology. It was provided in the

immediate aftermath of the 1976 PQ election in Quebec as a basis for reflections on how to refurbish Canadian federalism.

Chapter 7 proposes an informational and cybernetic approach to regulation that has provided some of the basic vocabulary that proved essential for the latter work on governance

Chapter 8 proposes a sketch for the redesign of the Canadian federal public service which would require a new philosophy of governance, and a network of new moral contracts.

Part IV builds on the notion of a socio-economy as an informational system. The issue was raised earlier in passing, but it represents a fundamental reframing of the economic approach – away from social physics and an object world, toward an approach built on the centrality of information and knowledge. This alternative approach, much inspired by the works of Leonid Hurwicz (1960) and Jacob Marschak (1966), stylizes the flip side of the world of production and exchange of goods and services as a communication system. Instead of focusing on the flow of goods and services, it focuses on the contents of the messages exchanged between actors, and on the characteristics of the communication system linking all those actors.

This approach has an immense heuristic power, for it opens the way to analyses that focus on cognition in the process of social learning, and key dimensions of governance (with the emphasis on pluralism, frame analysis, effective coordination, and the crucial importance of information, knowledge, and learning in it).

Chapter 9 celebrates the crucial work of Don Lamberton who was one of the key social scientists to develop significant insights into information economics. The fact that he trod hyper-prudently and felt the need to make accommodation with the neo-classical framework in good currency, is a testimony to the tyranny of conventional wisdom and ideologies in social sciences, but also to Lamberton's courage in so doing.

Chapter 10 provides a sketch of a promising framework for cognitive economics that might be used to rethink some of the current challenges. It attempts to formalize what an evolutionary cognitive paradigm might look like, and the new terrains and prescriptions that might ensue from an approach that stands in sharp contrast to the conventional paradigm.

The conclusion takes a moment to reflect on the next steps on the road to collaborative governance – and in particular at the central role in it for public intellectuals and the citizenry, and at the new importance of representations, evaluations and interpretations in the definition of conventions that go beyond coordination and aim at generating collaboration.

The demise of the public intellectual (and its displacement by columnistry and punditry) has been an echo effect of the social sciences having abandoned their central role to journalists – "les magistrats de l'immédiat" (as Jean Lacouture calls them). Together with celebrity activism, academic snobbery, and ideology, columnistry has debased the currency. The public intellectual needs to be brought back into active duty.

But the most important actor to be brought back into action is the citizenry. The re-engagement of the citizen as a producer of governance constitutes the most arduous task facing those arguing for collaborative governance. The citizen's distrust of officialdom is so profound that the citizen would appear to be only mobilized by localized crises that are easily capable of generating flaring violence.

The crucial dimensions in the next steps will mobilize expressive rationality and recognize the centrality of evaluation (ethics) and conventions. These are the two loci where collaboration will materialize. The arrangements likely to be embodied in the emergent conventions are going to have to meet the conditions of being within the boundaries of fairness, legitimacy and reasonableness.

There is a clear message of dissent that emerges from this book about the sort of governance thinking required. I feel that such dissent is not only healthy but necessary, and that one has to find ways to generate the negotiated compromise conventions required for effective collaboration. Failure to take seriously the sources of such dissent and to actively deal with the concerns raised is tantamount to sabotaging the very process of social learning that underpins good governance. This is not a view in good currency, but Cass Sunstein (2003) has shown why organizations and societies are far more likely to prosper if they welcome dissent. Consequently, it should be the spirit in which the reader enters this book.

The work reported here has been done with the help of friends and colleagues. From *mes vieux maîtres* (Albert Faucher and John Meisel), from Jean-Pierre Wallot (my historian colleague of some 40 years), from a host of younger colleagues also around the Centre on Governance (Dan Lane, Pierre Lecours, Christian Navarre, Lise Pigeon, Jeffrey Roy, Christopher Wilson, etc.), and from my INVENIRE partners (Robin Higham and Ruth Hubbard) – I have been blessed with much intellectual support, but also with constant criticism. Most of these colleagues and friends have disagreed with a sufficiently substantial portion of my babbling and scribbling that there is no need to repeat that they should not be tarred by association.

However, three of those colleagues cannot escape some responsibility: they have kindly allowed me to draw freely from three papers they separately co-authored with me, and must share responsibility for these segments of the book – Ruth Hubbard (for Chapter 4), Pierre Lecours (for the portion of the Conclusion dealing with ethics) and Lise Pigeon (for most of Chapter 8).

This work has been supported financially over the years by the Social Sciences and Humanities Research Council of Canada. For this I am most grateful.

References

W.T. Anderson, *All Connected Now*. Cambridge: Westview Press, 2001.

C. Argyris, D.A. Schön, *Organizational Learning*. Reading, MA: Addison-Wesley, 1978.

C. Barnard. *The Functions of the Executive*. Cambridge: Harvard University Presses, 1938.

P. Bourdieu, *Esquisse d'une théorie de la pratique*. Genève: Librairie Droz, 1972.

R. Caillois, *Méduse et Cie*. Paris: Gallimard, 1960.

R.P. Chait, W.P. Ryan, B.E. Taylor, *Governance as Leadership*. Hoboken, N.J.: Wiley, 2005.

M.S.W. Chwe, *Rational Ritual*. Princeton: Princeton University Press, 2001.

J. Dewey, *The Public and Its Problems*. New York: Henry Holt, 1927.

J. Dewey, *Liberalism and Social Action*. New York: Putnam, 1935.

H. Dreyfus, S. Dreyfus, *Mind over Machine*. New York : The Free Press, 1986.

M. Elliott, "Stigmergic Collaboration: The Evolution of Group Work" *M/C Journal* 9 : 2 (2006) (retrieved 08.Aug. 2008 from http://journal.media-culture.org.au/0605/03-elliott.php)

M. Emery, R.E. Purser, *The Search Conference*. San Francisco: Jossey-Bass, 1996.

B. Flyvberg, *Making Social Sciences Matter*. Cambridge: Cambridge University Press, 2001.

F. Fukuyama, *State-Building: Governance and World Order in the 21st Century*. Ithaca, N.Y.: Cornell University Press, 2004.

M. Gauchet, "Quand les droits de l'homme deviennent une politique", *Le Débat*, 110, 2000.

F.A. Hayek, *Scientism and the Study of Society*. Glencoe, Ill. : The Free Press, 1952.

A.O. Hirschman, *Development Projects Observed*. Washington, D.C. : The Brookings Institution, 1967.

A.O. Hirschman, *Exit, Voice and Loyalty*. Cambridge: Harvard University Press, 1970.

A.O. Hirschman, *Essays in Trespassing*. Cambridge: Cambridge University Press, 1981.

L. Hurwicz, "Conditions for Economic Efficiency of Centralized and Decentralized Structures" in G. Grossman (Ed.) *Value and Plan*. Berkeley: The University of California Press, 1960, 162-183.

B. Jessop, *Governance and Metagovernance: On Reflexivity, Requisite Variety, and Requisite Irony*, 2003, http://comp.lancs.ac.uk/sociology/soc108rj.htm

C.E. Lindblom, *Inquiry and Change*. New Haven: Yale University Press, 1990.

J. Marschak, "Economic Planning and the Cost of Thinking" *Social Research*, 33 (2), 1966, 151-159.

R. Martin, "The Design of Business" *Rotman Management*, Winter 2004, 7-11.

J. Meisel, G. Paquet, "Some Quantitative Analyses of Canadian Election Results: An Exercise in the Testing of Hypotheses", in J. Henripin & A. Asimakopulos (eds) *Conference on Statistics*, Toronto: The University of Toronto Press, 1964, 1-31.

J. Monnerot, *Les faits sociaux ne sont pas des choses*. Paris: Gallimard, 1946.

C. Morel, *Les décisions absurdes*. Paris: Gallimard, 2002.

D.C. North, *Understanding the Process of Economic Change*. Princeton: Princeton University Press, 2005.

G. O'Donnell, "Horizontal Accountability in New Democracies", *Journal of Democracy*, 9:3, 1990, 112-126.

G. Paquet, *Savoirs, savoir-faire, savoir-être: in praise of professional wroughting and wrighting*. A report prepared for Campus 20/20 – An inquiry into the future of British Columbia's post-secondary education system, July 31, 2006, 25p.

G. Paquet, *Deep Cultural Diversity*. Ottawa: The University of Ottawa Press, 2008a.

G. Paquet, "Pour une éthique prospective et reconstructive fondée sur les besoins" *Ethique publique*, 10:1, 2008b, 93-102.

G. Paquet, *Gouvernance: mode d'emploi*. Montréal: Liber, 2008c.

N. Rescher, *Process Metaphysics*. Albany: State University of New York Press, 1996.

N. Rescher, *Process Philosophy*. Pittsburgh: University of Pittsburgh Press, 2000.

A.G.L. Romme, "Making a Difference: Organization as Design" *Organization Science*, 14 (5), 2003, 558-573.

C.F. Sabel, "A Quiet Revolution of Democratic Governance: Towards Democratic Experimentalism" in *OECD Governance in the 21st Century*, Paris 2001, 121-148.

A. Saveri et al. To*ward a New Literacy of Cooperation in Business*. Menlo Park: Institute for the Future, 2004.

A. Saveri et al. *Technologies of Cooperation*. Menlo Park: Institute for the Future, 2005a.

A. Saveri et al. *Leveraging Technologies of Cooperation*. Menlo Park: Institute for the Future, 2005b.

D.A. Schön, *The Reflective Practitioner*. New York: Basic Books, 1983.

D.A. Schön, *Educating the Reflective Practitioner*. San Francisco: Jossey-Bass, 1987.

D.A. Schön, "The Design Process" in V.A. Howard (Ed.) *Varieties of Thinking*, New-York: Routledge, 1990, 110-141.

C. Spinosa, F. Flores, H.L. Dreyfus, *Disclosing New Worlds*. Cambridge: The MIT Press, 1997.

C.R. Sunstein. *Why Societies Need Dissent*. Cambridge: Harvard University Press, 2003.

P.M. Sweezy, *Monopoly and Competition in the English Coal Trade*, 1550-1850. Cambridge: Harvard University Press, 1938.

J. Tussman, *The Burden of Office*. Vancouver: Talonbooks, 1989.

Part I:

Early probing

Social science as a profession has evolved significantly over time. In the world of Adam Smith, much of it remained confounded with philosophy. It was only over the following centuries that there was an effort to disentangle the handling of broader questions from concerns about smaller technical issues, assigned or delegated to more narrow specialists in different sub-disciplines, purported to be better equipped to handle them.

In one sense, this diffraction of the "study of society" into disciplines – each armed with a particular *manière de voir* – may be said to amount to a normal division of labour, and most certainly to have helped the disciplines to develop into professions (Katouzian 1980). Yet this professionalization also led to the emergence of groups of disciplinarians that dealt with society in different and compartmentalized ways. After a while, the diverse groups came to have little to do with one another. Indeed, by the 20th century, these disciplinarians had developed into guilds having their own methods, their own rules, their own journals and their own criteria of what is meaningful work.

I arrived on the professional scene at a time when there was a hardening of the boundaries between disciplines. Questions that had led to the emergence of the social sciences in the first place were forgotten as specialists toiled on smaller and smaller and ever more specialized puzzles, often suggested much more by their instrumentation and their angle of vision than by the materiality or the seriousness of the problems at hand.

Persons of my generation were perplexed and somewhat disconcerted by this development. Most of the members of my cohort boarded the disciplinarian train, and were seduced (bamboozled?) by the methods borrowed from the experimental sciences. A minority could not easily contain their malaise, and strove painfully to find a middle ground between the old and the new perspectives: the old one starting with issues and problems, and trying to improve social coordination, sometimes in rather casual and clumsy ways, and the new one, quite reductive, ensnared by the logic of the discipline, and focusing on puzzles, often of little interest to anyone but the members of the tribe.

The two chapters in this section document preliminary efforts, in the 1970s, to develop the basis for an alternative paradigm based on systems thinking, likely to overcome the difficulties generated by the diffraction of social science knowledge (Vickers 1965, 1968).

Chapter 1 suggests different ways of dealing with ill-structured problems through experimentalism and a process-oriented analysis. Chapter 2 uses a different way of partitioning the socio-economy instituted process into sub-processes (demography, production and exchange, finance, distribution, ecology of groups, state sub-process), inspired by the work of Johan Akerman in the 1940s (Akerman 1944/1955), to generate insights into the overall dynamics when they are brought together

These rather simple ways of overcoming the disciplinary meltdown by process analysis, and by a meso-analysis of sub–processes (loosely associated to different disciplines, but meant to underpin an integrative analysis of the interactions among these sub-processes), may not appear earth-shattering. However, they have done much to help me look at society somewhat differently, and to organize my own process thinking in ways that have proved rewarding, even though they have not permeated the protective belt that surrounds the conventional wisdom.

My attempt to give these organizing ideas a second kick at the can may be futile, but I am convinced that they deserve it.

In closing, a forewarning is in order. Those papers correspond to a period when the conventional wisdom, based on a propensity to centralize and to rely on the state for guidance, was being questioned but remained somewhat hegemonic. The reader may detect the toxic influence of the conventional wisdom remaining present at this first stage on the road to collaborative governance. I have not attempted to fine brush off these juvenile Keynesian whiffs, but the reader is invited to exercise caution since many flats and sharps are applied to Keynesian-type arguments in the rest of the book.

References

J. Akerman, *Ekonomics Theori II*. Lund: CWK Gleerups Forlag, 1944 (traduction française Paris : Presses Universitaires de France, 1955).

H. Katouzian, *Ideology and Method in Economics*. New York: New York University Press, 1980.

G. Vickers, *The Art of Judgment*. London: Methuen. 1965

G. Vickers, *Values Systems and Social Process*. Penguin Books. 1968

Chapter 1

Ill-structured problems and experimental intelligence

*"Lecturing on navigation while
the ship is going down..."*
– W. H. Auden

Introduction

In his L. T. Hobhouse Memorial Lecture of 1957, Alexander Macbeath posed a question which is fundamental to all work in the social sciences: can social policies be rationally tested? I have implicitly answered the question with a cautious affirmative. This has allowed me to proceed to the next question of interest: how can it be done?

In the first section, I clarify the idea of social science and specify the boundaries of social policy, and I suggest that a new collaboration between researchers and policy makers is necessary if the ill-structured problems we are facing are going to be successfully tackled.

In a second section, I argue that one cannot separate the regulative (goal + control) from the innovative (intelligence + innovation) functions in policy-making, and that there is a need for a shift in favor of the latter. This leads to a redefinition of the role of social science research: social science must adopt experimental intelligence à la Dewey and transduction as its methods, and institution-building must play a stronger role in policy-making (Hughes 1965:52).

In the third section, I try to explain why social sciences have been so unsuccessful in shaping policy in Canada. My claim is that too often the expertise that many social scientists have brought to bear on social policy is largely bogus. Mishan has singled out transport economists (Mishan 1967: 97) as his preferred target. My point is that, to a certain extent, his argument can legitimately be extended to all social scientists.[1] This leads me to speculate on the optimal use of the social sciences for public policy.

The new interface researcher-policy-maker

Social science is a "practice": a set of procedures regarded in Wilson's words (1970: xv), as "the best way we know of investigating" social reality. However imperfect the current procedures may be, an archaeology of the social sciences would reveal that, since the nineteenth century, these inexact sciences have become more potent. (Helmer and Rescher, 1960) From the observation-only stage and the assemblage of information, to the construction of more and more complex classification schemes, to the development of functional relationships, the social sciences have matured. They have developed from empirical sciences into formal ones, from a body of information into a language of problem solution.[2]

In the words of Rapoport (1965: 208), "the making of social science... depends on the creation of scientific models to replace the metaphors in which so much discourse about social matters is still couched." Over recent years, the construction of such models has been the main activity of most social scientists, and they have moved steadily away from concern with superficial analogies to interest in more meaningful homologies.[3]

The language-of-problem-solution of social scientists

The language-of-problem-solution developed by the social scientist is often quite different from the unspecialized language in which citizens and other social actors couch their problems. This has led to charges of esoteric mannerisms and unrealism. To a large extent, these charges are well-founded. Since Kant, obscurity has acquired some respectability, and from the premise that "profound reasoning is difficult to understand", obscurity has often been taken as evidence of profundity. (Medawar 1967: 9-10).

But too much concern for strict adherence to all aspects of reality, and too much limitation on the development of a specialized language to deal with it, may grind the scientific inquiry to a halt. Da Vinci was unable to construct a flying machine because he was trying to produce it in the image of a bird. His planes resembled birds so much they could not fly. A bird with fixed wings and a propelling beak proved a much better simulator of the "real" thing than a straight copy.

The social scientist has to develop a set of concepts and categories which will enable him to proceed efficiently with his model-building. In the same way that the Inuit, in order to survive, require a wide variety of words to identify different types of snow, social scientists need an elaborate operational vocabulary for their problem-solving. The social scientist's activity amounts to the assemblage of information and the development of concepts enabling him to produce useful classifications and functional relations.

But, with the speeding up of technological change, and the emergence of a society which has become essentially temporary (Bennis and Slater, 1968), attention has shifted away from social functioning back to the social structure, with a view to using knowledge to effect organizational and institutional change.(Bennis,1964-1965)

The required collaboration of researcher and policy-maker

In this new context, the social scientist is not merely an observer of the social reality or some sort of diagnostician of malfunctioning in the system. He is a genuine social engineer designing new organizations and institutions. Social scientists are the new utopians (Boguslaw, 1965), whose function it is to redesign the social system in order to facilitate social change in a turbulent environment. (Emery and Trist, 1965)

But, if social scientists are to perform such a task, they need criteria by which to gauge their designing activity. Applied social science is a deliberate and collaborative effort of the researcher and the manager to improve the operations of the system. It is not sufficient for the man of knowledge to proffer a rational solution, for the owl to tell the grasshopper that, to avoid the severe pains of winter, he simply has to turn himself into a cricket and hibernate. (Bennis, et at, 1961: 3) This does not quite satisfy the client who might legitimately ask how one goes about performing such a metamorphosis.

The interface between the social scientist and the social policy maker has changed considerably as both the social sciences and social policy underwent radical changes in the period after World War II. For, as the social scientists turned themselves into social engineers, social policy emerged from the doldrums of welfare statism to take on a broader and more dynamic meaning.

Evolving notions of social policy and difficulties of collaboration

In the past, it was not easy for social scientists to collaborate with social policy makers, for policy makers appeared not too clear about the nature of their task. As late as 1965, T. H. Marshall could write "'social policy' is not a technical term with an exact meaning."(Marshall, 1965)

Although the exact meaning of "social policy" was unclear, the term was very clearly linked to the broad concept of the welfare state. This meant orientation, mainly in the name of charity and philanthropy, toward the well-being of those elements in society that were exposed to contingencies. (Frank, 1967) As we moved toward a post-industrial society, there was a need to go beyond this alleviative approach, and so the state redefined its action: away from a strictly passive and alleviative *post factum* approach, toward an active social engineering to ensure that each citizen gets fully "developed"[4]

This shift in the nature of social policy toward social development (i.e., toward a situation where the individual is perceived as having a right to maturation, learning, and extended adaptability, and in which social policy is directed at removing arrest, retardation, and waste) is now largely accepted, and has been promoted by diverse bodies, although usually in a diversity of idioms.[5]

In an attempt to define the boundaries of this new social policy — boundaries which go much beyond charitable gestures and welfare policies, but which obviously do not encompass all of public policy — and the common thread that unites all aspects of it, Kenneth Boulding (1970) has used a broad view of social dynamics, defined as a three-fold genetic evolutionary process. It involves a threat system (mainly studied by political scientists), an exchange system (mainly studied by economists), and an integrative system (supposedly studied by sociologists, social work and the like). According to Boulding, any concrete social organization can be regarded as an assemblage of processes of the three types, although the valence of each system may differ significantly from organization to organization.

The common thread that unites all aspects of social policy is the "integrative system": "this includes those aspects of social life that are characterized not so much by exchange in which a *quid* is got for a *quo*, as by unilateral transfers that are justified by some kind of appeal to a status, or legitimacy, or identity or community" (Boulding, 1967: 7) The problem is to recognize that "in any situation, there is an optimum degree of integration" (Ibid: 8), while acknowledging that we have very little theory of the over-all system and very little information even on its current performance.

We know more about the exchange system than about either the threat or the integrative system. Consequently, we can say more as social scientists about economic policy than about social policy, for instance. But the developmental philosophy *en émergence* provides us first with a useful dynamic guidepost. As long as social policy had no exact meaning, it was hardly surprising that we could generate no exact policy suggestions. Now that the notion of social policy is more clearly specified, we should be able to seek models of the "social market" in the same way as we have for the "economic market." Richard Titmuss (1968), in his usual candid way, has already volunteered an eight-point categorization of the task facing social policy makers – one that encompasses "not only goal-formulation but administrative processes, historical change, and methods of delivering, measuring and evaluating services and systems" – devolved to social science research in connection with social policy.[6]

Until now, the dialectics researcher-manager has been undermined by ill-specified conceptions from both sides. If this were the main reason for a poor inter-creation process between social scientists and social administrators, we might now have some hope. But this assumes that social scientists are able to make a positive contribution to the operations of social policy, and that what has prevented such a contribution up to now are mainly what Guetzkow (1959) calls "conversion barriers."

Social science research as an evaluative instrument: two broad approaches

In what ways can social science research be of help to the social policy administrator, given the present state of the art in the social sciences, and the elusiveness of the social policy situation? One could imagine a variety of types of research inputs and a diversity of devices to plug them into the policy process. Each such cross-classification would correspond to a specific theory of policy.

Since it is not our purpose to provide a primer on praxeology (Kotarbinski 1965; Kaufman, 1968), we will be satisfied to identify the policy-maker's major areas of concern without getting involved in an extensive discussion of the many ways in which these could be differently labeled.

Goal + control *versus* intelligence + innovation

One might identify the major areas of concern to the policy-maker under four headings, as per Wilensky (1967): goal setting; control; innovation; intelligence. A few words may be in order on the exact nature of these four categories of issues.

Goal setting raises the problem of the organization's objectives. There is in this context an optimum degree of secrecy. "The art of bluff and deception with respect to goals is part of the art of administration." But the real reason for embarrassment here is, in Gross's terms (1965), "the lack of well-developed language of organizational purposefulness."

Control has to do with getting the work done. It is more in line with operations analysis. To the extent that an objective function can be ground out by the goal-setters, a "rational" strategy can be produced. This rationality can be either technical or administrative. It is fair to say that up to now the process of control has been mainly reduced to the manipulation of so-called modifiable variables, so as to maximize some specified function subject to well-defined constraints.

While control refers mainly to an organization's problems of functioning, **innovation** refers to the system design, and to the change in the organizational structure and in the administrative arrangements. **Intelligence** refers to the problem of gathering, processing, interpreting and communicating the technical and political information needed in the decision-making process.

While the traditional approach to policy-making has largely emphasized the first two components, much of the recent literature has questioned the usefulness of such a focus and has tended to put more emphasis on the latter two components.

It would appear that the social scientists have come to realize that, for the time being at least, this second approach is more to the point, and for two interrelated reasons. The social sciences can neither properly reduce social policy to well-structured problems amenable to a simple control procedure, nor provide a language of organizational purposefulness which could help the policy-maker to clarify his goals *ex ante*. This makes the traditional approach somewhat less than helpful. However, an alternative approach, based on intelligence and innovation, has not really been fully spelled out yet. We suggest that enough elements are now available for us to attempt a preliminary synthesis. This would constitute a cybernetic theory of policy originating with the intelligence function, mainly process-oriented, and providing the goal setting (if any) *post factum*. The cornerstone of this theory of policy would be the notion of norm-holding.[7]

Ill-structured problems need a research strategy

If social development can be regarded as the norm (i.e., the broad direction of social policy) we are still very far from a set of precise targets which could be inserted into a function to be maximized, subject to constraints. The conflicts between the utopian cast of mind of the philosopher-king, and the piecemeal experimentation à la Lindblom, are still unresolved.[8]

It would therefore be premature to attempt a translation of this "sense of direction" into a set of specific goals which could then be subjected to operations-research type controls for their effective realization. A more realistic approach starts from the assumption that the problem of social policy is still largely ill-structured, recognizes that the social policy administrators have to operate in a rather turbulent environment, and seeks to define a philosophy of social policy which steers a course between mindless incrementalism and premature utopianism. This requires from the social sciences something more than the present set of operations-research type tools, which postulate the existence of well-defined goals and well-specified constraints. If the problem is ill-defined, it requires a research strategy adapted to it.[9]

Quasi-analytic methods and the learning process

Between the well-structured problem, requiring only the working out of an algorithm and the use of operations research methods, and the completely unstructured problem, based on the heuristic method of the classical social scientist drawing mainly on intuition, each case on its own merit, there is the whole field of the ill-structured problems, which calls for "a compromise between the well-structured methods of operations research and the unstructured method of the heuristic approach". This is the family of quasi-analytic methods suggested by H. I. Ansoff, (1960) [10]

The quasi-analytic methods are process-oriented, rather than outcome-oriented, as are the usual operations-research methods. This is the crucial difference: it emphasizes the continuous feedback between analysis and problem formulation, thus creating a self-correcting theory of organization.

Since the problem formulation itself is open, the evaluative function involves the designing of an information system to provide the medium for effective feedback between analysis and problem-formulation. The interplay among norm-setting, goal-setting, course-holding, control on functioning, and organizational and institutional innovations becomes fundamentally dependent on organizational intelligence. The medium of the monitoring device becomes a major factor in the shaping of the message. Instead of the standard surveillance, we are faced with a genuine learning process generating a self-organizing system.[11]

In this dynamic context of ill-structured problems, the notion of evaluation is completely changed. The difference between ends and means, between blueprints and little steps, between policy objectives and the social technology which is set up to pursue them, is blurred, and the social scientists involved in the policy process gain more power and more responsibility.[12]

Instead of a set of goals exogenously determined, the *desiderata* emerge from the exploration of the feasible. To explore, one starts with a highly tentative initial formulation and through a strong feedback mechanism learns, and then constructs a local plausible theory for the phenomena under study while erecting the social technology to steer the system and organize it, rather than simply regulating it.

This cybernetic formulation of policy-making is a learning process which hinges on the intelligence function.[13] There is, therefore, some urgency in the need to refurbish accordingly the concepts and the categories used by social scientists to provide the necessary instruments to operationalize this new primacy of the intelligence function.

Transduction, experimental utopia, and simulation

The "new social scientist" will require a good knowledge of a new conceptual framework, of new search processes, and of new testing techniques which take a fuller account of the nature of the problem at hand. This is not the place for a complete review of this arsenal, but it might be helpful to review a few of its pieces, if only to fix ideas. We shall say a few words about transduction, experimental utopia, and simulation – all of which are at the core of this revolutionized social science.

Transduction (what Roger Martin would call abductive reasoning) refers to an intellectual operation which differs from induction or deduction and which "élabore et construit un objet théorique, un objet possible et cela à partir d'informations portant sur la réalité ainsi que d'une problématique posée par cette réalité. La transduction suppose un feedback incessant entre le cadre conceptuel utilisé et les observations empiriques ... Elle introduit la rigueur dans l'invention et la connaissance dans l'utopie"[14]

This form of reasoning is congruent with the quasi-analytic method of Ansoff, and constitutes a valuable way to incorporate into the thought process the learning dimension which is crucial to the dynamic monitoring we are interested in. Instead of the ordinary model construction and statement of hypotheses, we have a form of reasoning which calls for feedback between problem formulation and analysis from a preliminary and highly tentative point of departure.

This formal procedure is fed, so to speak, by experimental utopia. If by utopia we mean the exploration of lateral possibilities (Ruyer, 1950: 9), experimental utopia refers to "l'exploration du possible humain avec l'aide de l'image et de l'imaginaire, accompagnée d'une incessante critique et d'une incessante référence à la problématique donnée dans le réel. L'utopie expérimentale déborde l'usage habituel de l'hypothèse dans les sciences sociales." (Lefebvre, 1961: 192). This method wishes to invent new forms, but they are new concrete forms; consequently, it uses variations around the theme defined by reality.[15]

In this process of transduction, properly fed by experimental utopia, the cost of exploring and of thinking may be much less than the cost of experimenting. One way to dramatically reduce such costs is to use simulation techniques,[16] which allow a research worker to try out his proposed technology on alternative artificially-generated environments, or to try out alternative social technologies in a given environment without having to conduct the "real" experiment. Enough experiments have been conducted for us to regard such methods as very reliable approximations.

A compendium of transduction-cum-experimental utopia-cum-simulation would appear to constitute a viable strategy of dynamic monitoring of social policy, which accommodates the ill-structured nature of the problem very well, the new trends in the social sciences, and the stronger role of innovation and intelligence in the contribution of social science to economic and social administration. It also leads to a superior approach to these eight tasks of social scientists suggested by Titmuss.

Redesigning as central function

The outcome of such dynamic monitoring will be a rather innovative learning process and an improving system design rather than a static information feedback.[17] This leads one to ponder on the type of redesigning of the present system of social policy which is likely to develop as this new dynamic monitoring becomes prevalent.

Many forms of approaches would appear to be possible: the formalist approach (based on the use of models), the heuristic approach (based on certain principles guiding actions), the operating unit approach (based on carefully selected people and equipment) and the ad hoc approach (based on the current situation).[18]

My contention is that the formalist approach appears unhelpful, or, if one is really optimistic, premature. The "muddling through"-cum-"seat-of-the-pants" techniques implied by ad-hocery are also rather unhelpful, if only because they are parcellary and myopic. The choice facing us in emergent situations and in a turbulent environment is therefore between the heuristic and operating units approach, rooted in a set of principles, or in a selection of flexible components. This latter solution clearly limits the evolution of the system unduly, as well as its capacity to deal with a changing environment (if the components' performance is reliable), or limits the controllability of the system (if the components are self-sufficient).[19] Heuristic system design would therefore appear to be *a priori* the preferred approach. The central task is for the social scientist to erect heuristic designs on the basis of the developmental principle as discussed earlier.

Can the social sciences demonstrate that the learning process triggered by such dynamic monitoring will lead to "better" results than those achievable by administrative rules of thumb? Boulding and many others suggest that such is the case. But since, as Boulding says (1967: 9), "we have very little theory of the overall system and practically no overall apparatus for collecting, processing and feeding back information," and since no good feedback apparatus exists between analysis and problem-formulation in social policy, there is little hope that the present haphazard and ad hoc practices will soon disappear.

It may well be that, as a transition strategy, one will have to rely on the operating unit approach: the involvement of key individuals ready to get close to where the action is, and interested in putting themselves in a position to get the ear of the prince. Indeed, one might say that this is now current practice. It may turn out to be the least objectionable way to effect those organizational and institutional changes necessary to improve social policy. While the involvement of social scientists as entrepreneurs in social change is not without creating some unease among the liberal-minded intelligentsia, it may turn out to be the only viable and effective strategy while we organize better ways for citizens to participate in social development. If the alternative is an organizational standstill in a period of accelerating change, I, for one, would accept this option as a second-best solution. It is hoped that the competition between these entrepreneurs in social change will prevent the system from being launched on a disastrous course, and on this, "my hopes are as good as your fears," as Macbeath would put it.[20]

Dynamic monitoring of social policy in Canada

The incredible ignorance that we have of the circumstances, the significance, and the effectiveness of social science research as an instrument to evaluate and to improve social policy is a shield behind which all possible positions can comfortably hide.

But, on the whole, if asked whether one can ascribe responsibility for great successes and failures in Canadian social policy (understood to be dealing with the integrative system) to social science research, one would have to say that the answer is no.[21] This is due to a number of factors: in part to the fact that too many Canadian social scientists have withdrawn to their Ivory Towers; in part because whenever they have jumped in, their expertise has too often proved irrelevant, if not completely bogus; and, in part to the fact that, when the few who had the capacity and will to monitor the system and to improve the social technology have become active, this has often not triggered important social improvements because of failures in the action programs, at the political and social leadership level, and in the functioning of institutions.

Why so much unsuccess?

While it is difficult to apportion blame among these three families of causes, social scientists would be ill-advised to ascribe all of the blame to the lack of political leadership. The effectiveness of social science research for social policy depends on the channels into which its results are plugged, and it is the responsibility of the social science research system to ensure that its output reaches the decision-maker, i.e., the person or group who has the policy levers. It is not sufficient for the social scientist to translate the problem into a language of problem solution and to solve it: he must also translate his answers into a language of persuasion, and ensure that it reaches the decision-maker. Given the serious lack of "social engineers" (so to speak) – brokers between scientists and practitioners – the social science apparatus is flawed.

Some may question this proposition by reciting a few success stories; others have argued that, while it may be factually correct, it is a misleading conclusion derived from an insufficient appreciation of the lag between social science expenditures in Canada and its impact on policy. Without denying the few success stories, or rejecting entirely the existence of long lags between ideas and policies, it would be scandalous to continue to pump additional money into social science research in the name of improvement to social policy without insuring that it will indeed provide some help. To do more of the same, without such assurance is not reasonable.

The solution, therefore, is not increased financial support, but a transformation of social science research to enable it to contribute to the evaluation and the improvement of social policy. Science, social or not, "is not only an exciting adventure for scholars and a technique for economic expansion, it is also an essential part of the social organism and must continuously evolve under the influence of social conditions" (Dubos, 1970: 17).

Experimentation

The emergence of a mood of experimentation is a good omen. The issuing of White Papers and the setting up of special committees of the House of Commons or the Senate on certain aspects of social policy, the spreading practice of task-forcing, and the greater use of planned non-permanent institutions to deal with certain issue domains have all contributed to providing some interplay between the analysis and the problem formulation. They also have prevented the premature and/or permanent crystallization of institutions, at a time when the issue area had been still insufficiently explored.[22]

But governments' willingness to experiment must be matched by a willingness on the part of social scientists to take part in these experiments. Before the government starts pouring additional money into social science research, and hiring a herd of social scientists, both parties must agree on the broad outline of an interface between the social sciences and social policy. "A new deal must be negotiated between the politician and the social scientist." (Lamontagne, 1969: 4837)

As to the content of this new deal, it might first entail the setting up of a forum where the guiding principles would be hammered out, and the norms set. Second, this new deal would require some loci both within and without government where the dialectics administrator-researcher could take place.

There exists a diversity of models for the sort of forum suggested above. Arthur Stinson (1968) reviewed a number of them, and he even delineated the contours of a Canadian Institute for Social Development. One might follow Bertrand de Jouvenel (1964) and sketch a "forum prévisionnel"; another possibility would be a Council of Social Values (Paquet 1968). In all cases, these forums would be future-oriented, and they would contribute to the expansion of the "arts de conseil" that de Jouvenel suggested would grow exponentially (de Jouvenel, 1964: 346) in the second half of the 20th century.

New loci for the policy multilogue

As for the locus where the dialectics administrator-researcher might unfold inside and outside the public administration, it calls for a system composed of different types of organizations dealing with various types of problems at different levels in specialized settings. In 1964, the Council of the Tavistock Institute of Human Relations prepared a document which might helpfully serve as a frame of reference in designing the optimal social science research machinery for Canada. This document spells out a useful classification scheme of the characteristics of the main types of research organizations, and puts forward a plausible and feasible system of institutions which could be established over the next few decades in Great Britain. This might constitute a useful point of departure for the elaboration of a Canadian mix of organizations likely to best meet our needs.

There already exist both within and outside of the government establishment a number of viable units with diverse vocations.[23] Their usefulness would be greatly enhanced by a grouping and balancing of the disciplines and activities into a set of only partially overlapping units covering the whole policy space (client-based units focusing on the research-services interface at the concrete level; university departments focusing on abstract work at the interface of research and teaching; special-issues institutes with a research-applications focus and dealing with generic problems). The different matching of outside units with inside commandos should ensure that the policy multilogue can be effectively carried out on the basis of this new deal between the social scientist and the social administrator, and of the coordination of these loci for the policy multilogue around a sort of Council of Social Values. Social scientists are bound to become more effectively present in the government operations in this way. It will remain for them to prove their usefulness.

Once we have better social science data and a refurbished social science arsenal on many fronts as a result of new loci, it might be time to produce an annual social report on the Canadian scene, one which would go much further than the premature one produced in the United States. (Olson, 1969; U.S. Department of Health, Education, and Welfare, 1969) This would generalize to the country as a whole "an orderly framework for our thought" on social policy. One might then even be adventurous enough to conceive of a Council of Social Advisors, along the lines suggested by Bertram Gross.

Conclusion: an experimentalist approach to accelerated change

Both social policy and social science research have evolved over the last few decades and their interface is not as clearly understood as one would like. Social policy encompasses the whole integrative system, and poses ill-structured problems to social scientists. If social science research has matured, its expertise still pertains almost exclusively to "established" rather than "emergent" situations. (Boguslaw, 1961)

There is now a pressing need to bridge this gap. The old division of labor between goal and norm-setting, control, evaluation, and innovation does not seem to fit present day policy-making processes. A new deal must be negotiated between the politician and the social scientist that might allow the social scientist to indulge in heuristic system design on the basis of only some guiding principles of social action. Recognizing fully the very tentative nature of his hypotheses, the social scientist would require strong feedback between his problem-formulation and the ongoing analysis. By a practical use of experimental utopia and simulation techniques, he could explore the lateral possibilities derivable from his original hypotheses, and examine their desirability.

This process-oriented analysis blurs the traditional difference between innovation and control-monitoring, but it appears to be the only effective response to the accelerated change which identifies our temporary society. Up to now, in Canada as well as in France (Crozier, 1970), research social scientists have had little impact on the conduct of social policy. This is largely due to their mal-adaptation. In a slow-motion society, one could study the functioning of institutions in a strict positivistic manner, but in a temporary society, social scientists' very mode of reasoning has to be altered, and priority must be given to experimentation. A few successful preliminary experiments in Canada have led us to believe that the time is ripe for what Crozier calls (Ibid: 17) "les premiers essais expérimentaux au niveau d'organisations ou d'institutions complexes". We have sketched some of the elements which must be considered in tackling the social policy system in this manner.

Endnotes

[1]   This is not to deny that the social sciences have made important breakthroughs over the last century. One could indeed point to major achievements in the twentieth century. For instance, see K. W Deutsch, S. Platt, D. Senghass (1971) who provide an analysis of 62 such advances since 1900. The issue here has to do with the usefulness and the effective use of such social science achievements to solve social problems and to design social policy.

[2]   For a simple and illuminating discussion of the stages of scientific activity, see Kuhn, 1963, Ch. 3.

[3]   "Le progrès de la connaissance consiste pour une part à écarter les analogies superficielles et à découvrir des parentés profondes, moins visibles peut-être, mais plus importantes et significatives...déterminer des correspondances souterraines, invisibles, inimaginables pour le profane:' (Caillois, 1960:9, 17) See also Kelly, 1963.

[4]   Eric Trist develops those ideas very clearly in the Proceedings of the Senate Committee on Science Policy, 1st Session, 25th Parliament, 1968-69, No. 39, March 29, 1969, pp. 4794-4820. This vocabulary has now passed into the government's language—see the White Paper on Unemployment Insurance, Ottawa, 1970.

[5]   See *A Comprehensive Statement on Social Welfare for Canada*, Canadian Welfare Council, May, 1967; also Manning, 1967. A review of the structure of benefits in different countries in the United Nations Yearbook shows that as the resources available increase (i.e., as the countries get richer) the mix of benefits shifts toward a relatively more development-intensive policy, although both components (welfare and development) are obviously higher in richer than in poorer countries.

[6]   Titmuss's eight points (1968: 22-23) read as follows:

"1. The analysis description of policy formation and its consequences, intended and unintended.

2. The study of structure, function, organization, planning and administrative process of institutions and agencies, historical and comparative.

3. The study of social needs and of the problems of access to utilization and patterns of outcome of services, transactions and transfers.

4. The analysis of the nature, attributes and distribution of social costs and diswelfares.

5. The analysis of distributive and allocative patterns in command-over-resources-through-time and the particular impact of the social services.

6. The study of the roles and functions of elected representatives, professional workers, administrators and interest groups in operation and performance of social welfare institutions.

7. The study of the social rights of the citizen as contributor, participant and user of social services.

8. The study of the role of government (local and central) as an allocator of values and of rights to social property as expressed through social and administrative law and other rule-making channels."

7   For an example of the traditional literature, see Lerner and Lasswell, 1951. As to the more recent directions, the importance of intelligence, the shift from goal-setting to norm-setting and holding and policy-making as a learning process, see Vickers, 1965.

8   A simple sketch of these polar approaches has been presented by Gordon, 1970 (Ch. 3). He titles this chapter very aptly— "Blueprints vs. Little Steps"

9   Ansoff (1960) specifies the adjustments to the method of analysis which are necessary when the problem is ill-structured. We shall refer to this very important paper later on.

10   It may be characterized in Ansoff's words as follows (1960: 230):

(a) It is process- rather than goal-oriented. Rather than comparing the likely outcomes of various alternative strategies, it emphasizes comparison of their characteristics (thus inferring likely outcomes);

(b) It utilizes qualitative judgments, embedded within the problem structure;

(c) It maintains continuous feedback between analysis and problem formulation, thus constructing a self-correcting theory of the business, as it proceeds. (The model of the whole cannot be made explicit in advance of the solution, but only in terms of symbolic relations between variables);

(d) It treats several (often mutually exclusive) business objectives simultaneously until a set of dominant alternatives is found;

(e) It divides strategic business problems into (1) external (concerned with the firm's opportunities in its environment) and (2) internal (concerned with the firm's strengths, and weaknesses); it divides each such problem further into its quantitative and qualitative sub-problems;

(f) It arrives at a family of solutions by successively narrowing the field of alternatives by means of eliminating criteria;

(g) It arrives at a final solution by applying some weighting procedure to the residual set of alternatives;

(h) It emphasizes comprehensiveness and validity by abstracting the real-life situation (rather than precision and mathematical formulation);

(i) It is neither well-structured (as the operations research approach), nor unstructured (as the heuristic approach), but rather ill-structured. It is thus methodical without being mathematically rigorous.

11   The self-organizing system is genuinely a learning system and as Sir Geoffrey Vickers puts it "the future of our society depends on the speed with which it can learn" (op. cit. p. 233) Much of this new function of organizational intelligence lies in the capacity it has to speed up the process. The idea of "experimental intelligence" and of "socially organized intelligence" was already clearly spelled out by John Dewey in 1935. Social scientists, however, abandoned the path of social

experimentation after the 1930s. Consequently, the interest of the policymaker diminished. According to Fred Harris (1970:3), commenting on the U.S. situation, "in 1938 the social sciences received 24 percent of total government expenditures for research. By 1950 this had diminished to about 8 percent, and for the last ten years the social sciences have been allocated between 3½ and 5 percent of federal funds for research".

12   Social policy becomes the nexus of social science and social ethics. Since the norm setting replaces in some way the old goal setting, social scientists must recognize their increased responsibility. However, the paucity of social-ethical reflections is such that much of this exercise is solely guided by a sort of "technological rationality" emerging from the modeling exercises themselves. This is the basis of the sharp critique proposed by Winter, 1966. For a primer on the ethics of large scale systems, see Churchman, 1968, Part III.

13   What is involved here is a dialectical process which eliminates the usual "chronological point at which the formulation ends and the data-gathering and analysis," and policy-making (we could add), begin. (Ansoff, op. cit., p. 242)

14   Lefebvre, 1968: 121. This refers to a form of reasoning which is in full accord with the quasi-analytical methods required by the ill-structured problems of social policy. Moreover, the idea has credibility because it has been supported by both theoretical and applied work. On the first point, see Mandelbrot (1953: 43); on the second front, see Lefebvre in *Du rural à l'urbain.* (Paris, 1970, pp. 129-140)

15   It is interesting to note that although the label is new, the process involved in experimental utopia is rather well rooted in the literature of the 1930s. A careful reading of John Dewey's *Liberalism and Social Action* (1935) reveals that "the method of experimental intelligence" and "social experimentation" in social policy had already been broadly sketched by the 1930s.

16   There is already an extensive literature on the subject. Over the wide range of viewpoints on it, we have picked three: de Jouvenel, 1964: 361ff; Barton, 1970; Naylor, 1971.

17   For an examination of the possible way in which one could formalize the process of development and the self-steering of a system, see Lange, 1965.

18   Boguslaw, op. cit. Note especially that heuristic does not have in this context its usual dictionary meaning. The word is taken here "to denote any principle or device that contributes to the reduction in the average search to solution" (p. 15)

19   For some reason, this approach (although I explicitly regard it as a second best) has been interpreted by some readers of this paper as the favored approach, the one which would obviously give maximum leverage to the expert who would be able to get the ear of the prince. Indeed, while it may be easier and desirable for an entrepreneur in social change to operate this way, it may be undesirable from the point of view of the system. But as a second-best procedure, it should not be discarded. On the other hand, "outside advisors" are not and cannot be regarded by healthy government organizations as anything more than a second-best answer to their problem of dynamic adaptation. See DesRoches, 1970.

20   On the new role of social scientists as entrepreneurs in social change, see Breton and Breton, 1969; also Davis and North, 1970. See also Bennis, 1964. It might be worth adding that in some sense this second-best approach has often proved a better way to plug social science research results of interest into social policy than the usual commission studies. Some of the comments of Dr. Otto Larsen on the effectiveness of the U.S. Commission on Obscenity and Pornography would tend

to support this view. Even if we were to be able to bring about a more open instrumentation for smooth social change and social development, it will be necessary to ensure that the dialectics researcher-manager is as close as in the case of the operating unit approach.

[21] David W. Slater has answered in the same manner to an analogous question posed about economic research and economic policy (1967). Since it is well recognized that both the economic theory and the economic information system are more sophisticated than the theories and information apparati in the other social sciences, Slater's conclusion is bound to hold a fortiori for the other social sciences. The question, I repeat, is not to deny that there is some social science knowledge that could be used, but to reiterate that, in the same way that the universities did not participate in the Renaissance, the social scientists have been and are of little use to social activists and social administrators in the designing of social policy. The problem was stated unambiguously by Martin Luther King (1968), "One reason some advances were made in the South during the past decade was the discovery by Northern whites of the brutal fact of Southern segregated life. It was the Negro who educated the nation by dramatizing the evils through non-violent protest. The social scientist played little or no role in disclosing truth."

[22] Neither the White Papers, nor the committees, nor the task forces, nor the creation of "temporary" departments (Department of Urban Affairs, for instance) are really a panacea. It constitutes, however, an opening of the dialectics researcher-manager to new possibilities. Social scientists have often not reacted at all to the challenge of the policy-maker in his White Papers; too often, they have used the task forces as vehicles to pursue their own (sometimes irrelevant) researches, rather than as a chance to explore anew a problem field and to provide the policy-maker with a new frame of reference; they have also used the new-born more impatient departments as more naive providers of research monies, without realizing what their precise vocation was. No autopsy of those experiments has been performed yet. The idea of a Council of Social Values (of a restricted sort) was first put forward by Hansen, (1960:91). I developed the idea a bit in a paper on "The Economic Council as Phoenix" (1968).

[23] A review of some of the existing institutions from the Canadian Council on Urban and Regional Research to the Canadian Council on Rural Development via the Institute for the Quantitative Analysis of Social and Economic Policy of the University of Toronto has been presented by Stinson (1968). Some of the very recent experiences in Ottawa (Treasury Board, Department of Finance, Unemployment Insurance Commission, Department of Housing and Urban Development), demonstrate that the politicians are more receptive to setting up a fifth column of social scientists close to policy-making.

References

H.I. Ansoff,. "A quasi-analytic method for long-range planning." In C. W. Churchman and M. Verhulst (Eds.), *Management Sciences—Models and Techniques*. London: Pergamon Press, 1960.

R.F. Barton, *A Primer on Simulation and Gaming*. Englewood Cliffs, N.J.: Prentice-Hall, 1970.

W.G. Bennis et al. (Eds.), *The Planning of Change*. New York: Holt, Rinehart, and Winston, 1961.

W.G. Bennis, "A new role for the behavioral sciences: effecting organizational change"*Administrative Science Quarterly*, 8, 1964, 125-165.

W.G. Bennis, P. E. Slater, *The Temporary Society*. New York: Harper and Row, 1968.

R. Boguslaw, "Situation analysis and the problem of action" *Social Problems*, 8, 1961, (Winter): 212-219.

R. Boguslaw, *The New Utopians*. Englewood Cliffs, N.J.: Prentice-Hall, 1965.

K.E. Boulding, "The boundaries of social policy" *Social Work*, 12, 1967.

K.E. Boulding, *A Primer on Social Dynamics*. New York: Free Press, 1970.

A. Breton, R. Breton, "An economic theory of social movements." *American Economic Review*, 59, 1969 (May): 198-205.

R. Caillois, *Méduse et Cie*. Paris: Gallimard, 1960.

Canada White Paper on Unemployment Insurance. Ottawa: Queen's Printer.

Canadian Welfare Council 1967. *A Comprehensive Statement on Social Welfare for Canada*. Ottawa:. Queen's Printer, 1970.

C..W. Churchman, *Challenge to Reason*. New York: McGraw-Hill, 1968.

M.Crozier, *La Société Bloquée*. Paris: Editions du Seuil, 1970.

L. Davis, D.C. North, "Institutional change and American economic growth: A first step toward a theory of institutional innovation" *The Journal of Economic History*, 30, 1970, 131-149.

B. de Jouvenel, *L'Art de la Conjecture*. Monaco: Editions du Rocher, 1964.

J.M. DesRoches, "The developing irrelevance of formal organization patterns" *Optimum*, 20, 1970, 6-12.

K.W. Deutsch et al., "Conditions favoring major advances in social science" *Science*, 171 (5 February), 1971, 450-459.

J. Dewey, *Liberalism and Social Action*. New York: G. P. Putnam and Sons, 1935.

R. Dubos, *Reason Awake: Science for Man*. New York: Columbia University Press, 1970.

F.E. Emery, E. L. Trist, "The causal texture of organizational environments" *Human Relations*, 18, 1965, 21-32.

L.K. Frank, "The need for a new political theory." *Daedalus*: 96, 1967.

H.S. Gordon, *Social Science and Modern Man*. Toronto: University of Toronto Press, 1970.

B.M. Gross, "What are your organization's objectives?" *Human Relations*: 18, 1965, 195- 216.

H. Guetzkow, "Conversion barriers in using the social sciences:' *Administrative Science Quarterly*, 4, 1959, 68-81.

A.H. Hansen, *Economic Issues of the 1960's*. New York: McGraw-Hill, 1960.

F.R. Harris (Ed), *Social Science and National Policy*. Chicago: Aldine, 1970.

O. Helmer, N. Rescher, *On the Epistemology of the Inexact Sciences*. Santa Monica, Calif.: The Rand Corporation, 1960.

C.L. Hughes, *Goal Setting: Key to Individual and Organizational Effectiveness*. New York: American Management Association, 1965.

A. Kaufman, *The Science of Decision Making*. New York: McGraw-Hill, 1968.

G.A. Kelly, "The expert as historical actor." *Daedalus*, 92, 1963.

M.L. King,. "The role of the behavioral scientist in the civil rights movement" *Journal of of Social Issues*, 1968.

T. Kotarbinski, *Praxeology*. Oxford: Pergamon Press, 1965.

T. Kuhn, *The Study of Society*. Homewood, Ill.: The Dorsey Press, 1963.

M. Lamontagne, *The Proceedings of the Senate Committee on Science Policy*. First Session, 28th Parliament. (29 March 1969): 4837.

O. Lange, *Wholes and Parts*. Oxford: Pergamon Press, 1965.

H. Lefebvre, "Utopie expérimentale: pour un nouvel urbanisme" *Revue Française de Sociologie*, 2 (juillet-septembre 1961): 185-193.

H. Lefebvre, *Le Droit à La Ville*. Paris: Editions Anthropos, 1968.

H. Lefebvre, *Du rural à l'urbain*. Paris: Editions Anthropos, 1970.

D.Lerner, H. Lasswell (Eds.), *The Policy Sciences*. Stanford: Stanford University Press, 1951.

A. Macbeath, *Can Social Policies Be Rationally Tested?* London: Oxford University Press, 1957.

B. Mandelbrot, *Lecture de l'expérience*. Paris: Presses Universitaires de France, 1955.

E.C. Manning, *A White Paper on Human Resources Development*. Edmonton, Alberta: Queen's Printer, Province of Alberta, 1967.

T.H. Marshall, *Social Policy*. London: Hutchinson, 1965.

P.B. Medawar, *The Art of the Soluble*. London: Methuen, 1967.

E.L. Mishan, *The Costs of Economic Growth*. London: Staples Press, 1967.

T.H. Naylor, *Computer Simulation Experiments with Models of Economic Systems*. New York: John Wiley and Sons, 1971.

M. Olson Jr.,"The plan and purpose of a social report:" *The Public Interest*, 15 (Spring 1969): 85-97.

G. Paquet, "The Economic Council as Phoenix" In T. Lloyd and J. McLeod (Eds.), *Agenda 1970: Proposals for a Creative Politics*. Toronto: The University of Toronto Press, 1968, 135-158.

A. Rapoport, *Operational Philosophy: Integrating Knowledge into Action*. New York: Harper, 1965.

R. Ruyer, *L'Utopie et les utopies*. Paris: Presses Universitaires de France, 1950.

D.W. Slater, "Economic policy and economic research in Canada since 1950" *Queens Quarterly*, 74, 1967, 1-20.

A. Stinson, *Canadian Participation in Social Development*. Ottawa: mimeograph, 1968.

Tavistock Institute of Human Relations, *Social Research and a National Policy for Science*. London: Tavistock Institute, 1964.

R.M. Titmuss, *Commitment to Welfare*. New York: Pantheon Books, 1968.

E. Trist, The Proceedings of the Senate Committee on Science Policy. First Session, 28th Parliament. (29 March 1969): 4794-4820.

United States Department of Health, Education, and Welfare, *Toward a Social Report*. Washington, D.C.: U.S. Government Printing Office, 1969.

G. Vickers, *The Art of Judgment*. London: Chapman and Hall, 1965.

H.L. Wilensky, *Organizational Intelligence*. New York: Basic Books, 1967.

B.R. Wilson (Ed.), *Rationality*. London: Oxford University Press, 1970.

G. Winter,. *Elements for a Social Ethic*. New York: Macmillan, 1966.

Chapter 2

MRI for an arterio-sclerotic socio-economy

"A ground-map whose central markers are 'affairs'..."

–Raymond D. Boisvert about the work of John Dewey

Introduction

The Canadian socio-economy of the 1980s shared with other advanced western socio-economies a number of difficulties: slow or sluggish growth, high rates of inflation, gross underutilization of resources, a slow rate of capital accumulation, very slow productivity increase, and difficulties in effecting the adjustments called for by changes in the world economy. But Canada had a number of specific features that exacerbated the difficulty of resolving these problems: it is a small, open, dependent, and balkanized economy of the northern hemisphere that has developed a relative specialization in the export of raw materials within the international division of labour.

Many have argued that our rich natural resources endowment more than compensates for these specific difficulties, but they remain a small minority of Canadians. If anything, the net effect of our wealth of natural resources may have been to induce Canadians to believe that there is no need for developing adjustment policies at all.

A *pessimisme mesuré* has emanated from most discussions of the likely performance of the Canadian economy in the last decades of the 20th century. However, two points may not have been sufficiently emphasized. The first is the dependent character of our economy, and the constraints this imposes on the capacity to transform the Canadian economy: Canada is tied to one major trading partner, a partner that happens to control a substantial portion of private decision-making in the Canadian economy, and with whom much of our trade is intra-firm trade, i.e., trade via imperfect markets or non-market channels. The second characteristic is the relatively high degree of dissonance in the Canadian economy and in its socio-cultural underground: regional and ethnic tensions mediated by a balkanized state and the omnipresence of bargaining as an increasingly important decision-making mechanism that reveals our dramatic inability to concert.

A conceptual framework of the Canadian socio-economy

In order to pull together the different strands of argument, one can stylize the Canadian socio-economy as a going concern, as an "instituted process" in the sense of Karl Polanyi, a macroeconomic real-life process, evolving through time and defined by changing structures, rules of operation, organizational arrangements, and institutions. A central question is to understand how the socio-economy gets instituted differently from place to place and from time to time. This leads to the further questions: to what extent the Canadian socio-economy is likely to change, and why and how one might wish to interfere with this evolution.

The central feature of this definition of the Canadian socio-economy is that it is a process operating through time. The dynamics of this process are to harmonize values, plans, and preferences on the one hand, with resources on the other, subject to the geo-technical and social constraints imposed by the physical and social world environments. At any point in time, this process works according to certain rules of operations, and unfolds within sets of institutions that may hinder, deflect, or even stall the process.

The central mechanism of adjustment of a socio-economy through time is investment. While transitory changes in demand are accommodated by changes in the rates of output, changes in permanent external and internal demand trigger a process of capital accumulation in certain sectors. Such capital formation carries with it the introduction of new technologies and of modern and most recent best techniques, and therefore some increase in productivity.

Consequently, when one wishes to gauge the capacity of a socio-economy to adjust and transform, one has to examine the forces that shape the size and composition of capital formation. This in turn brings into the picture a whole spectrum of factors: from the impact of state intervention, the importance of the distribution of income, the nature and efficacy of finance and credit instruments, to the social conditions and business climate likely to reduce uncertainty.

There seems to be a general agreement that Canada is likely to continue to experience low rates of investment for a variety of reasons. This implies a limited capacity to transform the economy, and, over the longer haul, slow growth, unused capacity, and waste.

The challenge is to search for the sources and causes of this lack of investment, and to remove the impediments to a greater capacity of the Canadian economy to transform itself. As we shall see, this in turn leads us in a number of directions.

Scanning six basic sub-processes

The world economy is being restructured: the new international division of labour threatens Canada, both in its traditional inefficient sectors (through the competition of the newly industrializing countries) and in its more sophisticated sectors (through keener competition from advanced countries).

Because its socio-economy is small and open, Canada has to transform as fast as possible, but because it is dependent and balkanized it is unlikely to do so quickly. While the Canadian sclerosis can be ascribed to some degree to important extra-territorial determinants in decision-making via the multinationals, it is more essentially due to a lack of consensus about what might be a collaborative strategy of transformation. Canada is paralyzed by internal dissent, and by a tendency to make every issue a bargaining issue at the federal-provincial level.

The ensuing "institutional sclerosis" of the Canadian socio-economy should retard the transformation of the Canadian economy sufficiently for its growth path to fall even more significantly below its potential growth path than had been anticipated – enough to trigger even a reduction in the potential growth path. In order to understand why this is the most likely scenario, and why this may not be one the Canadian economy is condemned to live through, it is essential to look at the set of forces that are reducing the Canadian socio-economy's capacity to transform.

One of the main difficulties in analyzing the Canadian economy is that it is very difficult to regard it as a totality. The very diversity and heterogeneity of the Canadian socio-economy make national averages meaningless, and reference to the "Canadian instituted process" is rather unhelpful since the Canadian sub-units are instituted quite differently from place to place. On the other hand, the provincial/regional partitioning that has become accredited in data collection and in the political arena overestimates to a great extent the degree of homogeneity within, and of heterogeneity between these parts.

It is therefore more useful to analyze the Canadian socio-economy as a complex structured game and to decompose it into more or less separable sub-games that are quite different from the provincial/regional realities. The sub-processes or sub-games discussed here do not exhaust the Canadian reality, but it can be said that they may be the most important sub-processes, and that any serious reconstruction of the Canadian economy would have to deal with them. What is observed as a region is the composite effect of these different sets of forces: as if the sub-games were superposed transparencies cumulatively constructing the spatial patterns.

The demographic sub-process — The labour force has grown fairly rapidly in the first half of the 80s as a result of the Baby Boom, before the deceleration of the late 80s. The slow growth in the demand for labour as a result of the low level of capital accumulation has generated a high level of frustration among new entrants into the labour force, and among the new generation of potential managers whose vertical mobility will be considerably reduced.

Not only is this likely to generate a high level of discontent, and serious inter-generational conflicts (as younger and more qualified cohorts are condemned to revise their expectations), but it is also most unlikely that this reduction in labour demand will not reduce the growth rate of wages and salaries. To the extent that pricing decisions are based in a large segment of the economy on a mark-up over some assessment of normal costs, or to the extent that existing institutions like marketing boards facilitate the transmission of cost increases into price increases, one may expect continued inflationary pressures.

It remains very doubtful whether the ageing of the population and the increase in the average level of experience of the labour force will generate an upward pressure on productivity levels sufficient to counteract the reduction in the rate of capital accumulation, and the shift of activities towards the tertiary sector. Moreover, one may expect labour mobility among regions to continue to be curtailed.

The financial sub-process — The financial process is the set of activities and institutions regulating the mopping-up of savings, and allocating investment funds throughout the economy. The implicit assumption in good currency has been that our financial process is indeed very efficient, and that it is not the source of any significant impediments to the investment activities in Canada. But in the face of the evidence revealed by the hearings in connection with the decennial changes to the Bank Act, it is a rather surprising assumption. It may also be that, given the fact that so much of Canadian investment is financed through retained earnings, it is not perceived as a matter of paramount importance.

The fact is that the structure of our financial system is such that it has not really acted in the most efficient way to stimulate investment and capital formation in Canada. The financial system is suffering from a great deal of institutional sclerosis, and it would benefit immensely from increased competition. Moreover, the present institutional structure does not handle many financing functions, especially with regard to risk capital, well or at all.

It is not unfair to say that the snail's pace at which Canada has modified its financial system has left it somewhat out of pace with the needs of the day. The revision of the Bank Act every decade is entirely unreasonable in an economic world that is constantly in a process of change. Consequently, one might point to the inadequacies and the quasi-monolithic character of our financial system as one of the causes of the very slow growth of capital formation in Canada. The system is inefficient in mobilizing savings, and in allocating them through the Canadian economy in such a way as to increase the size and efficient allocation of investment in Canada. Experimentation with new financial institutions should boost the capital formation in small and medium-sized enterprises.

The production and exchange sub-process — Until the 1980s, economic activities have located in Canada, not so much as a result of comparative advantages, but as a result of protective tariffs, as part of the spatial penetration strategy of foreign firms, and as a result of a multitude of tax holidays and subsidies by federal, provincial, and municipal governments. It is hardly surprising that one might have found *ex post* a miniature replica of the US economy in Canada, and a consistent burden of inefficiency, generated by short production runs and inefficient use of capital equipment in general.

The pressures from the transformation of the world economy will get stronger over the next few decades, but much decision-making in manufacturing still remains the preserve of foreign firms. Such extra-territorial shadow on the Canadian economy entails that there is little hope that a game plan for the restructuring of Canadian industry or some rationalization and positive adjustment will emerge soon.

One of the main reasons why no game plan is likely to emerge has to do with the nature of all discussions about the production and exchange process. The organization of production and the notion of productivity are only vaguely understood concepts. Commentators continue to divide the economy into very broad sectors (primary secondary, tertiary, or resource-based, non-resource-based activities) which are entirely inadequate for the definition of a strategy of selective development.

What is required is an entirely new set of statistical measurements of economic activities at the meso-level: that is, at a somewhat greater level of dis-aggregation if one might hope to be able to find out which clusters of activities should be retained and encouraged, and which ones should be abandoned. These new measurements are especially important at a time when broad measurements of a macroscopic sort would appear to indicate that a process of de-industrialization is in progress. Currently, it is not really possible for one to analyze these phenomena with the existing statistical categories.

For instance, even though the great bulk of the active population is in the so-called "service sector", and even though there has been a dramatic shift in most economic sectors from energy-intensive material production to information-intensive and knowledge-intensive production, we lack a really useful partitioning of the "service activities" going beyond existing output measures, which hide more than they reveal. In the same vein, steel as an industry is hardly the same creature that steel was 30 years ago; research, marketing, and other forms of knowledge-intensive activities have become much more important within the industry without being usefully registered in our data book.

In an economy with a high degree of concentration, with a high degree of foreign control, and with little incentive to promote productivity and efficiency, it is likely that the signals emanating from the external environment will not be picked up. And if they are picked up, it is unlikely that the necessary co-ordination between the public and the private sector will materialize to develop a useful economic strategy or game plan for the transformation of the Canadian economy.

Currently, neither the knowledge nor the ability needed to undertake a concerted effort in this direction exists in the Canadian economy, unless a major and immensely destructive catastrophe is looming.

The distribution of income and wealth sub-process — The distribution process is a force which is at centre stage, nationally and internationally: developed and developing countries oppose one another in global forums; regions and social groups oppose one another within Canada. In Canada, concern about distribution has tended to overshadow concern for growth and productivity since the 1960s.

The 1960s was the decade when new social rights were propounded and legitimized through various legislations, with the consequence that distribution of income and wealth ceased to be a more or less automatic consequence of the socio-technical production and exchange process.

It became popular to put distribution goals up front, and to argue for adjustments of the production and exchange process to realize certain distributional goals.

The result of the autonomization of the distribution of income and wealth was that distribution issues were discussed in terms of "fairness" and "justice" through bargaining processes that refused to be weighed down by considerations of efficiency, productivity, growth, and progress. Indeed, distribution goals have come to be defined without regard to the best way to ensure the full utilization of the socio-economy's productive capacity. It is unlikely that this will be altered unless a major crisis is looming.

Indeed, if anything, distributional issues will plague more and more of the Canadian debates, between regions, between the provinces and the federal government, and between labour and management. The trend has been shown by labour who argued forcefully in the 1970s for the last and, in a sense, the ultimate basic social right in which to anchor distribution entitlements – the social right for all to share in the increased national wealth without regard to any contribution to that increase, or "participation à l'enrichissement collectif." In all likelihood, this will remain centre stage throughout the next while, and the bargaining will become even more acrimonious as slower economic growth leads to slower growth of the overall pie available for distribution.

The state sub-process — The post-World War II period has seen an elevation of the state to the role of grand definer of the common good. And yet the state does not speak with one voice in Canada. The last 50 years have witnessed a genuine fragmentation of the Canadian state, and the development of stronger bureaucracies at the provincial level has led to the development of province-building policies that have contributed to the acceleration of the process of balkanization already in progress.

In Canada, the economic storms of the 1970s, together with the overly ambitious distributional roles that the state has volunteered to shoulder, have led to a proliferation of interventions and regulations in Canada. The burden of regulation is probably higher in Canada as a result of the larger number of activist governments. This process has led to a systematic overloading of the state, and consequently to management failures, and to a decline in the population's confidence in the legitimacy of government.

These failures have led to competing regulatory activity, a growing lack of willingness to harmonize policies, and to a real antagonism between the different portions of the Canadian state. This was exacerbated by some unwillingness, on the part of the federal government, to experiment with policies that would have given a greater say to the provinces. This centralized mindset has turned out to be the main source of the federal-provincial antagonism.

Governments have demonstrated sufficient difficulties with dispatching their responsibilities that the question "can governments govern?" has been a theme for public discussions in Canada since the 1970s. While many utopians continue to dream of states righting all wrongs, most observers (although few are allowing themselves to say in a loud and clear voice) have come to believe that governments have neither the capacity to govern in a world where power, resources and information are widely distributed, nor the imagination, knowledge, and will to do so.

Whether or not this is because federal governments have come to believe that the government that governs least governs best, or whether it is that they feel that social consensus is so low in Canada that any such strategy would be doomed, is not entirely clear. In any case, it may be expected that the Canadian state will remain balkanized, and ineffective in dealing with the country's economic difficulties.

The ecology of groups and their motives — One of the key reasons why any national consensus is unlikely to materialize is the high degree of dissonance in Canadian society. What used to be regarded as a mélange of regional, ethnic, linguistic, social, and occupational groups, forming an open and pluralistic society, has become a fragmented, divided, balkanized, and disjointed society. While this is obviously a phenomenon that has affected other societies, it might be said that Canadian society has been more profoundly hit. The basic social cohesion has been eroded and public spiritedness or even enlightened self-interest are not ideas in good currency.

This has generated a motivation crisis: a chasm between the need for motivation, demanded by our production and state process, and the motivation supplied by the socio-cultural system. This has also led to an increase in our inability to deal in a concerted way with the difficulties that threaten our socio-economy. Canadian society has broken down into a number of bargaining societies with a very limited interest in expending resources for the collectivity, but very keen to confront the system with exorbitant demands.

One may expect some heightening of the level of dissonance as the frustrations of the baby-boom cohort and the blossoming of the regional consciousnesses and province-building policies reach new heights: the emergence of a sort of "conflictive equilibrium" – a situation where each group would have had time to realize that it cannot rid the system of its opponents, and that it will have to live with them and compromise to achieve its own objectives. However, such an outcome will take some time to evolve, and it is unlikely that Canadian society will have completed such a learning process soon.

One of the main reasons why collaboration will be slow in developing is that Canadians appear to have lost confidence in the possibility of increasing their welfare through greater collaboration and integration.

Some have seen in this dispersive revolution some harbingers of greater regional patriotisms or local commitments. This is one possible scenario with a not insignificant probability since populist leaders have actively fuelled the flame of localism in response to the propensity to centralize and control. But there is also a decline in commitment to communities (proximate or diffuse), so what may ensue is an absence of commitment to the collectivity and even to the more proximate communities, and a lack of any sense of strong interdependence. This is bound to impair the capacity to adjust and transform of the Canadian economy, for market relationships depend on non-market norms.

Conclusions

Serious blockages exist in all of the basic sub-processes examined. One is left with a sense of drifting, with a sense that the balkanized and dependent Canadian socio-economy will not find ways to provide itself with the socio-political mechanisms necessary to effect its transformation without a long period of chicanery and cantankerousness. Our institutional sclerosis will take a long time to shake off.

This does not mean that technically the solutions to the Canadian malaise do not already exist. But Canadians have neither the will nor the ethos necessary to enact them. We know that the investment process is central in the transformation of our socio-economy, and that our institutions require modification in order to facilitate increased investment and to guide the allocation of investment through the system.

The size of the investment flows could be increased by refurbishing our financial system. It may also be necessary to recognize that the wage determination process, together with the growing importance of distribution claims (without regard for efficiency), is in need of control to prevent the excesses of the bargaining society. We also have at our disposal the institutional basis for a system of collaborative governance, of which the Conference Board and similar organizations would be an integral part. What is missing is the sort of social institutions or mechanisms capable of coordinating the private investment plans made by different groups of decision-makers within the economy.

The idea of a "new social contract" would call for a revolution in the minds of Canadians. This may be feasible later, but, in the meantime, we need, at the very least, to refurbish our social technology in each of the sub-processes, to be able to cope satisfactorily with the challenges in store for Canada in the decades ahead.

But the road to collaborative governance is bound to be long… and there is little hope to reach that destination until a number of mental prisons have been destroyed.

Part II

Questioning assumptions

Imagining alternative provisional ways to tackle wicked problems was useful but not sufficient to challenge the cosmology in good currency. Some of its foundational assumptions had to be called into question.

The different chapters in this section question a number of propositions taken for granted that may be regarded as consequences of the someone-in-charge ideology, and of the mystifying vocation of the presumed potentate to guide society in the name of shared values – state-centrism, the refusal to consider solidarity organizations as effective complements to market and state, and the futile search for elusive charismatic leaders.

The two culprits behind those mental prisons are two mistaken assumptions (1) that someone is in charge, must be in charge, and (2) that such leader can be guided by shared values. In contrast, our view is that nobody is in charge in a world where power, resources and information are widely distributed, and that shared values are a myth in a pluralistic society.

The first point has been made forcefully and persuasively by Harlan Cleveland (2002), but it has also been demonstrated in a variety of studies that have documented the extent to which, in our complex and ever changing world, no potentate can claim to have all the power, resources, and information required to be fully in charge. The second point has been made equally persuasively by Joseph Heath (2003): he shows that the mythical shared values are based on the false presumptions that social integration is achieved through value consensus, that shared values make people more cohesive, and that the state exists to promote these values.

From these false premises, conventional wisdom has been led to invoke a variety of other derivative assumptions – that the state is the fulcrum of such big G governing, that solidarity and altruistic collaboration in civil society is both utopian and superfluous, and that charismatic leadership is an essential ingredient of good governance.

The case for state-centricity is criticized in the context of a debate around the so-called "model" of Canadian public administration. The case against the unimportance of solidarity organizations aims at demonstrating that selfless collaboration is a powerful integrator. The case against the mythological discussion of leadership is used as the basis to propose a new perspective focused on the centrality of stewardship.

There are many more assumptions that would need to be challenged. But these may be regarded as central, and the more so because they have become generally accepted as truisms by social scientists to such an extent that many of them are no longer even aware that they are making such assumptions, and most certainly do not recognize their toxicity.

References:

H. Cleveland, *Nobody in Charge*, San Francisco: Jossey-Bass, 2002.

J. Heath, *The Myth of Shared Values in Canada*. Ottawa: Canadian Centre for Management Development, 2003.

Chapter 3

State-centricity as dogma

*"...a body politic is a group of persons
sharing a common set of habits and customs..."*

– Joseph Tussman

Introduction

Iain Gow is a senior and highly respected member of the public
administration research community in Canada. His views on many
issues correspond to the canonical views of that community. Such is
the case about the importance of the state. The occasion of an exchange
with Gow about his model of Canadian public administration revealed
the full extent to which state-centricity, centralization, and shared
values are at the core of the canonical literature. This chapter draws
from my contribution to this exchange. It is not meant to malign Gow
(a researcher for whom I have high regards, and that I consider as a
friend), but, through a critical evaluation of his stand on certain specific
issues, to indict a dogma in good currency in the public administration
community.

Iain Gow (2007) did not like the characterization of his model of
Canadian public administration that is presented in R. Hubbard and
G. Paquet's recent book – *Gomery's Blinders and Canadian Federalism*
(Ottawa: The University of Ottawa Press, 2007). In particular, he did
not like being branded as a defender of strong state-centric governance
by the federal state.

A reader might read Gow's clarification of his position in the December
2007 issue of www.optimumonline.ca. There, he has synthesized
the broad features of his model of Canadian public administration (as
he has "found it in the literature", to use his words), re-proclaimed that

59

it is effective and should remain intact, and defended it against the emergent alternative model that Hubbard and Paquet's book claims to be more desirable.

Why does Gow regard his own model as satisfactory?

Because the Westminster model (of which it is an *image d'Epinal*) is neat and tidy (hierarchical, accountable, transparent, oversight-heavy); because, in it, elected officials are purported to be in charge; because the state plays a transcendent role in defining the public interest on the basis of shared values (equality, equity). Moreover, he regards the way the system has been operating in Canada as an echo of a vibrant tradition of moderation and pragmatism, with a strong tolerance for ambiguity.

A contrario, Gow finds fault with those who argue for less state-centricity, more decentralization, more subsidiarity, more participation, more collaboration, more partnerships, and more consensus-seeking, because all those elements have a downside: they make things more complicated, and as a matter of consequence are seen as dangerous for they might not work.

Gow therefore compares an idealized and idyllic Westminster model with an emergent messy template in the making. Gow lionizes the Westminster model, and is in denial vis-à-vis its real-life dysfunctions. He denounces the strategic state alternative as preachy and advocacy-based, while he claims that his model is nothing of the sort.

I do not intend to debate the relative merits of these two positions. What is of interest here is the set of assumptions on which Gow (but also many other eminent colleagues) base their argumentation. So the use of Gow's name in the rest of the chapter should be read as nothing more than the reference to an author who has articulated the canonical view in a particularly clear and unambiguous way.

Questionable state-centric assumptions

First, Gow suggests that Hubbard and Paquet are naïve in "romanticizing" the citizen, hints that civil society is n-times more likely to defend indefensible causes than good ones, questions the idea that anything consensual about major decisions can emerge in our fractured society, and concludes that mass collaboration and self-organization cannot work.

Second, Gow proposes that the state is the sole legitimate vehicle to elicit what the public interest really means, that the public service *in toto* staunchly serves as guardian of core values (equality and equity), and that the state apparatus in place is the only instrument on which to rely to protect the fundamental requirements of Canadian democracy. So state-centricity is seen as mandatory.

Third, Gow suggests that there are many reasons to believe that decentralization, public-private partnerships (P3s), subsidiarity, etc. will not work as well as the old hierarchical system, that these arrangements will fail to provide the requisite accountability, transparency, and equity that are regarded as essential, that in any case "the state assumes the greater part of the risk in these arrangements", and that pressures to recentralize is bound to prevail.

Fourth, Gow therefore explicitly aligns himself with many other specialists in public administration who say that any reduction in the size of the state can only mean an impoverishment of governance (Rouillard et al 2006 – Foreword by J.I. Gow), and builds his argument unabashedly in favor of state-centricity on this foundation – not so much because of its greater effectiveness, efficiency, and economy (although he hints at these dimensions at times) but mainly and recurrently because of the egalitarian guarantee it provides.

Four assumptions that need to be challenged

(1) The assumption of the incompetence of the citizen is not new. It has served from time immemorial to legitimize the overtaking of governing by the so-called better informed elites. This was at the core of the debate between Walter Lippmann (1922) and John Dewey (1927), and the debates have continued until today (Critical Review 2006).

For Lippmann, the average citizen is like a deaf spectator sitting in the back row of a sporting event: he does not know what is going on, why it is happening, and lives in a world he does not understand and is unable to direct. For Dewey, the basis of democracy is not the competence of the citizen, but conversation: the citizen need not have more than "vital habits" – the ability to follow an argument, grasp the point of view of another, expand the boundaries of understanding, debate the alternative purposes that might be pursued.

Gow would appear to lean toward the Lippmann view of the world, and to interpret the body politic as a group of individuals under the domination of a single power, while Hubbard and Paquet lean toward the Dewey side, and interpret the body politic as a group of persons sharing a common set of habits and customs (Tussman 1960: 4-5). Gow would appear to be pessimistic about the citizen playing any governing role while Hubbard and Paquet suggest giving a louder voice to the citizens: open-source governing would involve the citizenry as a pivotal component of governance.

Gow's prospective pessimism appears to be countered by the growing evidence of successful mass collaboration that has accumulated: it would not appear to require anything like ultra-competence, and has proved very effective (Sunstein 2006; Tapscott and Williams 2006).

(2) The Hegelian notion of the omni-competent state defended by Gow depicts the state in a way that is exactly the obverse of the way in which he describes the citizenry. The state is purported to play a transcendent role and to be the agent of transfiguration of society. For those holding this view, (1) only politics, through the process of conflicts among parties and collective adversaries, can lead to a meaningful taking-into-account of the common good; (2) the state is the centre of the public sphere, and the privileged locus of the conflicts between power groups; and (3) since the body politic is squarely reduced to the power game, any relativization of the role of the state can only be regarded as a deplorable erosion of the "political", even though the state is said to have generated a "primat de la représentation des acteurs sur la résolution des problèmes qu'ils posent" (Gauchet 1998:123).

This elevation of the state to such a transcendent status translates into a required state-centricity because it is the source of the articulation of the public interest and the common good. In the process, both politicians and bureaucrats are promoted to a level of holiness commensurate with their sacred status.

Less state-centricity, more decentralization, more subsidiarity, more participation, more partnerships, or more consensus-seeking, constitute different forms of weakening of the state, and, because of it, are dangerous. They all threaten the coherence of a system that acquires and maintains its coherence through the state.

(3) It is true that all these initiatives to empower the citizen, and to return to him the burden of governing, generate problems of coordination. But these are operational problems. And managerial inconvenience cannot seriously be regarded as a determining or persuasive argument in favor of hyper-centralization and uniformity.

This leads those bent toward state-centricity to unfairly denigrate what have been effective coordination principles and mechanisms.

For instance, subsidiarity is a basic principle of organizational architecture for those arguing in favor of decentralization. It suggests that the decision-making should be delegated as much as possible to the most local level where the problem can be satisfactorily resolved. According to this principle, one should not delegate to a higher level of government anything that can be handled effectively by a lower order of government. One would hardly recognize this complex principle of social architecture in Gow's definition in his original paper, where he defines subsidiarity as something "which seems to mean 'look after yourself' ".

In the same manner, in dealing with public-private partnerships (P3s), it is assumed that the state has automatically and irretrievably to shoulder the greater part of the risk, when this is strictly a matter to be negotiated with other parties – a matter that can be taken care of by due diligence in negotiation.

(4) While there are some references to effectiveness, efficiency and economy in the discussion of the state-centric model, the main reference point is to core values that focus mainly on equality and equity. This is problematic.

Plural societies (and Canada is one) are societies that explicitly recognize that individuals and groups are motivated by different values, and that they can legitimately have different value systems. To pursue their different objectives, they require positive freedom: capacity and opportunity to actively and effectively pursue these values, and promote the elimination of the constraints or unfreedoms that prevent them from doing so. Moreover, plural societies deny that there are any constantly overriding values (Kekes 1993 : 19).

So as Joseph Heath (2003) has argued, shared values are a myth in Canada.

In a deeply diverse and pluralistic society, it is impossible to identify what the shared values are because individuals and groups have very different notions of good life. The best one can hope for – especially in a turbulent world where the means and ends of individuals and groups are continually redefined as the result of evolving circumstances – is agreement on some *principles* that are likely to preserve the neutrality of the state vis-à-vis these different notions of the good.

This confusion between values and principles (and the consequent excesses that this confusion has generated) is most flagrant in the case of the notion of "equality" which has become interpreted (wrongly and most unhelpfully) as meaning that each person or group must be treated identically. The basic principle of equality calls only for the state to be neutral vis-à-vis different preferences, and the different projects of individuals and groups. It does not in any way require that uniformity be enforced (Heath 2003: 28).

Egalitarianism is a basic philosophy that states that "all human beings should be treated with equal consideration unless there are good reasons against it." (Kekes 2003:1). Given the extraordinary variety of human conditions, and the differences in talents, capacities and projects, it is difficult to understand why this cautious presumption has come to be interpreted as an imperative for *identical* treatment, and for arrangements that would make rights and resources more equal to be considered as a foundational pre-condition and imperative for progress.

Such a philosophy allows one principle (equality) to take precedence over all others, at the expense of all others, and ordains indiscriminate compassion for any person claiming to be at a real or imagined disadvantage, on the basis of an optimistic faith that every human being is by nature equally worthy, and that bad political arrangements generating non-uniformity of treatment are evil. As a result, it is argued by egalitarians that the search for absolute equality should guide our design of social architecture and political arrangements.

Practical reasoning usually escapes from such absolutism, and generates *in situ* reasonable responses, even if problems have not been completely theorized. Trade-offs between different principles are arrived at pragmatically. This is how utopian egalitarianism gets tamed in the real world into some form of *equability* — a principle that calls for a sustained effort to eliminate unacceptable or especially troublesome or destructive inequalities.

One observes no such caution on the part of state-centrists. Shared core values are assumed to exist, and, at the end of the day, it is considerations of equality that bolster the argument in favor of state. If egalitarianism *stricto sensu* is the guiding principle, massive redistribution is the rule, and, in order to be able to so redistribute, the "goods" are to be first channeled to the center.

State-centricity, centralization, and the dominium of the central government flow naturally from these assumptions.

However, Gow is uncomfortable with the argument unfolding as we have just done. Even though he dislikes subsidiarity, he seems uneasy with the conclusion that he is irremediably forced to draw from this anti-subsidiarity stance – conclusions leading to federal state-centricity. Indeed, he calls it a "distortion" of his position, and yet the whole logic of his argument leads in this direction.

This explains, in part, why the Canadian model of public administration had a glorious reception in the bureaucratic circles in Ottawa. It provided the logical foundations for the political philosophy that inspired the governance regime over most of the last few decades.

Since 2006, the bulk of the Ottawa bureaucracy has remained deeply anchored in the state-centric view of the world, but even some of the stalwarts of the previous regime have begun to change their tune (Bourgon 2007): the weight of evidence is such that the argument for a less state-centric and a more decentralized governance has to be acknowledged and given appropriate attention. It is not sufficient to discard it as simply a "mode".

Conclusion: an unrepentant experimentalist

Academic debates are both an exercise in critical thinking and an art form. When conducted between individuals who have the greatest amount of personal respect for each other, they may become treacherous if, unwittingly, one or the other of the discussants is led to make points in such a way as to draw blood.

It was never my intention to misrepresent or to malign the Canadian model of public administration, but only to ensure as much clarification as possible. As an unrepentant experimentalist and social learner, I believe that critical thinking aims strictly at exposing the underpinnings of what has become canonical for eminent members of the public administration academic establishment.

The fact that specialists in public administration are unreceptive to the message that state-centricity may be toxic is however hardly surprising. Indeed, they are unlikely to allow the state to be deprived of its rust-proof core character without a fierce fight: what would Hamlet be without the Prince of Denmark!

References

J. Bourgon, "Responsive, Responsible, and Respected Government: Towards a New Public Administration Theory" *International Review of Administrative Sciences*, 73: 1, 2007, 7-26.

Critical Review, Democratic Competence – Special Issue. 18 (1-3) 2006.

Dewey, J. *The Public and Its Problems*. New York: Henry Holt, 1927.

M. Gauchet, *La religion dans la démocratie*. Paris: Gallimard, 1998.

J.I. Gow, *A Canadian model of public administration?* Ottawa: Canada School of Public Service, 2004.

J.I. Gow, "Whose model is realistic, whose unrealistic?" www.optimumonline.ca 37 (4), 2007.

J. Heath, *The Myth of Shared Values in Canada*. Ottawa: Canadian Centre for Management Development, 2003.

R. Hubbard, G. Paquet, *Gomery's Blinders and Canadian Federalism*. Ottawa: The University of Ottawa Press, 2007.

J. Kekes, *The Morality of Pluralism*. Princeton: Princeton University Press, 1993..

J. Kekes, *The Illusions of Egalitarianism*. Ithaca: Cornell University Press, 2003.

W. Lippmann, *Public Opinion*. New York: Macmillan, 1922.

C. Rouillard et al. *Reengineering the State*. Ottawa: The University of Ottawa Press, 2006.

C.R. Sunstein, *Infotopia*. New York: Oxford University Press, 2006.
D. Tapscott, A.D.. Williams, *Wikinomics*. New York: Portfolio, 2006.
J. Tussman, *Obligation and the Body Politic*. New York: Oxford University Press, 1960.

Chapter 4

Solidarity organizations as under-rated option

*"Connection, not affection,
is the defining characteristic of a community"*

–Samuel Bowles (2004: 474)

Introduction

Unrequited transfers are gifts and contributions of all sorts that, by definition, entail no *quid pro quo*. These sorts of transfers, through which people, or groups of people, give help and advantages, may be inspired by all sorts of motivations, and they may bind donors and recipients in reciprocal relations or not. The central feature of these transfers is that they are other-regarding or altruistic. Very diverse forms of solidarity organizations and institutions have emerged to govern such transfers. In this chapter, we will use *philanthropy* or *gift* interchangeably to connote the relationships, arrangements, and organizations underpinning such unrequited transfers

There is a good deal of neglect of, and a fair degree of suspicion about gift organizations. Over time, citizens have developed a much greater trust in the reliability of the *quid pro quo* market exchange and state coercion as coordination mechanisms than in the power of altruism and giving.

Yet this presumption may be unwarranted.

From Richard Titmuss (1970) to Francis Fukuyama (1995) to Elinor Ostrom (1990, 2005), many have shown that the gift/solidarity relationship is a very powerful coordination mechanism that can work (under certain circumstances) as effectively and efficiently as the price mechanism or coercion. Indeed, solidarity arrangements can often carry out coordination tasks that neither of the other two mechanisms can accomplish. (Gintis et al 2005).

We know that, in small groups and under restrictive conditions, gift and solidarity do work. What is less clear is to what extent and under what conditions these findings can be generalized to broader and looser situations.

This paper attempts to fill a portion of this gap.

In section 1, we quickly review the broad range of coordination mechanisms in good currency, and explain where the gift relationship fits. In section 2, the existing literature that seems to make the case for solidarity as coordination mechanism is examined briefly. It was first developed on an ad hoc basis from limited empirical studies, but, in more recent times, behavioral scientists' experimental work has shown that other-regarding behavior and ensuing collaboration are much more prevalent and potent than had been previously presumed. In section 3, we reflect on three broad legacies (charity, commons, and *honneur*) on which philanthropic organizations have been built, and identify the different sets of constraints and blockages that these three strands face. In section 4, we suggest a conceptual framework to deal more directly with the governance challenges with which these strands are confronted. In section 5, we put forward some modest general propositions that may provide guidance in the governance of the solidarity sector. The conclusion reflects briefly on the speculation in good currency that solidarity governance is likely to become more important in the future.

Solidarity in perspective

Self-interest is at the core of economics. Economics is mainly built on the assumption that the only things that matter are self-regarding preferences: concerns about personal gains or losses, and not what others gain or lose. There is some work done at the margin of conventional economics that deals with other-regarding issues like positional goods, reputation, etc. (Hirsch 1976; Klein 1997), but most of this work presents other-regarding dimensions as "instrumental" in pursuing self-regarding preferences. In effect, economics has an autistic quality.

As a result, it is generally concluded in the economic literature that, unless external constraints or incentives are in place or are imposed, less collaboration than might be warranted ensues, and the collectivity suffers.

This approach is unduly restrictive and occludes the possibility that individuals might be much less autistic than is usually assumed. Work that takes this latter position, such as the Post-Autistic Economics Network (www.paecon.net), remains still somewhat marginal within the economics discipline, but it has been gaining more attention in recent times.

But presuming that other-regarding motivations exist, and speculating or theorizing about them, cannot suffice. To be able to argue convincingly that individuals behave in other-regarding ways, one must show that such behavior is observed, explain why it emerges, and be able to point to the consequences it entails.

On these three fronts, some progress has already been made.

First, the existence of other-regarding behavior has now been amply demonstrated experimentally (Gintis et al 2005).

Second, such behavior (and the institutional arrangements in which it is embedded) appears to have three important sources: the first one (charities) has roots in tradition and religion; the second (commons) is mainly ascribable to some awareness by actors of their transversal sharing of facilities and of the interdependencies that such a situation entails; the third (based on a logic of *honneur*[2]) has to do with a commitment to do something one is proud of as a result of one's own status or sense of identity (Hanley 2000; Graeber 2007:32).

Thirdly, these three sets of activities or arrangements have given rise to different types of pure and mixed organizations that neither need be nor are governed in the same manner. This has had an impact on the fabric of society: the growth of organizations built on other-regarding behavior has been both a substitute for and a complement to the other two standard mechanisms of integration – quid pro quo exchange of self-regarding individuals, and coercion based on power relations often rooted in the state.

This impact on the fabric of society will be felt in two major ways: through the production of social capital generated by other-regarding activities and permeating the whole of society; and through the coalescence of an instituted solidarity sector (formal, independent, not-for-profit, self-governed) that transforms the division of labor among the private, public and civic sectors.

Solidarity within the institutional order

Depending on the composition of the population, its ethnic and socio-cultural traits, the conventions of the different groups, and the pattern of power, resources and information they share, a collectivity may evolve quite different patterns of coordination of its activities.

Indeed, it is the very valence of these different mechanisms and the

2 *Honneur* might be expressed as "honour/pride"

nature of their *métissage* that defines the fabric of the overall govern-ance process.

To map out this terrain, Boulding (1970) used a simple triangle, with each of these integrating mechanisms (*quid pro quo* exchange, coercion, and solidarity) in its purest form at one of the apexes; all the inner ter-ritory represented organizations and institutions embodying different mixes of these mechanisms.

The three sectors need not maintain the same valence and a similar weight through time. In Canada, a century ago, for example, the state portion was quite limited, and the scene was dominated by the other two sets of organizations. From the late 19th century to the 1970s, governments of liberal democracies throughout the Western world grew in importance. At the zenith of the welfare state in Canada, almost half of the measured activities fell into the general ambit of state and state-related sector. More recently, there has been a vigorous counter-movement of privatization and deregulation that has caused a reduction of the public sector, and a reverse shift of the boundaries among sectors (Paquet 1996-97).

Of course this rough-and-ready stylization is not meant to suggest that a given particular characterization holds for a socio-economy *in toto*, or even for a whole sector: different sub-national and sectional entities may reveal arrangements that vary considerably. For example, in Canada, the relative distrust of the state and the relative robustness of civil society in Alberta are in sharp contrast to the situation in Quebec, where reliance on the state has been much more important, and philanthropy plays a significantly-lesser role. In the same manner, organizations dominated by the logics of charity, commons or *honneur* solidarity organizations may not be instituted in the same manner everywhere.

There has been a tendency in more recent times for an ever-larger number of mixed institutions, blending these different mechanisms (e.g., market-based public regulation, public-private-social partnering, corporate social responsibility etc.) to develop as instruments to provide the necessary signposts and orientation maps in our new confused and confusing world. This has translated into a much denser filling in of the Boulding triangle. Institutions have emerged that are capable of providing the basis for cooperation, harmonization, concertation, and even co-decision involving agents or organizations from the three sectors (Burelle 1995; Laurent et Paquet 1998; Hubbard and Paquet 2002).

Finally, it should be noted that the mix of charities, commons and honneur solidarity arrangements is startlingly different from one country to the next. This is often deeply rooted in history, beliefs and traditions, and translates into significantly different configurations of institutions and organizations (D'Iribane 1989; D'Iribarne et al 1998/2002; Bevir and Rhodes 2006).

Instituted solidarity and the links to the other two sectors

Although the dynamics that underpin the texture of the Boulding triangle have not been explored in as much depth as might be desirable, it is already clear that the fabric of any socio-politico-economic system is defined by a mix of these three families of mechanisms (both formal and informal) that ebbs and flows according to times and circumstances

In different countries, the solidarity sector has been crowded out at times and in places by the market and state sectors. But it has also been allowed to gain a greater dominium when fiscal crises forced the state to evacuate certain domains of activities, or when market forces have proved incapable of sustaining a presence in some areas. In other circumstances, developments in state and market sectors have resulted in meaningful support for solidarity organizations. Indeed, each integration mechanism has, on occasion, been a substitute for and a complement of the others, depending on circumstances.

This sort of *conflit/concours* relationship of the solidarity sector with the other two has left it vulnerable, both to the virus of hyper-competition that has often weakened the private sector, and to the virus of bureau-cracy that has often paralyzed the public sector.

It has also generated a good deal of uncertainty about the contours of the solidarity sector. Unlike the market and state sectors that engage all citizens to a great extent, the "organized" portion of the solidarity sector (which we agree is only the tip of the iceberg) engages only one quarter of the population (in the form of recorded philanthropy of one sort or another), and a much smaller portion of the population in a very significant way. A relatively small core of citizens represents the bulk of these activities. This helps to explain why the solidarity sector is so easily occluded.

The *métissage* of organizational forms and the blurring of the bound-aries among sectors have had significant impacts as well.

The solidarity sector has often had to adopt the style, language and organizational strategies preferred by markets and states in its efforts to be successful in obtaining support from them. This has "tainted" the endeavour (some would say) since it has meant (1) much scheming vir-tuously and competition in fund-raising activities that has offended and repelled the base; (2) a professionalization of the staff that has tended to shift power away from boards, volunteers, and donors to permanent staffers, further alienating the base; and (3) a bureaucratization of the "third sector" in efforts to improve relations with the state (e.g., through state-voluntary sector accords) which has contributed to extinguishing some of the effervescence of the base.

The solidarity sector has therefore benefited on the one hand from the disillusions generated by statism and neo-liberalism. But it has also been weakened by the direct competition of state and market, and by their indirect encroachment through a modification of its *modus operandi*. The net effect on solidarity organizations and social capital is not always clear (Putnam 2002).

The case for solidarity

In the introductory chapter of Gintis et al (2005), a most useful summary of experimental evidence is presented that demonstrates that (1) in various game contexts (ultimatum game, public goods game, etc.) a predisposition to contribute to a cooperative endeavour exists, and (2) that a small fraction of strong reciprocators is able to invade a population of self-regarding types, with the result that high levels of cooperation ensue. Such experiments also show however, that while a mix of mechanisms (incentives, coercion, solidarity) may at times be the source of greater cooperation, it may also lead to toxic results.

Solidarity is contingent

These paradoxical results are ascribable to the fact that solidarity is fundamentally conditional and that, depending on the context, the different integration mechanisms may be substitutes or complements.

On the one hand, the existence of better information, more robust monitoring, and fail-safe mechanisms may generate more solidarity; but, on the other hand, fines, subsidies, and sanctions may be leading to exactly the obverse.

Therefore, the case for solidarity can only be made in a contingent way: it may be likely to be successful only if certain conditions are met, if certain principles, mechanisms, and auxiliary conditions are in place, also and depending upon context and circumstances. In fact, one of the most important elements that differentiate solidarity from quid pro quo exchange coercion as mechanisms of integration is its relatively greater dependence on context.

One can already gain some sense of what contextual forces may foster solidarity: solidarity is often much more efficient and effective as a coordination mechanism when the task is qualitative, when a meaningful contract is hard to negotiate, when the conflicts of interest are limited, and when the distribution of benefits is not too unequal (Gintis et al 2005; Ostrom 2005).

Solidarity is not simply the result of encapsulated self-interest

Economics, like any robust paradigm, has a vibrant immune system. Faced with the unrealism of the pure and perfect competition assumptions, it was quick to invent "contestable markets" that did not require all those taxing conditions, and yet performed the same challenge function. In the same manner, attempts at hollowing out solidarity led some to postulate that solidarity was simply the result of an individual taking the interests of another person to heart and encapsulating them in his/her own preference function (Hardin 1991).

In that version, solidarity is simply an exotic notion of self-interest.

This reductionist version has the advantage of eliminating the need for any explanation for solidarity outside of sheer self-interest maximization. Yet this artifice does not quite work: it is a subterfuge that eliminates the problem at hand by suggesting that the individual may have self-interest in selflessness *per se* (Cook, Hardin, Levi 2005: 5ff). The reason this over-complicating of the preference function of the individual does not work is that it simply pushes the problem one step back. It leaves entirely unexplained why and when self-interest in selfishness and unselfishness might prevail.

Solidarity as the result of embeddedness, frame and habitus

If solidarity is not simply an exotic form of self-interest, neither is it a mechanical bond, à la Durkheim. It is the echo effect of the sociality of a collection of persons or groups that is rooted in history, beliefs, and traditions – their capacity to invent social glue that can help them coalesce in stable and functional ensembles (Baechler 1994:21).

Sociality helps define the way in which individuals and groups are embedded in the broader social context, how the "frames of reference" they inherit from such a context influence their decision-making, and how such settings forge predispositions to act in certain ways (Tversky and Kahneman 1981; Bourdieu 1977).

And so, depending on the texture of the environment, certain behaviours will be differentially appreciated. Accordingly, individuals and groups will take decisions that vary greatly, and the predispositions that emerge from such habitualized experiences through time will help forge an habitus, a culture that triggers different patterns of reactions and behaviours. The logics of charity, commons, and honneur solidarity organizations will be differentially framed. Consequently, one does not need to invent exotic preferences: individuals and groups operate differently as a result of the context they face. Such a context is both enabling and constraining. It defines the corridor of what is permissible, fostered, and encouraged in an organizational context at a certain time, but also of what is not (Mesthene 1970: 48-50).

Building on three legacies – charities, commons, and *honneur*

The world of solidarity organizations is "diverse, fragmented, complex, territorial, ill defined and less influential in terms of public policy making than it might be" (Hanley 2000:1). These very features are inherent in the nature of the solidarity sector, and efforts to herd these "cats" may in fact impair the sector's dynamism.

The particularly difficult and perplexing aspect of the challenge of the solidarity sector is that it draws from a pool of quite different motivations, and that it takes many institutional forms[3].

The logic of redistribution from the rich to the poor (charities), the logic of co-operation when there is a common pool of resources in which many share (commons), and the *logique de l'honneur* leading citizens to contribute to the community (as a matter of honour, pride, gratitude, and status that commands to do good for the commonwealth) are complex. They are rooted in some mix of (1) a profound need to be regarded as a good person, that is at the core of moral development; and (2) social pressures not entailing necessarily threats or penalties, but reinforcement or unpleasantness (Kohlberg 1981; Ireland and Johnson 1970).

Three logics and three institutional strands

Patrick Hanley (2000) has examined the root sources of the first two families of solidarity organizations: (1) the charity logic – which entails volunteering on behalf of strangers, a concept derived from thousands of years of religious tradition – where the focus is on the needs of others, and (2) the commons logic – involving volunteering on behalf of "people like us", in order to find rules, norms, laws, rights and obligations capable of helping us to live together more comfortably. These two logics have generated different strands of solidarity organizations.

The third one – the *honneur* logic – appears at first to be more difficult to pin down in our modern world. It has to do with the mix of social pressures and motivations at the core of the urge *d'être à la hauteur des attentes*, as an echo of status.

It also explains a variety of patterns of behavior: why elites and members of the noble professions feel the urge to give; why persons

---

3 It is a mix of social pressures and motivations that shapes solidarity institutions – sort of World 3 creatures, à la Popper that are the outcome (often unintended) of this dialectical interaction between World 1 (context) and World 2 (values and plans). So the logic of solidarity institutions cannot be reduced simply to motivations (Popper 1972).

are so easily offended when altruistic or collaborative gestures are met with immediate offers of compensation (Richebé 2002, 2003), and why professionalism and professional pride (*la logique compétence*) can do so much more than financial incentive reward systems to promote efficiency and effectiveness in private and public bureaucracies (Favereau 2004).

Anthropologists have even explained the extraordinary contribution of citizens to the world war effort in the 20th century (and in particular the effort of the lower classes) as perhaps the only way for some members of these groups to exercise their right to do good as citizens (Graeber 2007).

This noble sense of *honneur* is easily discounted in the public discourse of the day, and yet, this is a strong feeling that may also explain why, in many organizations, members of the support staff often contribute more significantly (and yet anonymously) than the executive staff to certain fund-raising campaigns like the United Way. It is not done simply as a matter of charity, or to contribute to the commons, but *pour l'honneur*.

i.   The logic of charity is built on ministering to the needy and the downtrodden. It is about one group willingly trying to help another. This is the rationale for organizations like charitable trusts, philanthropic and faith-based organizations. The basic components are the focus on *others*, the existence of *have-nots* who *need assistance*, and the *moral obligation of the haves to help*.

It is the tradition that has led to the emergence of the welfare state as a meta-organization that has claimed the responsibility to structure and formalize, through the state, the amateurish ways in which this kind of assistance was provided by diverse solidarity groups in earlier times. The approach is *top-down* and *centralizing* for it would not be possible to redistribute between groups of haves and have-nots unless the funds were first brought to the center.

This approach has acquired a new garb and softer faces under the rubric of "sharing communities" but the redistribution imperative has imposed a centralized mindset on it, and, in their relationship with the state, these solidarity organizations are under constant threat of being overrun by the state in the name of efficiency.

ii.   The logic of the commons is quite different. It connotes the means by which people within a community work together for mutual benefit. This is the rationale for community organizations, help groups, advocacy groups, micro-credit groups, and the like. The basic components are the focus on *us* not others, on the *benefits of solidarity as a method of coordination*, and on the *effectiveness of horizontal reciprocal coordination*.

This tradition has to do with the effectiveness of collaborative governance as compared to other ways of coordinating. It is *horizontal* and *non-centralizing*, and it does not mesh at all well with state intervention. Indeed, there is a congenital distrust of the state-centric arrangements in this tradition, and a premium is put on independence and autonomy.

iii.   The logic of *honneur* is neither *us-them* based, nor *us-us* oriented; it is rooted in a sense of *me-all* obligation based on status, on a sense of pride and competence that defines my identity.

In certain cases, it is articulated as gratitude to country or tribe (Buckley 1990). This sense of pride based on identity is the source of selflessness that explains why in times of war individuals are willing to give their lives for their country.

It is the solidarity of those who often have nothing to give but themselves, their time and life. It underpins an extraordinary sense of worth and reveals the emptiness of taylorism that proposes to organize the division of labour strictly through incentive reward systems based on threats and financial gratifications. There are things money will not buy easily: as Favereau suggests, firms have long understood that they cannot operate without professional pride – "rendre la coopération rationnelle est une façon irrationnelle de produire de la coopération" (Favereau 2004: 33). [making co-operation rational is an irrational way of producing co-operation]

Many solidarity organizations are shaped by a single dominant logic – a mindset or worldview, or conceptualization of the organization, and of the tools to accomplish its goals and make decisions, that acts as a filter to determine what information is relevant or not, and what is important (Prahalad and Bettis 1986). But many are built on a mix of *assistance*, *coordination*, and *honneur* logics. As a result, they experience tension between the different logics when, for instance, pursuing somewhat subversive objectives (autonomy, independence and advocacy) while at times reluctantly attempting to secure support from the state (directly or indirectly, through charitable status for tax purposes or straight grants or contributions to finance part of their operations), or from the private sector.

Three sets of organizational challenges

Charity-based solidarity organizations may proclaim their independence, but they easily welcome arrangements that would stabilize their funding, even when the state (through grants, contributions and contracts) puts these organizations in a form of dependency.

These solidarity organizations have embraced a certain degree of formalization and welcomed the creation of government-voluntary organizations "accords", but also attempted at the same time to minimize their accountability and to defend their independence.

Commons-based solidarity organizations do not refuse state funding. Indeed, some demand it vehemently, and rationalize their claims to "state obligations" by references to greater efficiency, historical treaties, particular governance requirements, etc., but they forcefully resist any sort of general framework accord that would impose constraints on their activity, and they resent accountability frameworks.

Honneur-based solidarity organizations are even less formalized. They are based on a passion to serve often generated by particular circumstances that provoke an urge to contribute to the commonweal, "a kind of nobility no less aristocratic for being widespread and universally accessible" (Buckley 1990: xxi).

A sort of fundamental decentralized mindset underpins these "noble" operations, and takes on a subversive quality. It becomes anti-state-centric, and counts on design principles that are based on relationships rather than rules. It also underpins a propensity to under-design in order to allow the system to remain innovative and resilient, and to emerge as it should. This is clearly revealed in the idiosyncratic nature of the diverse foundations created by philanthropists.

Different blockages

The different strands of solidarity organizations have had to overcome important blockages, the most important of which flow from the dynamic conservatism of state-centric politicians and bureaucrats. These state actors, building on a strong Hegelian view that the state is a transcendent creature that embodies the true will of the people, have argued that the welfare state is uniquely positioned to perform the charity role, that it is also best placed to govern the commons, and that it does not need to count on whimsical honor codes and the like, inherited from the *Ancien Régime*.

Counting on charity, collaboration, or an honor code has come to be regarded as *passé*: indeed, these very words have lost their lustre in modern times, and their references have come to be embalmed as antiquated values.

The result is that the state sector has opposed any decentralization, and invested a good deal of effort over the last decade trying to "reorganize" the solidarity sector to make it fit state institutions. It has also used its coercive power to shape the community-commons-honors solidarity organizations (when they emerge) in a top-down way. When there has been resistance to these top-down pressures, the state clerisy has often vilified the resilient bottom-up initiatives as utopian, or as agents of balkanization.

This strategy of encapsulation and containment has been particularly clear in the recent UK 2006 Charities Act, coming into effect in 2008.

Under this new law, the ambit of charities-based solidarity organizations is so greatly increased as to encompass the commons-based and even some honor/professional endeavors, and to sanitize them.[4] This effort to coerce the solidarity sector into a harness of hierarchy and bureaucracy has pleased some segments of the solidarity sector clerisy no end (for this group has been offered a place at the state table), but it has not always served the sector itself well.

In particular, it has often contributed to demobilizing the supporters of charity organizations, to de-voice and de-claw commons organizations, to demobilizing elites and citizens, and to disenchanting pride and *honneur*.

A conceptual framework

Governance is best defined as effective coordination when power, resources and information are widely distributed.

In the case of the solidarity sector, the governance challenge might be usefully categorized under six headings:
- what are the relevant dimensions of the context within which it operates?
- what constitutes the minimal quality of information required for solidarity to crystallize?
- which principles guide the governance of solidarity organizations?
- what sort of design is likely to be most effective?
- what are the auxiliary conditions needed for solidarity organizations to play their full potential role?
- how does one ensure operational goodness-of-fit of all the above?

This is stylized in Figure 1.

---

4 Main charitable purposes (Charities Act 2006): prevention or relief of poverty. Plus advancement of: education; religion; health or the saving of lives; citizenship or *community development*; arts, culture, heritage or science; amateur sport; human rights, *conflict resolution or reconciliation or the promotion of religious or racial harmony or equality and diversity*; environmental protection or improvement. And relief of those in need by reason of youth, age, ill-health, disability, financial hardship or other disadvantage; advancement of animal welfare, promotion of the efficiency of the armed forces of the Crown; or the efficiency of the police, fire and rescue services or ambulance services; and any other purposes charitable in law (i.e., including everything that is currently charitable).

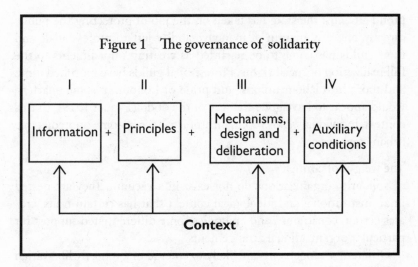

We will not attempt in this chapter to provide a detailed grammar of the different principles and rules pertaining to each family of solidarity institutions. Our objective is more modest: to identify the ways in which the response to the six questions above might help in meeting to a greater or lesser extent the governance challenges of the different solidarity organizations – the charities, the commons, and the *honneur/professional* organizations.

In the case of charities, matters of participation, accountability, independence and funding generate much precariousness because of (1) a small and declining demographic base, (2) loose, diffuse, and improvised organizational forms, (3) a tug-of-war between a will to be independent and the growing dependency on the state, and (4) unstable funding.

In the case of commons, the demographic base around commons is often more stable, focused and deeply motivated, accountability to the government, or to any external body is challenged, staunch independence is the ultimate goal, and unconditional funding from traditional sources both vehemently demanded (in the name of efficiency) and often equally vehemently refused by those who hold the purse-strings (in the name of equity or sheer uniformity).

In the case of *honneur* organizations, the binding pride of many meso-groups or individuals has been dramatically eroded by the bureaucratization of the professions and kindred groups. Indeed, the state in Quebec has now created L'Office des Professions, which has forced them into a rigid mould. While the nobility of the "vocation" has survived in some groups, the rise of the new ideology of social rights has dramatically diminished the importance and influence of elites, professions, and proud citizens: the state has taken on the job of protecting the public directly, and any margin of maneuverability left to professionals and their guilds has come to be regarded as creating impediments to the full realization of social rights. Professional guilds have morphed more and more into labour unions, and pride or honour, in some quarters, would appear to have gone the way of the dodo (Paquet 1979). In this context, individual *honneur* philanthropists have become unpredictable urban cowboys.

The weight of context

Solidarity organizations do not exist in a vacuum. They are nested in an institutional and ideological context that has certain traits, creates certain constraints, and embodies some differentiated support for particular organizational arrangements.

Different arrangements are likely to emerge in a robustly libertarian milieu and in a state-centric jacobine context (Hollingsworth 1993). This explains the different organizational textures of the arrangements in Alberta and Quebec, for instance. In a jacobine environment, a social housing project will naturally be state-designed and governed. In a less statist environment, it is quite conceivable to have a governing apparatus that is characterized by a high degree of decentralization, community governance, and obligational networks.

The nature of the context, like the fabric of the corporate culture in good currency in a given country or region, is not calcified in perpetuity. It changes slowly, and not always in predictable ways. So the *zeitgeist* must be factored in when trying to understand the structure and governance of solidarity organizations. The point has been made very well by Laforest and Phillips (2001) when they compared government-solidarity organizations relations in Quebec with what takes place in the rest of Canada.

The context also has an important impact on the emergence of commons and *honneur* organizations. For instance, the legal framework often makes it much easier to organize a commons governance structure, or a cooperative, in certain jurisdictions than in others: it can be put together in hours in certain cases, while it may take months or years in others, thereby stimulating or discouraging these initiatives.

In the same spirit, the sociality of certain socio-economies recognizes, celebrates and encourages certain heroic contributions more readily while, in some other settings, the egalitarian ethos is such that any action involving bravura is unlikely to generate any appreciation, and indeed, may provoke snarl and scorn. The way in which a person who has experienced a business failure is regarded in different societies is quite telling: in some places, it is a sign of irreparably tarnished reputation, while in others it is a sign of courage, boldness, and resilience.

The differential sort of reaction to "social entrepreneurship" is bound to have an impact on the emergence of *honneur* initiatives, in particular: they are unlikely to spring up in a context where they are likely to generate negative reactions.

The centrality of accurate information

Nothing drives home more effectively the fundamental importance of the accuracy of information in the emergence of effective governance than the Condorcet Jury Theorem – one of the most interesting results in modern social theory, throwing light on how many minds produce knowledge. This theorem – in a formulation borrowed from Sunstein (2006:25) – states that the probability of a correct answer by a majority of a group increases toward 100% as the size of the group increases *if each person in the group is more likely than not to be correct.*

The theorem is based on simple arithmetic, but is a justification of democracy. It depends however, on the crucial condition that individuals are informed and competent enough that each is more likely to be correct than not. Otherwise, the probability for the group to be correct decreases towards zero as the size of the group increases.

If groups were made up of uninformed and incompetent persons who are more likely *not* to be correct, deliberation would not elicit the information that the members have, but rather amplify the errors of the members, and produce cascades and polarizations where the blind lead the blind to extremes (Sunstein 2006: 75).

The sort of self-governance that prevails in solidarity organizations is very vulnerable to such information and competence failures. In charities, commons, and *honneur* organizations, the information + competence requirement is of central importance. Yet it is likely to be neglected, with the result that solidarity organizations' deliberations and governance tend to go awry.

This may explain why solidarity organizations, built on single issues that are based on solid common knowledge (focused local specialized charities), or on solid information systems (even in commons as large as the Gulf of Maine) thrive, while others, where information is quite vague or dominated by ideology, tend to fade away. Such a solid information base very often helps to develop the basis of trust that enables the group to proceed with more and more demanding and taxing collaborative efforts (Paquet 2005a).

Principles

To fix ideas, one may start with some of the principles most often listed as being at the core of good societal governance: (1) legitimacy and participation (2) responsiveness, effectiveness and efficiency; (3) accountability and transparency vis-à-vis the public, as well as institutional stakeholders; (4) fairness and equability.

Solidarity organizations and institutions need to adhere to these principles if they are to survive, but they need more: like democracy, they require more than procedural neatness. They are built on commitment and reliability: other-regarding concern is the main driver at the motivation level, but at the institutional level, the crucial dimensions are reliability, consistency, trustworthiness. These call for nothing less than constructing a reliable "machine" out of unreliable parts.

The search for reliability and stability explains the drive toward the institutionalization of solidarity. But it is also its Achilles' heel, since formalization may discourage participation and self-governance, and trigger calcification and crystallization in a sector that needs to evolve and to innovate as much as the other sectors.

It has been suggested that such reliability is built on trust and bonding capital. Solidarity organizations are not necessarily or even usually a form of "bonding capital" built on high trust. Rather, they are a form of "bridging capital". They build on the strength of weak ties, and do not necessarily require reciprocity or trust. Bridging organizational capital is less constraining: bridging is bonding lite (Putnam 2002).

This does not mean that the level of trust "in the context" is not important. But there is no simple linear relationship between levels of trust and solidarity organizations.

On the one hand, high-trust societies may just as easily foster tribal bonding networks generating negative externalities and exclusion. On the other hand, a general climate of trust may indeed foster a higher capacity to form stable networks, and a general atmosphere of distrust may hinder such efforts.

Trust and distrust are therefore important factors, but not likely to generate determinacy.

It has been argued that, over the recent past, Western democracies have drifted into an age of greater distrust, that distrust fuels defiance and that, as a result, citizens act differently and in a more defiant and obstructive way (Rosanvallon 2006; Hardin 2006).

At the socio-political level, this has meant: (1) increased surveillance, vigilance, and monitoring of the official state apparatus; (2) a greater development of a capacity by civil society to stop, block, derail and sabotage the political process (forcing it to back off, to withdraw planned legislation, and the like); and (3) an increased pressure to force the political and state process to face their accountabilities in front of courts or adjudication bodies.

The citizens have not become more passive as some might be tempted to argue on the basis of turn-out statistics in official elections. Rather, they have chosen to express themselves, to get involved and to intervene in a different (and Rosanvallon would say *impolitical*) way – generating a *contre-démocratie* geared to reducing the power of the state process.

This has encouraged a greater effervescence in civil society, a greater ebullience of social movements and emergent publics, à la Hine-Angus (Hine 1977; Angus 2001). But more importantly, it has led to the emergence of new principles in the design of the governance of organizations: independence, experimentation, openness, and social learning. Such dynamic and open-ended principles tend to perturb the staunch defenders of traditional representative democracy.[5] And, yet, for practical reasons, this sort of subversive thrust has remained relatively tamer in solidarity organizations than might have been expected.

The necessary proximity of charity to other sectors – closeness to the state looking to offload certain services and to the private sector as a source of funds – and of *honneur*/pride organizations with the state (honour and pride do not exempt persons and groups from being willing to gain tax exempt status) have quickly generated a compensatory call for the state to engage in more monitoring, oversight, prescription, and performance measurement of their activities.

This has made keeping true to their ideal principles an increasing challenge for daring solidarity organizations. As for commons, they would appear to have been spared the odium of unintelligent accountability only to the extent that they have avoided the temptation of searching for access to state largesse above and beyond their cherished independence.

Design

The requirements of "proven" good governance demanded from solidarity organizations have called for appropriate mechanisms, design, and deliberation spaces being put in place to ensure that persons empowered with basic information and competence can engage in the process of cumulative social learning as effectively as possible. And yet solidarity organizations are too often "a collection of small boutique programs, or pilots auditioning for government support" (Husock 2007:21).

---

5 For an intriguing view of the malaise generated by the word *open*, see K.G. Banting et al *Open Federalism – Interpretations, Significance*. Kingston: Institute of Intergovernmental Affairs 2006.

How then can independence, experimentation, openness, and social learning – with the built-in requisite amount of emergence – be translated into real life?

In general, for both charities and commons, the only effective way to meet this challenge is a design of a "federal" sort – allowing parts (chapters) to operate with as much independence as possible so as to be able to be nimble and creative, while remaining, as a whole, as coherent as necessary to demonstrate that they can meet the basic good governance requirements to attract both venture capital and sustaining support. This calls for clear purpose, succinct approach, outcome measurements, and enthusiasm for reporting regularly on their progress (Husock 2007:22).

In addition, charity organizations must be able to help design, manage, and work in partnerships and collaboration with hierarchical bureaucratized organizations from other sectors. This calls for new and enhanced infrastructure, processes, and competencies, in order to counter criticisms that their cost of operations are too high, and that their capabilities reveal significant gaps.

For commons, Elinor Ostrom (2005) has drawn from her case studies of commons reciprocity organizations, a list of internal design principles, including:

- the need for a clear definition of the stakeholders, of their rights and responsibilities
- the requirement for clarity in the benefits received and contribution to sustaining costs
- the participation of those involved in making key decisions
- the production of reliable performance monitoring information
- a graduated system of sanctions for errors and infractions, and
- the presence of local conflict resolution mechanisms.

On the *honneur*/pride solidarity organizations front, the new celebration, by the new gentility of money, of *gratitude* vis-à-vis community and society (of which Bill Gates is only the most prominent) has given philanthropy more lustre than it has had for decades.

Whether this resurgence is temporary or not is unclear, and whether this form of solidarity can lend itself to rules of institutionalization remains to be seen. But it may signal at least that one should not confuse such initiatives with charities: as in the case of social movements, the underpinning "moral contract" is immensely more ambitious, and the organizational form more experimental and idiosyncratic.

Auxiliary conditions

Auxiliary conditions are often necessary to overcome the practical blockages facing solidarity organizations. This has as much to do with the ideological climate as with the legal and bureaucratic systems. There may be a need for very specific contraptions both (1) to ensure that the appropriate level of solidarity activity is unleashed, and (2) to provide the contextual security zone that will allow the desirable experiments to proceed and succeed.

In the first case, there may be a need to put in place an infrastructure of information and forums to allow the knowledge base and the getting-together technologies (required for some issues to be tractable by solidarity organizations) to emerge.

Such capacity building is not necessarily costly, but it may require some essential contextual support. The emergence (and at times the transformation) of solidarity organizations entails a change of kind in these organizations that is often effectively opposed by their traditional governors. A nudge from the outside may be required.

This may call for a formal process of periodic external evaluation that the solidarity organizations impose on themselves as part of their governing apparatus. This self-imposed mandate and governance review has proved immensely useful in the case of certain basic legislations in providing a periodic moment to review the adequacy of the mission, governing structure, and decision-making process in light of the evolution of the context and priority needs.

In the second case, what has to be fought is the burden of inertia and risk-aversion that prevents much experimentation. Organizations must be given permission to experiment. Intelligent accountability may require a definition of the corridor of "normal-times" conditions, when organizations are allowed to conduct their affairs without much intervention from the outside, but also a definition of what is meant by "abnormal times" when fail-safe mechanisms would kick in. This might provide the sort of contextual security zone that is required for sceptics to accept experimentalist community governance arrangements.

Some operationalization difficulties

Translating these requirements into operational terms is no simple task. In all types of solidarity organizations, shortcomings in implementation capabilities are often the Achilles' heel of their governance and management.

i. The zones of tension are many: participation, independence, performance, accountability, and funding. These five elements are significantly intertwined, and in each case, the resolution of the difficulties calls for a refurbishment of the governance and management of solidarity organizations and, most of the time, for the emergence of new mixed/pluralist forms of organization.

Some innovations are intellectually appealing, but practically unlikely to succeed. The temptation by Husock et al to search for the equivalent of a *stock market for nonprofits* is both inspiring and somewhat romantic. It is more likely that, in the medium term, one will have to scheme virtuously: to agree to build on the new interest of citizens in getting involved in their own commons community, and less on the eroding charity-based motivations, and wait to see if the nobility of purposes is experiencing a permanent revival.

The different families of solidarity organizations will have to innovate in different ways to survive and thrive, but they are likely to have to do it in collaboration with the private and state sectors.

In the case of the commons, the governing is made easier by the realization of the impossibility of getting away from the sharing. The central issue has less to do with funding and more to do with *performance* and *accountability*. This puts a premium on governance, enforcement, and compliance.

It is through a mix of formal and informal arrangements – Mobius-web governance as Rosenau would call it (2003) – that such governing is best achieved. And it need not be based of necessity (as some fear) on close proximity. Moreover, since the common-property resource often has a most important interface with the other sectors (in environment, for instance, but also in health, with the emergence of self-care), forms of co-governance involving the three sectors may be expected to emerge.

In the case of charities, *participation* and *funding* are the crucial dimensions, and in both cases the rapport with the state is fundamental. Participation is crucial and depends much on the margin of maneuverability allowed or be encouraged by the state; and funding is almost always (directly or indirectly) the result of state largesse (tax incentives and the like). Consequently, charities may have to make the Faustian bargain of a symbiotic relation with the state, with the clear possibility spelled out that they may, in so doing, lose their soul.

In the case of *honneur*/pride solidarity organizations, the challenge is *participation* and *performance*: the new gentility of money often shuns any visibility to avoid being plagued by unwanted requests for help, and many either leave the traditional professions where such largesse was a tradition, or never take part in their formal organizations. Moreover, in both cases, there is little doubt that any action on their part is often perceived and advertised by third parties as self-serving.

This may call for a change in the culture of the elite organizations and a re-affirmation of professional values (and connected oaths of office) that have ceased to be as omnipresent as they used to be. But such a bootstrap operation is unlikely to be instituted. The Gates and Buffetts of this world are unlikely to be mobilizable by any *encradrement* – they will remain idiosyncratic. Those inhabited by a logic of *honneur* fear more than anything the notion of a state *encadrement* (the very *encadrement* that has largely killed the sense of pride, honor, and social responsibility of professionals).

ii.   Yet it would be unwise to suggest that refurbished governance arrangements, introduced subtly and *sotto voce*, cannot make a difference. Difficult as the task may be, a transition strategy for solidarity organizations would help if it could focus on two major complementary initiatives.

The first should focus on *performance*, in order to ensure that the governance apparatus is capable not only of keeping the system under control, but also of providing a real impetus to explore, to adopt an experimentalist attitude, to constantly search for new and better ways to do new things, and to constantly reinvent both goals and means. This is a long-run focus constantly feeding the need to adapt and adjust in the short-term.

The second should focus on *conformance*. It is supervision, regulation, and accountability in order to ensure that capabilities are in place to keep the ship afloat and to steer it in the directions that have been ascertained as the most promising by the governing board. This is mainly a short-term focus, but one that cannot be satisfied with simply operating in a routine way: it must focus on dealing with all the apparent weaknesses in the existing arrangements that may prevent good steering, and correct them.

It is not unfair to say that conformance work is less risky, and therefore less stressful, so it has a tendency to gobble up much of the authorities' attention and time in most organizations. This is the case, in particular, for solidarity organizations where the board members represent a very diffuse community of stakeholders that do not speak with a strong performance-oriented voice because the very notion of performance is not easily clarified and measured. In these organizations, full-time staff has a great deal of latitude in choosing whether or not to inform the board fully on matters of performance, and they are more clearly monitored on the conformance aspects of the operations. So the fiduciary and trustee roles (and those insuring that things are done right) are often well dispatched, but it is not always clear whether it has been ascertained beyond reasonable doubt that the organization is doing the right thing (Garratt 1996).

In the case of commons, the degree of ignorance of the partners is significantly less than in the case of charities, so one may legitimately expect that performance concerns will be better aired and assessed. In the case of charities, the matter is more perplexing. Products (as defined by staff) often give an illusion of success and much effort goes into "sell(ing) donors the sizzle rather than the steak" (Friedman 2007:49). In the case of elite and professionals or groups on the basis of status – often poorly informed – despite all the good intentions, even the sizzle is sometimes not there.

Conformance is not sufficient and good dynamic performance requires generative governing. In the case of solidarity organizations, the sort of rigor that produces generative stewardship can only come from a transformation of the very notion of what governing boards must do, and what the governing rules should be (Chait et al 2005).

Generative stewardship is a matter of survival for all solidarity organizations. Collaboration of board and staff is required, but it can only materialize through a reinvigoration of the role of the boards, and a more experimentalist and innovative way for them to do their work. The boards must become truly exploratory, through the use of prototypes and serious play, if the solidarity organizations are to innovate and transform themselves as they should (Schrage 2000).

The governing board has to become bold, catalytic, intellectually playful, inventive, and to provide generative thinking in this complex and yet fluid environment, instead of allowing itself (1) to be completely absorbed by routine technical roles in a world where the very nature of the mission of solidarity organizations is constantly challenged and redefined, or (2) to be totally manipulated by the full-time bureaucracy, and fall prey to the calcification of the role of the organization around its past activities – becoming a myopic and unduly narrowly focused functional system instead of a learning system, and being so captured by dynamic conservatism so as to run the risk of becoming irrelevant. Schön (1971) has richly documented the cost of dynamic conservatism and the sad stories of solidarity organizations becoming crusaders without a crusade.

In the case of charities, boards have to fight fiercely not to be encapsulated by their full-time staff. As a result, they have not naturally been an engine of innovation. In the case of commons, generative and innovative governance is usually much more readily adopted, as a result of the deeper involvement of interested parties. In the case of honor/pride organizations, the danger is the obverse of what it is in the case of charities: stellar boards are likely to be less attentive to operatives than they should, because of the very forcefulness of the key persons acting as the driving force.

Modest general governance propositions

Given the numerous caveats sprinkled throughout this chapter, it is clear that one can only be very tentative in spelling out modest general governance propositions about solidarity organizations.

We have put forward a set of hypotheses that would appear to suggest some priority work in some areas.

i.   One of the most important results of our exploratory work has been the full extent to which the solidarity organizations are *context-contingent*. The same mechanisms and the same tools are likely to generate quite different results, depending on the context. This brings forth the need to probe the causal texture of the environment further.

This sort of research program was celebrated in the 1960s by Frank Emery and Eric Trist (1965), but it has not been in good currency for quite a while. The particularly important sensitivity to context in solidarity organizations has given it new currency. Emery and Trist had proposed a typology of environments (random-placid, clustered-placid, disturbed-reactive, turbulent) that called for different types of organizations. What is required is a much more fine-grained typology of the same ilk in the analysis of voluntary organizations.

Such a work would focus on the different mega-communities (i.e., public spheres in which organizations and people deliberately join together around a compelling issue of mutual importance, following a set of practices and principles that will make it easier to achieve results). What might be useful is a macrosocial mapping of the *mega-community* and its dynamic underground (i.e., the critical elements for a thriving mega-community[6] , Gerencser-style):

- understanding the problems to be resolved, the necessary players and partners, and the ways in which they affect one another;
- partners willing to listen, learn and, understand;
- designing and customizing suitable cross-sector arrangements; and
- learning from experiments and effective collective monitoring of progress.

---

6 M. Gerencser et al "The Mega-community Manifesto" www.strategy-business. com 16.08.06 (10p.)

ii.   The terrain of solidarity organizations and their subversive character have changed dramatically over the last little while.

First, as the demand for solidarity organizations grew in response to both state and market failures, the capabilities of the so-called "third sector" appear to have been eroded. In the case of charities, the problem has been a *quantitative* one (decline in the *civic core* of citizens involved). In the case of commons and honour organizations, the decline has more of a *qualitative* flavour: the construction of solidarity organizations has suffered from a growth of distrust in modern societies (Hardin 2006; Rosanvallon 2006).

Second, and maybe for the same reasons, there has been a shift in the *pressure to build more solidarity organizations*. At first, in the post-World War II period, circumstances have called for more and more commons-based organizations and a lesser emphasis on charity-based organizations, as the welfare state invasion proceeded, and as honour organizations lost their lustre. More recently, in the post-Thatcher world, the pressure has been upward across the board.

But the key foundational components have changed. One has a sense that the focus is becoming less on principles-based organizations dedicated to helping *them* – a matter about which we knew quite a bit – toward organizations dedicated first and foremost to helping *us* and *all* (1) based on sophisticated social architecture and designs that are still in their infancy, and (2) a better understanding of the socio-psychological dimensions that have not been well explored.

Third, it has become clear that new solidarity organizations often tend to emerge from social movements (Hine 1977; Angus 2001). These organizations have a *diagnostic importance*, and often develop into a force that can influence opinion within the broader society: "they make questionable what has previously not been questioned and thereby open up larger areas of social life to public discussion, decision and action" (Angus 2001:65).

In a world of powerlessness, apathy, and distrust, solidarity organizations are at the core of this process of discovery of community and identity. This makes them somewhat subversive, and it explains why dynamic conservatism in the organizations themselves (and in the state sector) is so strongly countering them: these organizations are becoming agents of social change.

iii.   The growing complexity and deeper diversity of the context has led to a particularly important increase in the *variety of the solidarity communities*. This has led to a burgeoning of organizational innovations and to an explosion of different experiments. This complicating of the *terrain des opérations* has led to some balkanization, and much overlap, in the coverage and extension of the different solidarity organizations. Perhaps more importantly, the growing and deepening interdependencies have multiplied the loci of potential commons.

Solidarity organizations have mostly continued to focus exclusively on their fiduciary/technical and analytical/strategic roles, they have often not graduated to true generative governing – i.e., putting in place the creative grappling, grasping and sense-making that are the true underpinnings of learning and discerning, even though this is exactly what is required in this new context.

This cultural transformation of the composition and role of boards is unlikely to materialize unless more emphasis is placed on intelligent accountability (O'Neill 2002) with less of a focus on the superficial transparency that may tend to deter experimentation and make solidarity organizations even more risk-averse.

iv.   Not only have the textures of mega-communities and the solidarity organizations grown richer, but the relevant domain over which the charities, commons and honour organizations have begun to spread has grown significantly as a result of the increased interdependencies. What used to be parish-based or quasi-tribal in scope has come to encompass much broader socio-technical realities. Both territories and social entities involved have emerged on a new scale, and this has called for the construction of new organizations built on weaker links.

Meso-scale solidarity organizations, where they have emerged, have generated new challenges. Becoming more spread out and more diffuse has meant facing difficulties of mobilization but has strengthened peripheral informal monitoring and learning. On the other hand, bureaucratization has often ensued.

Governing by network is the solution, but this calls for new competencies: aligning goals, providing oversight, averting communication failure, coordination of multiple partners, overcoming information and capacity deficits, etc. (Goldsmith and Eggers 2004).

These are matters that have not been mastered by solidarity organizations.

v.   Solidarity organizations have also tended to blend different principles of integration, and to become more and more hybridized. The futility of the search for independence and autonomy has become more and more apparent. The new ongoing *métissage* has generated new interdependencies among sectors, and made it much less likely that pure solidarity organizations can work in isolation from market and state.

This erosion of a single and powerful dominant logic has had un-intended consequences of some import.

The first is a growth of hyper-competition as a natural consequence of the takeover of the solidarity organizations by staffers and bureaucrats. But they are not alone. In this age of growing distrust of the state, citizens are choosing to get involved in *impolitical* ways, and solidarity organizations are a magnificent instrument for ideologues to mobilize emergent publics.

Second, this triple helix (hypercompetition, bureaucratic efforts to replace politics with administration, and some hijacking of solidarity organizations by radicals) has made the governance of solidarity organization, much more complex, and may explain why solidarity organizations have often lost their sense of purpose and ceased to be the agents of prototyping and serious play.

Conclusion

It has been argued by Gintis at al that the role of solidarity organizations is bound to increase over the next little while.

This argument is based on three basic assumptions.

First, citizens are not as badly informed nor as willingly inactive as is presumed: they will distrust the state more and more, and will choose to take their affairs into their own hands more and more often, albeit perhaps in a manner that may be more obstructive than previously.

Second, there is a propensity by a number of citizens to act in other-regarding ways, and a high probability (even if the reciprocators are not a majority) that such an attitude will pervade the rest of the community and crystallize around commons issues like environment and the like.

Third, discontent about the failures of market and state is growing, and combined with the conviction that auxiliary conditions will likely emerge that will favor experimentation with solidarity organizations, these forces will translate into the emergence of a very loose regulatory framework that will both facilitate and reassure citizens that these new solidarity organizations can do a great deal of good and that citizens are protected because these creatures are under control.

There may be a number of blockages on the road to this tamed world of solidarity organizations, and many slippages that may derail the dynamics, but it would appear that the general trend toward a greater presence of solidarity organizations is at least a credible possibility. This, however, is likely to require a significant transformation of the existing solidarity groups, and that, in turn, raises many crucially important questions:

Can solidarity organizations adjust more effectively to the new variegated context?

Can they graduate to generative governance?

Can they meet the challenges of meso-organizations and the new centrality of weak ties?

Can they re-invent a new blend of charity, commons and honours?

Can the reciprocators regain the control of their organizations from the sociocrats?

Can dynamic conservatism be overcome?

Can solidarity organizations become a main vehicle of social change?
   Underpinning many of these questions is a redefinition of a few words:
1. if solidarity organizations are to prosper, *proximity* has to take a different meaning. Distant proximities are required. This is the world that Rosenau (2003) has begun to explore;
2. *commons* has to become a way to frame many questions that used to be framed in terms of charity or honour;
3. the cognitive and subversive nature of *solidarity* organizations is at the root of emerging publics and social change: it has to be harnessed, not suppressed by the power structure.

References

I. Angus, *Emergent Publics*. Winnipeg: Arbeiter Ring Publishing, 2001.
J. Baechle, *Précis de la démocratie*. Paris: Calmann-Lévy-Unesco, 1994.
K.G. Banting et al, *Open Federalism*. Kingston: Institute of Intergovernmental Affairs, 2006.
M. Bevir and R.A.W. Rhodes, *Governance Stories*. London: Routledge, 2006.
K.E. Boulding, *A Primer on Social Dynamics*. New York: The Free Press, 1970.
P. Bourdieu, *Outline of a Theory of practice*. Cambridge: Cambridge University Press, 1977.
S. Bowles, *Microeconomics – Behavior, Institutions, and Evolution*. New York: Russell Sage Foundation, 2004.
W.F. Buckley jr *Gratitude*. New York : Random House, 1990.
A. Burelle, *Le mal canadien*. Montréal : Fides, 1995.
R.P. Chait et al. *Governance as Leadership*. New York : Wiley, 2005.
K.S. Cook, R. Hardin, M. Levi, *Cooperation without trust?*. New York: Russell Sage Foundation, 2005.
P. d'Iribarne, *La logique de l'honneur*. Paris : Seuil, 1989.

P. d'Iribarne et al. *Cultures et mondialisation*. Paris : Seuil, 1998/2002.

F.E. Emery and E.L. Trist, "The Causal Texture of Organizational Environments" *Human Relations*, 18, 1965, 21-32.

O. Favereau, "Trois considérations critiques sur les rapports entre l'éthique et la théorie économique" in M. Canto-Sperber (sld) *Éthiques d'aujourd'hui*. Paris : PUF, 2004, 25-36

J. Friedman, "There is no Substitute for Profit and Loss" *Society* 44(3) 2007, 48-53.

F. Fukuyama, *Trust – The Social Virtues and the Creation of Prosperity*. London: Hamish Hamilton, 1995.

B. Garratt, *The Fish Rots from the Head*. London: HarperCollins, 1996.

M. Gerencser et al "The Mega-community Manifesto" www.strategy-business.com 16.08.06 (10p.) 2006.

H. Gintis et al (eds), *Moral Sentiments and Material Interest*. Cambridge: The MIT Press, 2005.

J.T. Godbout, *La démocratie des usagers*. Montréal : Boréal, 1987.

S. Goldsmith and W.D. Eggers, *Governing by Network*. Washington: The Brookings Institution, 2004.

D. Graeber, "Army of Altruists" *Harper's* 314 (1880) 2007, 31-38.

P. Hanley, *Third Sector and State Partnerships: Perspectives from the New Zealand Community Sector* (Deakin University, Melbourne) 2000, 12p.

R. Hardin, "Trusting Persons, Trusting Institutions" in R.J. Zeckhauser (ed) *Strategy and Choice*. Cambridge: The MIT Press, 1991, 185-209.

R. Hardin, *Trust*. Cambridge: Polity Press, 2006.

V.H. Hine, "The basic paradigm of a future socio-cultural system" *World Issues*, April-May 1977, 19-22.

F. Hirsch, *Social Limits to Growth*. Cambridge: Harvard University Press, 1976.

R. Hollingsworth, "Variation among nations in the logic of manufacturing sectors and international competitiveness" in D. Foray and C. Freedman (eds) *Technology and the Wealth of Nations*. London: Pinter, 1994, 301-331.

R. Hubbard, G. Paquet, "Ecologies of governance and Institutional Metissage" www.optimumonline.ca 31(4), 2002, 25-34.

R. Hubbard and G. Paquet, *Gomery's Blinders and Canadian Federalism*. Ottawa: The University of Ottawa Press., 2007

H.A. Husock, "Stock Market for Nonprofits" *Society* 44(3), 2007, 16-23.

T.R. Ireland and D.B. Johnson, *The Economics of Charity*. Blacksburg: Center for the Study of Public Choice, 1990.

D.B. Klein, *Reputation*. Ann Arbor: The University of Michigan Press, 1997.

L. Kohlberg, *The Philosophy of Moral Development*. New York : Harper & Row, 1981.

R. Laforest and S. Phillips, "Repenser les relations entre gouvernements et secteur bénévole : à la croisée des chemins au Québec et au Canada" *Politique et Sociétés*, 20 (2-3), 2001, 37-68.

P. Laurent, G. Paquet, *Epistémologie et économie de la relation : coordination et gouvernance distribuée*. Paris/Lyon : Vrin, 1998.

E.G. Mesthene, *Technological Change*. New York : Mentor Books, 1970.

O. O'Neill, *A Question of Trust*. Cambridge: Cambridge University Press, 2002.

E. Ostrom, *Governing the Commons*. Cambridge: Cambridge University Press, 1990.

E. Ostrom, *Understanding Institutional Diversity*. Princeton: Princeton University Press, 2005.

G. Paquet, "Professional Guilds and New Socials Rights" in J. Dufresne et al (eds) *The Professions: their growth or decline?* Montréal: Critère, 1979, 199-210.

G. Paquet, "The Strategic State" *Ciencia Ergo Sum* 3(3), 1996,257-261; 4(1), 1997, 28-34; 4(2), 1997, 148-154.

G. Paquet, *The New Geo-Governance – A Baroque Approach*. Ottawa: The University of Ottawa Press, 2005a.

G. Paquet, *Gouvernance: une invitation à la subversion*. Montréal : Liber, 2005b.

K.R. Popper, *Objective Knowledge*. Oxford: Oxford University Press, 1972.

C. Prahalad and R. Bettis, "The Dominant Logic: A New Linkage between Diversity and Performance" *Strategic Management Journal*, 7, 1986, 485-501.

R.D. Putnam, (ed) *Democracies in Flux*. Oxford: Oxford University Press, 2002.

N. Richebé, "Les réactions des salariés à la 'logique compétence': vers un renouveau de l'échange salarial?" *Revue française de sociologie* 43 (1), 2002, 99-126.

N. Richebé, "La gestion et la rémunération des compétences peuvent-elles inciter les salariés à coopérer? Réflexions sur le paradoxe de la coopération" *Document de recherche*, ESC Nantes, 2003.

P. Rosanvallon, *La contre-démocratie*. Paris : Seuil, 2006

J.N. Rosenau, *Distant Proximities*. Princeton: Princeton University Press, 2003.

D.A. Schön, *Beyond the Stable State*. New York: Norton, 1971.

M. Schrage, *Serious Play*. Boston: Harvard Business School Press, 2000.

C. R. Sunstein, *Infotopia*. Oxford: Oxford University Press, 2006.

R.M. Titmuss, *The Gift Relationship*. London: Allen & Unwin, 1970.

A. Tversky and D. Kahneman, "The Framing of Decisions and the Psychology of Choice" *Science* 211, 1981, 453-458.

Chapter 5

Stewardship versus leadership

"Every time we attribute everything to leadership,
we are no different from the people in the 1500s who
attributed everything they did not understand (such as
famine and plague) to God"

–Jim Collins

Introduction: problems with leadership

The notion of leadership is not unlike the ink blots on the slides used in a Rorschach test: one may read almost anything into these meaningless spots, and project into them any fantasy.

This weasel word –leadership– is popular for two main reasons.

First, leadership is anchored in the notion of hierarchy: it assumes that someone is in charge, and that he/she is responsible for the guidance of the organization, and responsible and accountable for anything good or bad that may ensue from such guidance.

Second, leadership has mystical dimensions. It ascribes to the leader exceptional qualities the source of which is somewhat mysterious, and a power of seduction that cannot be entirely explained by rational means.

The attraction of such a notion lies fundamentally with its reassuring power: someone clairvoyant and wise is (or should be) in charge, and will take the organization to the promised land, sparing the rest of the crew the need to worry about where the ship is going. The followers can wallow in *servitude volontaire*.

The fact that in the real world nobody is in charge, and that these exceptional qualities are so elusive, makes the discussions about leadership somewhat surreal. Such discussions quickly slump into circularity and seek intellectual comfort in tautology. The leader is identified as a person who has leadership qualities, and these leadership qualities are said to be the capacity of the leader. Leadership is not unlike phlogistics for proto-chemists who centuries ago explained inflammability by the existence of a flammable substance in objects.

Yet a whole literature has burgeoned around the notion of leadership, and it has become associated with a wide range of disparate properties purported to invest particular individuals with particular capacities to take charge. Indeed, a certain scholarship claims to have identified those properties, and some management schools are unashamedly claiming to be able to inject them into willing souls like steroids.

In the rest of the paper, I underline the inadequacy of this notion, and suggest replacing it by the alternative notion of stewardship – one that would appear to be better adapted to a networked world (Goldsmith et Eggers 2004) where nobody is in charge because power, resources, and information are widely distributed (Cleveland 2002). The notion of stewardship has the added benefit of not requiring any mystical garb, and of being based on certain understandable mechanisms. This chapter explores those mechanisms.

A word ending in *ship* and dressed in mystical garb

In English, the words ending in *-ship* are part of a family of expressions connoting a capacity to exercise a complex activity – like entrepreneurship or citizenship. These words are congenitally fuzzy. They define the contours of a complex of behaviors, activities, and relations – a nebulous entity that can only be approximated, but which corresponds to a dynamic, a set of activities oriented toward change, transformation, and geared to accomplishing something.

The popularity of these expressions is ascribable to the fact that they lend some firmness to incompletely theorized realities. Conversely, it also explains why they allow dramatically different interpretations to blossom and to become accredited.

In the case of leadership, the true believers associate the word with some sort of aura of clairvoyance-cum-influence: the leader sees things better than others, has uncommon communication capacities, and commands the unconditional following of the masses. Cynics are rather skeptical about the existence of such clairvoyance, and suspend their judgment in the face of the constant reference to some sort of charisma – a word that connotes the same occult powers that were invoked to explain that rats and children were mesmerized by the pied piper in the Grimm brothers' tale.

The followers do not believe that it is irrational to follow the leader, because he knows things the rest of the group does not know. We follow Warren Buffett because he is better informed than we are, more competent, and because he obviously has good reasons for doing things even though we do not fully understand them. It is a matter of faith.

In the traditional model of leadership, the root of this asymmetry is based on some sort of enlightened guidance capability embodied in the person of the leader. This is the presumption in good currency, even though organizations evolve in the absence of an enlightened person-leader. (The determining influences on an organization may emerge from diverse sources – random events, culture, systemic gridlock, a multiplicity of sources of innovation, etc. – that cannot be related to any presumed leader.)

This traditional approach to leadership drifts quickly into magical thinking when it rationalizes search processes for a leader with these mystical personal qualities that one is purported to be able to transport from one situation to the other like the turtle carries its shell. This has generated a whole literature – from the nice photographs of Charles Handy's *The New Alchemists* (1999), to the self-help texts for sale in airports that promise all comers a recipe to become such a mystical leader in just a few lessons.

The intent here is not to deny that there are exceptional individuals who are able to inspire their colleagues. Rather it is to denounce a literature built on pop psychology, that appears to be about as sophisticated as biology used to be when it classified animals according to the number of legs. Such an approach contributes to keeping the attention away from the modern realities of stewardship in a world of networks where nobody is in charge, and power, resources and information are widely distributed.

A primer on stewardship in a world of "small-g"

The central hypotheses underpinning governance as stewardship are that in modern organizations nobody is in charge, and that stewardship is *un effet de système*. Therefore, it depends on the nature of the system in question. And since there has been a change in the nature of the system – a drift from Big-G government to small-g governance in all organizations – there has been a change of kind in the nature of stewardship (Paquet 1999; Hubbard & Paquet 2007).

In the world of Big-G, hierarchy was the order of the day, and some individuals or groups claimed (legitimately or not) to be in charge. They issued orders and inert agents were supposed to obey to the best of their abilities. This was the world of *servitude volontaire*.

In the new world of small-g, nobody is in charge, and the different stakeholders have a portion of power, resources, and information. As a result, collaboration and effective coordination are the new imperatives. This collaboration occurs through conversations and communications in which active agents are experimenting (each in their own way) in the full consciousness that their action will trigger unintended consequences, and that their intended outcomes may not be the realized outcomes. Self-organization forces complement deliberate interventions: sometimes, it amplifies their impact; at other times it neutralizes or distorts them.

In the public sector, a massive redesign of the governing apparatus, as a result of the drift from a welfare state to a strategic state (Paquet 1999), has generated forceful resistance within the technocracy (often emboldened by a citizenry not eager to lose generous state protection) to new arrangements calling for a lower valence for the state, more inter-sectoral partnerships, and more mass collaboration – all initiatives seen as reducing the power of the powerful, including the upper levels of the state bureaucracy in place, and demanding a greater personal responsibility of the citizenry. The same wave of transformation has hit organizations and institutions in the private and social sectors, with the same resistance from the managerial class.

Despite such resistance, stewardship has been transformed in all sectors. Coordination has become the pivotal feature. It can materialize through one person in small groups, like a boat with eight rowers – through the light touch of the coxswain. In more complex organizations, nothing but the equivalent of an automatic pilot will suffice: an ensemble of mechanisms assuring the requisite dynamic coordination (Paquet 2007).

In the small-g world, each stakeholder needs to contribute to the stewardship through working at continually improving the automatic pilot. As a result, any lack of critical thinking or vigilance on the part of any stakeholder or member may result in less effective experimentation, poorer prototypes being developed, less effective social learning, and therefore in a governance regime that is less effective than it might have been (Argyris & Schön 1978, Schön & Rein 1994).

The governance regime (i.e., the ensemble of mechanisms making up the automatic pilot) ensures stewardship, and commands a new level of responsibility for all the parties involved. This new responsibility of all parties involved makes those who are not continually making full use of their critical thinking, and are not tinkering with the governance regime in real time, complicit in the fiascos that may ensue as a result of their sins of omission.

Stewardship: components and guideposts

Stewardship is an echo effect of the governance regime, and the governance regime may be regarded as an attractor, the cruising regime that crystallizes temporarily in the absence of major disturbances.

One can analyze the governance regime in its three components: (1) the emergence of the governance regime as attractor; (2) the process through which there is or is not rallying support for it, and it acquires legitimacy or not; and (3) the capacity on the basis of this focal regime to generate the requisite amount of coordination, resilience, innovation, overcoming and accomplishment. The challenge is to explain how the stewardship emerges without needing to be personalized, and how it generates resilience and high performance or catastrophes – for there is no guarantee of success.

Emergence of governance regimes

In certain cases, where the situation is relatively simple, an attractor emerges organically. The contextual pressures generate some anomie in the agents. This leads them to search for guideposts, and a focal regime emerges to resolve the tensions among the different points of view. In the case of a pure and perfectly competitive situation, a price system will become the focal regime, as was experienced in the desolate world of POW camps in the 1940s, where the fact that each prisoner was receiving a Red-Cross type standard ration which did not necessarily match his/her pattern of preferences generated a situation that gave rise to generalized trading within the POW camp with cigarettes used as currency (Radford 1945). In a total panic, a crowd movement becomes the reference point (Dupuy 1992). In both cases, coordination emerges without the need for any personalization.

In more complex cases, the governance regime emerges in more circuitous ways: effective coordination connotes sets of principles, norms, rules, mechanisms, and protocols, around which the expectations of agents converge, and around which decision-making and implementation get defined (Paquet 2005a : 76-78). Such a regime may crystallize quickly when the organization is relatively small. Communities of practice gel; for instance, the board of directors of a small high-tech startup company brings together quite naturally the inventive engineer, the angel financier, the potential important buyer of the new widget, etc. This forum undertakes the stewarding function.

In more complex organizations (private, public, social) the governance regime wears a more formal attire (more legalistic, constraining), and the board is more stylized, but the same logic is at play.

In these complex cases also, Chait et al (2005) show that the governance regime is not playing the simple role of financial sentinel (Type I governance) but is also the place where the points of view of the different stakeholders get integrated (Type II governance). An effective governance regime goes further and is the locus of discernment, of meaning-making, provides the mental map of the organization, of its environment, its mission, its projects, and proposes the sort of transformations, innovations, and reframing likely to bring the organization beyond its limits, to renew itself (Type III or generative governance). This generative governance unfolds through a robust multilogue, much experimentation, prototyping and social learning, and the collaborative congealing of nothing less than a community of meaning (Michael 1993; Schrage 2000; Martin 2000, 2004, 2006, 2007).

Support and legitimacy

In order for the focal regime to be able to resolve all those tensions in a creative way, it must generate a rallying effect that bestows legitimacy. What must emerge is nothing less than a culture, *une manière de voir* that establishes the basis of a collective intelligence that facilitates collaboration.

How is this collective intelligence constructed? It is through communication and deliberation. A focal regime underwrites a structure, certain rituals, mechanisms that facilitate interactions by stabilizing anticipations. This is the visible face of the governance regime that triggers a rallying movement, or a movement of rejection, through the dual logics of synchronicity and cascades (Sunstein 2006).

This movement of contagion may materialize through reasoned discussion and justification, but it may also operate through surprise mechanisms – like modes and fads – via the media that may either dampen the cascade or amplify its impact and generate a movement of polarization (Guillaume 1987, 1989). These mechanisms of propagation are relatively poorly understood, and may generate governance regimes that are idiosyncratic, fragile, and often surprising (McCann & Selsky 1984; Bikhchandani et al 1998; Barabasi 2002; Strogatz 2003; Sunstein 2006).

Only when a governance regime is in place can it be said to be performing well or not. Obviously, the focal regime must make sense of the situation, but it must most importantly have a *great adaptive capacity* (Bennis & Thomas 2002: 45). This capacity does not emerge from the *properties* of the governance regime (that would be usable in all situations and transportable from one situation to another), but from the *capacities* of a regime that are revealed *in situ*, in a precise context and particular circumstances (DeLanda 2006). It is the wave that determines if the governance regime as *surfer* has the required capacities.

Effective coordination: uncertain

Do these difficulties condemn all efforts at designing a good governance regime to fail? Some, like Lindblom (1990), think so; others are more optimistic, and believe that this is not the case, and that one may soon be able to gauge, to engineer, and to nudge into existence the right mix of *capacities* likely to generate good governance and good stewardship in different contexts. However, for the time being, most observers are satisfied to list the important *properties* of persons-leaders (Badaracco 2006; Martin 2007, to name just a few), and there has been little attempt to sort out the *capacities* likely to generate goodness-of-fit for governance regimes, and therefore effective stewardship.

One can reasonably suggest however that the principles of good governance likely to generate that sort of dynamic adaptative steward-ship would have to make good use of the following reference points: inclusion, subsidiarity, multistability, and experimentalism (Paquet 2005b: ch.8). In each case, these reference points must obviously be interpreted taking into account each particular context, but they cannot be ignored.

i. Longitude: the inclusion-subsidiarity axis

The first two reference points have to do with the best way to assemble the potential partners when power, resources and information are diffracted, and to structure their coordinated work. The key idea is to include as many of the meaningful stakeholders as possible in the decision-making process (inclusion), and to design the decision-making apparatus in such a way as to allow those closest to the situation to take the decision (subsidiarity). From this ensues the principle of as much decentralization as possible, but only as much centralization as necessary.

Such a participative and distributed governance regime should ensure continuous social learning, quick self-correcting feedback, creative conflict resolution, and the existence of shared responsibility mechanisms in order to generate the right mix of reliability and innovation.

In the words of Simons (2005), proper alignment for the organization requires that the spans of control (hard) and support (soft) – on the supply side of resources – be adequate to meet the obligations imposed by the spans of accountability (hard) and influence (soft) – on the demand side of resources.

ii.   Latitude: the multistability-experimentalism axis

The other two reference points deal with the resolution of tensions between exploitation and exploration (March 1991). The principle of multistability is important in the architecture of open systems. It suggests that the best way to stabilize a differentiated system is to partition it into sub-systems in order (a) to immunize the system as a whole from the impact of broad shocks that could destabilize it completely, hitting it as a whole; and (ii) to be in a position to delegate to a portion of the organization (best able to handle the shock) the adjustment job that is called for.

Multistability also facilitates experimentation and innovation by allowing them to proceed *par morceaux*. Innovation is creative destruction, and thereby destabilizing. A good governance regime will be fundamentally *experimentalist*, capable of engaging the organization in new avenues, but safely and prudently – i.e., engaging it tentatively, partially, and often *par morceaux* (Sabel 2001, 2004); Schrage 2000). This form of attentive experimentalism is an essential condition for Type III governance.

iii.   Sextant: blockages, sabotage and failures

Despite the fact that these reference points will help in nudging an adequate governance regime into existence, and in ensuring effective stewardship, there is no assurance that such an outcome will prevail. There are systemic blockages that may prevent such emergence: an important one being the gridlock fragmentation of ownership powers that may well prevent the assembly of what every stakeholder knows is a winning combination (Heller 2008).

There are also acts of sabotage: passive sabotage as a result of neglect, lack of vigilance or sheer incompetence, or active sabotage by powerful vested interests that may see immense benefits for their clan in ensuring that some effective governance regime and stewardship do not materialize (Hubbard & Paquet 2009).

Perhaps more importantly, governance failures and ineffective stewardship may evolve because of cognitive dissonance, and a refusal to factor in (even in a tentative way) the dynamic of context and the power of self-organization that are bound to produce surprises (good and bad). These occurrences cannot be ignored, and must be dealt with opportunistically.

This factor is most important not so much because of any inherent destructiveness in self-organization *per se*, but because the very existence and importance of self-organization is occluded, denied, and therefore not fully (or even partially) taken advantage of.

The unbearable denial of self-organization

In a world where nobody is in charge (Cleveland 2002), stewardship emerges from a good matching of the structure of governance and the dynamics of the context – together with a full awareness of the underlying forces of self-organization that are constantly unleashed. But a mental block exists with reference to self-organization.

Mitchel Resnick (1994) has analyzed that blockage with much subtlety. He shows that it corresponds to a profound sentiment in humans who (i) do not understand creative mechanisms like randomness (that opens new avenues of exploration), positive feedback (that amplifies the impact of a minor shock), emergence ascribable to interactions among agents (as in the case of traffic jams), etc.; (ii) refuse to acknowledge the very notion of self-organization; and (iii) cling to explanations that assume that complex realities must be orchestrated by a *deus ex machina*, and refuse to accept that there is not a leader to claim responsibility or to shoulder the blame.

This is the sort of reaction one expects from young children (who are naturally animists). Resnick tells a story about Rachel (the very young daughter of a friend of his) who has a theory about rain: clouds rain, she suggests, because the thunder orders them to (Resnick 1994: 147). For children, there must be someone in charge. But adults and scientists have the same mental blocks. This explains the difficulty of communicating the messages of Adam Smith (market and the invisible hand) and of Charles Darwin (evolution), who have proposed theories that do not require that anybody be in charge. The same skepticism awaits works that suggest that CEOs and orchestra leaders may not be as indispensable as is usually presumed (Cleveland 2002; Semler 1989; Seifter and Economy 2001).

It is only by disclosing the basic mechanisms at work in the governance of organizations that one may unveil the workings of the automatic pilot, and that one may hope to dispel these mental blockages (Spinosa et al 1998). In this sense, the flow of studies of leadership in the traditional literature is counter-productive: they contribute to keeping alive the tradition of mysticism, instead of showing how the basic mechanisms of stewardship work.

Some studies of complex systems, like ant hills or synchronized flocks of birds, show the way: complex coordination exists without an ant-in-chief or a leader bird (Resnick 1994). This is also the case for human organizations, as in the case of a leaderless orchestra, (Seifter & Economy 2001) or the governance of aircraft carriers operations (Pool 1997). It is only through an examination of a very large number of such cases of complex organizations, where there is stewardship without a leader, that one may hope to break the spell that gets both experts and lay persons to fall prey to the propensity to search always and everywhere for a deus ex machina.

But this demolition work cannot suffice. One must also find ways to open the minds to the ways of self-organization (Axelrod & Cohen 1999; Johnson 2001; Tapscott & Williams 2006). This is bound to be a daunting task. For the time being, the theories of self-organization of Smith and Darwin are said to be believed, but it is often more from fear of ridicule than as a result of their theories being fully understood, even by the educated public.

Stewardship as process

The crucial difference between properties and capacities raises questions about how one may expect to improve the practice of stewardship since "adequate" properties may not suffice. This calls for a dynamic sense of stewardship as process, as the result of on-going social learning based on individual and collective capacities, affordances, and innovation.

As we have shown elsewhere (Paquet 1999, 2005), social learning is triggered by anomalies noted and taken seriously. This is best captured by the social learning cycle à la Boisot (1995). Collective intelligence is defined by Pierre Lévy as "une intelligence partout distribuée, sans cesse valorisée, coordonnée en temps réel, qui aboutit à une mobilisation effective des compétences" (Lévy 1994:29). Such intelligence is continuously producing new knowledge and sharing it with all the partners, for its main purpose is social learning and the effective mobilization and coordination of the continually growing competencies of all the partners.

Social learning

In an effort to identify the major obstacles to social learning (and therefore to guide the process architecture interventions), Max Boisot has suggested a simple mapping of the social learning cycle in a three-dimensional space – the *information space* – which identifies an organizational system in terms of the degree of *abstraction, codification,* and *diffusion* of the information flows within it. This three-dimensional space defines three continua: the farther away from the origin on the vertical axis, the more the information is codified (i.e., the more its form is clarified, stylized, and simplified); the farther away from the origin laterally eastward, the more widely the information is diffused and shared; and the farther away from the origin laterally westward, the more abstract the information is (i.e., the more general the categories in use) (Boisot 1995).

The social learning cycle is presented in two phases, with three steps in each phase: phase I emphasizes the cognitive dimensions of the cycle, phase II the diffusion of the new information.

In phase I, learning begins with some scanning of the environment, and of the concrete information widely diffused and known, in order to detect anomalies and paradoxes. Following this first step (s), one is led in step 2 to stylize the problem (p),posed by the anomalies and paradoxes, in a language of problem solution; the third step of phase I purports to generalize the solution found to the more specific issue to a broader family of problems through a process of abstraction (at). In phase II, the new knowledge is diffused (d) to a larger community of persons or groups in step 4. Then there is a process of absorption (ar) of this new knowledge by the population, and its assimilation so as to become part of the tacit stock of knowledge in step 5. In step 6, the new knowledge is not only absorbed, but has an impact (i) on the concrete practices and artefacts of the group or community.

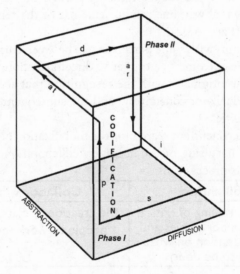

Figure 1
Learning cycle and potential blockages.
Source : Max Boisot, 1995, pp. 237, 190.

In Figure 1, one can identify the different blockages through the learning cycle. In Phase I, cognitive dissonance in (s) may prevent the anomalies from being noted, epistemic inhibitions of all sorts in (p) may stop the process of translation into a language of problem solution, and blockages preventing the generalization of the new knowledge, because of the problem definition being encapsulated within the *hic et nunc* (at), may keep the new knowledge from acquiring the most effective degree of generality. In Phase II, the new knowledge may not get the appropriate diffusion because of property rights (d), or because of certain values or very strong dynamic conservatism which may generate a refusal to listen by those most likely to profit from the new knowledge (ar), or because of difficulties in finding ways to incorporate the new knowledge (i).

Interventions to remove or attenuate the negative effects of such blockages always entail some degree of interference with the mechanisms of collective intelligence. In some cases, like the modification of property rights, the changes in the rules appear relatively innocuous, but entail interfering with the affairs of the mind: correcting social learning blockages modifies relational transactions, and therefore the psycho-social fabric of the organization.

Framework for stewardship in action

If one had to stylize the stewardship process through social learning in a sequential way, one might make use of the template used by practitioners (Parr 2002).

Stage A begins with some perceived gap between current reality and some desirable outcome as a trigger to direct attention toward initiating action. This originates with the recognition that action is required (either individually or collectively) and the subsequent exploration of action possibilities.

Stage B is a concurrent search for the mobilization of required partners, and the nurturing of the necessary collaboration. This dual and interactive sub-process calls for

Mobilization	Collaboration
the correct framing of critical issues and opportunities and focusing attention on what needs to be done	the creation of platforms for people to work together
the communication of key information likely to inspire, rally and motivate a broader set of people to take part in the diverse networks	the development of new relationships capable of generating tangible results and thereby of changing mindsets, and encouraging creative thinking

Stage C has to do with efforts to sustain change through creating and renewing institutions, and re-igniting the process by refocusing on new challenges and opportunities. This entails much conceptual refurbishment, and efforts to agitate and rekindle the social learning process through reframing the very notion of what is possible.

What is required is a capacity for the organization to learn, i.e., to reflect on its own experience, to make sense of it, and to retool, restructure, and even to reframe the basic questions facing the organization in order to generate effective ways to discern and grapple with the generative challenge of learning. These requirements have been spelled out by practitioners of reflexive governance. They may be summarized as follows: knowledge integration and learning by doing; capacity for long-run anticipation of systemic effects; adaptivity of strategies and institutions; iterative experimental and participatory definition of broad directions; and interactive strategy development (Drath & Palus 1994; Voß et al 2006).

Competencies

Since dynamic adaptation is the core process, such stewardship action requires competencies that need to be nudged into existence, not only by leveraging the existing forces of self-organization, but also by harnessing them somewhat.

These required competencies may be divided into five categories (Michael 1993; Hughes & Weiss 2007):

(i) contextual (embrace uncertainty and error, building bridges, reframing, improvise, adapt, overcome (in the manner of Clint Eastwood's Heartbreak Ridge);

(ii) interpersonal (consultation, negotiation, deliberation, conflict resolution, facilitation, brokering, preceptoring, educating, animating, changing roles);

(iii) enactment (enabling, empowering, responsiveness, creativity);

(iv) systems values (ethics of interconnectiveness and interdependence, removing obstacles, freeing others to act better);

(v) staying the course while rocking the boat (imagination, experimentation, responsibility to explore, emphasis on sins of omission, learning by prototyping)

These capacities are not only individual, but collective, in the sense that rules of interaction among individuals generate emerging properties that derive from the dynamics of situations, not from the heads of actors. The interaction order (in the language of Goffman) generates a sort of collective intelligence, a sort of social mind (Goffman 1959; Johnson 2001; Rheingold 2002: 179).

The dual (individual and collective) capacities are obviously interacting and confronted with a context that affords "action possibilities" and not others. Whether these affordances are real or perceived is of less relevance than the fact that they limit the realm of possibilities. In particular, the context generates affordances that individuals and collectivities perceive or learn to perceive. Learning to perceive affordances is a key kind of perceptual learning (Gibson 1982; Norman 1999).

"Affordances are not fixed properties: they are relationships that hold between objects and agents… to discover and make use of affordances is one of the important ways" to deal with novel situations (Norman 2007: 68-69).

Learning to perceive affordances better or developing ways to improve such perception is the substance of social learning, and is at the core of innovation and innovative design. This is the way in which the automatic pilot is improved.

Stewardship dynamics

The dynamic of stewardship focuses on information and communication. But it need not be, as mentioned earlier, only through the head of actors: it may equally emerge from the context and situations. All the dimensions explored earlier are important (components, guideposts, process, framework, competencies) but they remain incomplete unless one can add some enabling resources – like the use of the mega-community, the development of common knowledge, and the full appreciation of the forces of synchronization – that are at the core of self-organization, and constitute the sort of glue that makes these other components hang together.

This is not the place to probe these matters at great length, but they cannot be ignored altogether.

i. Megacommunity

Stewardship entails cooperation, and has to take into account the various points of view coexisting within the mega-community process and involving divergent interests and developing partnerships based on trust, in which parties may jointly pursue somewhat different objectives.

A mega-community – i.e., "a public sphere in which organizations and people deliberately join together around a compelling issue of mutual importance, following a set of practices and principles that will make it easier to achieve results" (Gerencser et al 2006) – entails a requisite amount of both trust (institutional, inter-organizational, and interpersonal) and social capital.

As we mentioned in the last chapter, in practice, Gerencser et al have identified four critical elements for a thriving mega-community: (1) understanding the problems to be resolved, the necessary players and partners, and the ways in which they affect one another; (2) the presence of partners in a listening, learning and understanding mode; (3) designing and customizing of suitable cross-sector arrangements; and

(4) experiments: learning from them, and effective collective monitoring of progress.

People and groups potentially affected by, or involved in, stewardship are by definition players in the mega-community. For all of them, their interests in it (and views of it) will tend to be framed by the mindset that dominates the culture in good currency in the socio-economic context. Their opinions will evolve to some extent as time passes, and will change to a greater or lesser degree as a result of external influences.

Partners have quite different expectations. In the private sector, the main interest is the profitability likely to ensue if additional efficiency and effectiveness are value-adding. From the public sector point of view, even though the public good is readily invoked, bureaucrats, elected officials, political opposition, and the unionized public service may have diverse interests, and may not see things the same way. This is bound to have an impact on the nature of the negotiated contracts. The not-for-profit mindset is no more univocal. Board members, paid permanent staff members, and volunteers may pursue different objectives that will shape their direct involvement and choices in the process of enhancing stewardship.

The media also play a special role as opinion-molders, to the extent that they influence the frames of reference of both the mega-community and the particular actors, and help to shape their perspectives.

ii. Common knowledge

Another set of forces that is most important in the dynamics of stewardship is common knowledge. Chwe (2001: 98-99) has shown that "coordination is often achieved through adaptation and evolution and implicit communication, but often people explicitly communicate" in order to solve problems. He shows, looking at how common knowledge emerges, that it is often through communicative events like rituals, ceremonies, and other cultural practices. He thereby shows how the problem of indeterminacy in coordination can be resolved by common knowledge through rituals. It thereby indicates ways in which intervention might nudge people toward coordination through generating common knowledge, and allowing choices to be made by actors on that basis (i.e., allowing self-organization to proceed).

This approach explicitly leverages the cultural and informational contexts likely to generate effective self-organization.

iii. Synchronization

Yet another set of forces at work in the dynamics of stewardship has to do with synchronization: the fact that, for reasons that are not always clear, humans, like animals, would appear to fall into synchronized behavior in self-organized ways (traffic flows, applause, etc.). Strogatz (2003) has thoroughly reviewed the existence of synchronization in animal and human worlds: the spontaneous outbreak of coordinated or herd or mob behavior, with certain thresholds (or mix of thresholds for different groups) defining tipping points where mass synchronization occurs (Granovetter 1978; Watts 2002).

Strogatz has shown that, in the animal world, spontaneous coordination is omnipresent (fireflies flashing in unison, flocks of birds flying in formation, etc.). It has also been shown that synchronization occurs in the material world of lifeless things like clocks. In the human world, group think, coordination of menstrual cycles, etc. are also well documented. In the same way, synchronization materializes in group behavior, and we are beginning to understand the mechanisms underlying such generation of order out of chaos when certain thresholds are reached. This illustrates in a simple way the forces of self-organization that need to be taken into account.

Such forces of synchronization need not generate orderly coordination. Often they generate heart fibrillation or mobs. But understanding such forces is fundamental if one ever hopes to find the equivalent of a defibrillator at the social level

The dynamics of stewardship underpinning the metaphor of the automatic pilot needs to be understood as a mix of mechanisms, many of which are designed with certain purposes in mind, but many of which are simply the result of self-organization, either triggered by common knowledge, or as unintended consequences of context, situations and experimental interventions, or as a result of synch.

While this definition of stewardship does not promise the simplicity of the literature on imperial leadership, it has the advantage of defining a program of research that is immensely more promising and realistic. It escapes from the simplistic anthropomorphic images of governing, by recognizing both the full extent to which mechanisms can be put in place capable of nudging the organization in preferred directions, and the full extent to which experiments with prototypes to tinker with complex non-linear systems are likely to generate important unintended consequences as a result of the self-organization it triggers. Such an approach does not promise success in governing organizations, but it provides an insight into the ways in which governing works.

Conclusion

How can one refocus research away from leadership toward stewardship, toward questions like how focal points emerge, how their legitimacy gets established by contagion, how coordination through experimentation, prototyping, serious play and social learning contributes to developing an improved governance regime in symbiosis with the self-organization of the context, and how effective governance provides effective stewardship?

Primarily, in the first instance, by casting doubts on the chivalrous stories in good currency, and suspicion on their alchemists, but also by showing that one can usefully replace their magic potions with mechanisms. This quest began a long time ago with the intriguing work of scholars like the Nobel-Prize laureate Thomas Schelling (1978), who have made a career of showing how some complex social phenomena can be shown to be the outcome of relatively un-mysterious mechanisms; or like Leonid Huwicz (another Nobel prize winner, in a different genre) (Hurwicz & Reiter 2006).

But one must also be bolder and agree to deconstruct complex social phenomena, to dare to put forward hypotheses as fascinating, intriguing, and perplexing in such areas as those that have been proposed in dealing with the animal world.

One must succeed in generating for human organizations something like what Resnick has done to explain the creation of a single central cemetery in ant hills. He has shown that if an ant follows two simple rules – (1) if you stumble on a dead brother, and you are unburdened by a dead brother, take him on, and (2) if you stumble on a dead brother, and that you are already carrying another dead brother, dump him – it is possible to show by simulation of thousands of notional ants that they will construct a central cemetery without the need to assume that there is any foreman-ant.

This is the challenge of research in organization and coordination science in the next round: a sort of deconstruction of black-box notions and concepts into their component mechanisms.

Can one, with the existing tool box available, disclose the foundations of stewardship in all sorts of different contexts? To a certain degree, one most certainly can. And the hypothesis at the core of this paper is that the answer lies in a better understanding of governance regimes, of the dynamics of self-organization, and of the interactions between these two sets of forces. However, it may be that the work cannot be completed without much conceptual refurbishment: a new lexicon, new

Prgect

analytical tools, and a new paradigm (Resnick 1996; Axelrod 1997; Parket & Gallagher 2007).

References

Argyris, C., Schön, D.A., *Organizational Learning: A Theory of Action Perspective*, Addison-Wesley, 1978.

Axelrod, R. *The Complexity of Cooperation.* Princeton University Press, 1997.

Axelrod, R., Cohen, M.D., *Harnessing Complexity – Organizational Implications of a Scientific Frontier.* The Free Press, 1999.

Badaracco Jr, J.L. *Questions of Character.* Harvard Business School Press, 2006.

Barabasi, A.L. *Linked – The New Science of Networks*, Perseus, 2002.

Bennis, W.G., Thomas, R.J. "Crucibles of Leadership" *Harvard Business Review*, 80 (9), 2002, 39-45.

Bikhchandani, S. et al, "Learning from the Behavior of Others: Conformity, Fads, and Informational Cascades" *Journal of Economic Perspectives*, Vol. 12, No. 3, 1998, 151-170.

Boisot, M. *Information Space: A framework for learning in organizations, institutions and culture.* London: Routledge, 1995.

Chait, R.P. et al, *Governance as Leadership*, Wiley, 2005.

Chwe, M.S.Y. *Rational Ritual.* Princeton University Press, 2001.

Cleveland, H. *Nobody in Charge*, Jossey-Bass, 2002.

DeLanda, M. *A New Philosophy of Society*, Continuum, 2006.

Drath, W.H., Palus, C.J., *Making Common Sense*, Center for Creative Leadership, 1994.

Dupuy, J.P. *Introduction aux sciences sociales – Logique des phénomènes collectifs*, Ellipses/Ecole Polytechnique, 1992.

Gerencser, M. et al. 2006. "The Mega-community Manifesto" www.strategy-business.com 16.08.06, 2006, (10p).

Gibson, J.J. "A Preliminary Description and Classification of Affordances" in E.S. Reed & R. Jones (Eds) *Reasons for Realism.* Hillsdale N.J.: Lawrence Erlbaum & Associates, 1982, 403-406.

Goffman, E. *The Presentation of Self in Everyday Life.* Garden City, N.Y.: Doubleday, 1959.

Goldsmith, S., Eggers, W.D., *Governing by Network*, The Brookings Institution, 2004.

Granovetter, M. "Threshold Models of Collective Behavior" *American Journal of Sociology*, 83, 1978, 1420-1443.

Guillaume, M. "The Metamorphoses of Epidemia" in M. Feher, S. Kwinter (eds) *Zone 1/2 : The Contemporary City*, The MIT Press, 1987,

Guillaume, M. *La contagion des passions – essai sur l'exotisme intérieur*, Plon, 1989.

Handy, C. *The New Alchemists.* Hutchison, 1999.

Heller, M. *The Gridlock Economy.* Basic Books, 2008.

Himberger, D. et al."When there is no cavalry" *Strategy + Business*, 48, 2007, 10p.

Hubbard, R., Paquet, G., *Gomery's Blinders and Canadian Federalism*, University of Ottawa Press, 2007.

Hubbard, R., Paquet, G. "Design Challenges for the Strategic State" in A.M. Maslove (ed) *How Ottawa Spends 2009-2010*, McGill-Queen's University Press, 2009.

Hughes, J., Weiss, J. "Simple Rules for Making Alliances Work" *Harvard Business Review*, 85 (11), 2007, 122-131

Hurwicz, L., Reiter, S. *Designing Economic Mechanisms*. Cambridge: Cambridge University Press, 2006.

Johnson, S. *Emergence*. Scribner 2001.

Lindblom, C.E., *Inquiry and Change*, Yale University Press, 1990.

March, J.G., "Exploration and Exploitation in Organizational Learning", *Organization Science*, 2, 1991, 71-87.

Martin, R. "The Death of Heroic Leadership" *Rotman Management*, Fall 2000, 5-7.

Martin, R., "The Design of Business" *Rotman Management*, Winter 2004, 7-11.

Martin, R., "Designing in Hostile Territory" *Rotman Management*, Spring-Sumer 2006, 4-9.

Martin, R. *The Opposable Mind*, Harvard Business Review Press, 2007.

McCann, J.E., Selsky, J. 1984. "Hyperturbulence and the Emergence of Type 5 Environment" *Academy of Management Review*, 9, 460-470.

Michael, D.N., "Governing by Learning: Boundaries, Myths and Metaphors" *Futures*, 25(1), 1993, 81-89.

Norman, D.A. "Affordances, Conventions and design" *Interactions*, 6(3), 1999, 38-43.

Norman, D.A. *The Design of Future Things*. Basic Books, 2007.

Paquet, G. *Governance Through Social Learning*, The University of Ottawa Press, 1999.

Paquet, G. *The New Geo-Governance – A Baroque Approach*, The University of Ottawa Press, 2005a.

Paquet, G., *Gouvernance: une invitation à la subversion*, Editions Liber, 2005b.

Paquet, G., "Organization Design as Governance's Achilles' Heel" www.governancia.com, 1 (3), 2007, 1-11.

Parker, S., Gallagher, N. (eds) *The Collaborative State*. London: Demos, 2007.

Parr, J. et al. *The Practice of Stewardship*. Alliance for Regional Stewardship, 2002.

Pool, R. "When Failure in not an Option" *Technology Review*, 100(5), 1997, 38-45.

Radford, R.A. "The Economic Organization of a POW Camp" *Economica* 12 (48), 1945, 189-201.

Resnick, M. *Turtles, Termites and Traffic Jams*, The MIT Press, 1994

Resnick, M. "Beyond the Centralized Mindset" *Journal of Learning Sciences*, 5 (1), 1996, 1-22.

Rheingold, H. *Smart Mobs*. Cambridge: Perseus, 2002.

Sabel, C.F., "A Quiet Revolution of Democratic Governance: Towards Democratic Experimentalism" in *Governance in the 21st Century*, OECD, 2001, p.121-148

Sabel, C.F., "Beyond Principal-Agent Governance: Experimentalist Organizations, Learning and Accountability" in E. Engelen and M. Sie Dhian Ho (eds) *De Staat van de Democratie. Democratie Voorbij de Staat*. WRR Verkenning 3, Amsterdam University Press, 2004, 173-195.

Schelling, T.C., *Micromotives and Macrobehavior,* Norton, 1978.

Schön, D.A., Rein, M., *Frame Reflection*, Basic Books, 1994.

Schrage, M., *Serious Play*. Harvard Business School Press, 2000.

Seifter, H., Economy, P., *Leadership Ensemble: Lessons in Collaborative Management from the World's Only Conductorless Orchestra*, Times Books, 2001.

Semler, R. "Managing without managers" *Harvard Business Review*, 1989, 76-84.

Simons, R. *Levers of Organization Design*, Harvard Business School Press, 2005.

Spinosa, C. et al, *Disclosing New Worlds,* The MIT Press, 1997.

Strogatz, S., *Sync – The Emerging Science of Spontaneous Order*, Hyperion 2003.

Sunstein, C.R., *Infotopia*, Oxford University Press, 2006.

Tapscott, D., Williams, A.D. *Wikinomics*. Portfolio, 2006.

Voß, J.P. et al (eds) *Reflexive Governance for Sustainable Development*. Cheltenham: Edward Elgar, 2006.

Watts, D.J. "A Simple Model of Global Cascades on Random Networks" *Proceedings of the National Academy of Sciences* USA 99, 2002, 5766-5771.

Part III

Sketching and designing

Questioning unwarranted assumptions will not suffice either. The central challenge of governance is design. The particular difficulties created by the design process are that it calls for a different rationality: its purpose is to explore worlds that do not yet exist. Consequently, it demands skills quite different from the ones in good currency in conventional positivistic analysis (Romme 2003).

This sort of social architecture work has to take into account plumbing and engineering considerations: one cannot construct an edifice that would not respect these constraints. But these considerations do not dictate the nature of the built outcome. Social architects have to be guided by Hirschman's possibilism – the discovery of paths, however narrow, leading to outcomes that appear to be foreclosed on the basis of probabilistic reasoning alone.

The core task of organizational design is to disclose new worlds. For organizations are worlds: they are a totality of interrelated pieces of equipment to carry out a specific task (such hammering in a nail). These tasks are undertaken for some purposes (like building a house); and these activities bestow those accomplishing them with identities (like being a carpenter) (Spinosa et al 1997: 17). This is the sense in which one speaks of the world of medicine, business, or academe.

However, there is more to organizations than the interconnection of equipment, purposes, and identities. Spinosa et al use the word "style" to refer to the ways in which all the practices are coordinated and fit together in an organization. Style is what coordinates action, what makes certain kinds of activities and things matter. In a way, style is an echo of culture: it pertains not only to the way coordination is effected, but also to the way we effect change.

In their study, Spinosa et al (and many others) show how economic, social and political entrepreneurs are those who spot disharmonies between what seem to be the rules in good currency and what would appear to be the sort of practice likely to be effective. They detect anomalies. Those anomalies create puzzles. The reaction to puzzles is often to ignore them and pursue the on-going tasks as usual, instead of recognizing that the anomalies are creating mysteries, and that what is needed is a way of understanding mysteries, the search for "guidelines for solving a mystery by organized exploration of possibilities" (Martin 2004:7).

Effective governance regimes become aware of marginal practices (or alternative ways to re-tool, re-structure, and reframe their activities according to principles heretofore not regarded as necessarily of central interest) and tend to become involved in lateral thinking: articulating the problem differently, cross-appropriating ways of doing things elsewhere and adjusting them to the task at hand, reframing the very notion of the business one is in along different lines.

This is the world of prototyping, of experimentation, of serious play, of organization design. In all areas (economic, political, social) organ-ization design redefines the style of the organization.

The difficulty is that this type of world disclosing activity or inquiry – based on empathy (for one always designs for somebody else), on holistic problem-setting (solution-focused strategies, looking for what works), and prototyping (not waiting until one has the best solution, but starting with anything promising, prototyping it, getting feedback, playing with it, and learning in that way) – Tim Brown quoted in Martin 2004:11) – is not what higher education is organized to foster, and, as a result, the skills required are not necessarily cultivated (Paquet 2006).

This explains why the design work is done so poorly (Paquet 2007)

In this section, we present three exercises in critical thinking about design. The first one (Chapter 6) is a reaction to events which chal-lenged the suitability of Canadian federalism as it stood. The second one reframes the notion of regulation through an informational perspective (Chapter 7). The third one (Chapter 8) suggests an agenda for change for the federal public service, and a new covenant of moral contracts to define the burden of office of federal public servants.

References:

R. Martin, "The Design of Business" *Rotman Management*, Winter 2004, 7-11.

G. Paquet, *Savoirs, savoir-faire, savoir-être: in praise of professional wroughting and wrighting*. A think-piece for Campus 2020 – An inquiry into the future of British Columbia's post-secondary education system 2006 (available at http://www.campus2020.ca/EN/think_pieces/)

G. Paquet, "Organization Design as Governance's Achilles' Heel" www.governancia.com, 1 (3), 2007, 1-11.

A.G.L. Romme, "Making a Difference: Organization as Design" *Organization Science*, 14 (5) 2003, 558-573.

C. Spinosa, F. Flores, H.L. Dreyfus, *Disclosing New Worlds*. Cambridge: The MIT Press, 1997.

Chapter 6

Federalism as social technology

"Il n'est pas trop tôt pour cueillir le fruit
dont l'ignorance est la saveur"

– Joe Bousquet

Introduction

The conventional economic approach is rooted in a methodology of radical individualism. Starting with the assumption of rational monads operating in given and constraining environments, economists view the economy "as a sequence of acts of economizing, i.e., as choices induced by scarcity situations" (Polanyi 1968). Everything is "traced back to individual motivations with mind as the operative entity" (Robbins in Seckler 1975). Economists then attempt to reconstruct collective social phenomena and the texture of human economies from a hierarchy of microdecisions by individual actors.

There is a fundamental reason for taking exception to this framework, which dissolves human economies into marginal adjustments by rational independent monads with stable objectives, and operating within well-defined constraints. One cannot reconstruct the rich and changing texture of human economies exclusively from the perspectives and choices of those micro-managers.

An alternative approach is to present human economies as essentially relational, as nets of ongoing relations between persons, groups, and environment defining a game process with a characteristic generating function (in the sense that statisticians use the term). This approach, which owes much to the work of Karl Polanyi, presents the economy as "instituted process of interaction between man and his environment". The emphasis is on coordination, and on the transcending importance of the organizational and institutional aspects of the economy.

This alternative approach entails a change in the stylization of the economy from a network of physical flows of transactions and transformations, triggered by the consumption and production programs of the rational monads to a view of the economy as an information system. The economy as an information system is defined by the nature and the pattern of messages exchanged. These acquire a relative autonomy vis-à-vis individuals, very much like a language vis-à-vis the specific individuals using it, and contribute to shaping the structure of the economy, i.e., the network of actors, their activities, and their valences (defined by bundles of property rights).

The underlying system of communication, by making possible various types of behavior and actual instances of such behavior, tends to modify them over time.

This perspective on the economy makes it possible to suggest overall characterizations of economies as "instituted process", and allows the problem of finding the best economic organization to degenerate "into the problem of choosing the optimal information system" (Marschak 1966).

The socio-economic process

This inversion of perspectives not only directs attention to organizations, institutions and information as fundamental for an understanding of the economic game. It also underlines the process of intercreation between organizations and institutions, and information flows – each one helping to shape the other.

Adaptation and adoption
This comes about through a dynamic which composes the forces of adaptation by the parts or actors in the economy (an adjustment emphasized to the exclusion of almost everything else by the conventional approach) with the forces of adoption by the whole, which are less often mentioned.

The process of adaptation is familiar to all, and constitutes the basis for much of conventional economics: economic actors modify their program of consumption and production to bring them into line with environmental constraints in the name of self-interest, and their messages are modified accordingly. The process of adoption corresponds to a process of economic natural selection: the causal texture of the environment, and the structure and rules of operations of the system as a whole, generating institutional information and bestowing differential probability of survival on different parts, given their characteristics (Alchian 1950).

In the experience of all human economies there are many rounds of adaptation and adoption, and these rounds generate changes in the nature of the instituted process. At any stage, through the confluence of unintended consequences and unforeseen short-circuiting, the environment or the information system acquires new traits (Hirschman 1967) by a process of sedimentation, with the result that new "institutional information" (Newman 1976) – information supplied by the institutional structures and the whole to the component parts – is generated. A different adoption process ensues, and different adaptive behaviors are triggered in turn. The adaptation/adoption process triggers not only a change in the relations between parts and in the informational/institutional structure, but also, through cumulative causation, an erosion of parts and their valences/rights. The organizational form of the game acquires different features, and discontinuous and irreversible changes in the economic process are generated, as inequalities and asymmetries make the former organizational form less viable.

A particular sequence may generate modifications, not only in the type and quality of institutional information, but also in the formal rules of the game *stricto sensu* and even in the tacit or informal agreements on which the game is built. This in turn entails either the development of new ways to play the game of cooperation/conflict, or a breakdown of the game altogether. (Akerlof 1970)

A macroscope

One cannot understand the dynamics of that game, and usefully intervene in it, on the basis of the image provided by the conventional approach. A microscopic analysis may provide some explanation of the change in institutional arrangements ("that govern the ways in which these units can cooperate and/or compete") (Davis/North 1971) through the examination of differential costs of transactions. This is the basis of what might be called frictional economics. However, when what is at stake is an explanation of changes in the institutional environment ("the set of political, social and legal ground rules that establishes the basis for production, exchange and distribution"), frictional economics fails. What is required is a more macroscopic approach.

Such an approach has characterized Canadian economics in the Innis tradition, a tradition which "aimed at establishing the broad inter-relations between geography, economics, and political and social change" (Berger 1976). One might add technology and culture: other forces that helped shape the Canadian instituted process in an Innisian framework (Neill 1969). The main point in explaining this characteristic function of the institutional environment is that it is not the result of a conscious design, but has just grown as the undesigned result of social actions, as unintended consequences of rational actions (Popper cited in Seckler 1975).

True, some institutions in the socio-economy and its underground have been consciously designed, but it is a minority. To be able to make utterances about the process which defined a going concern like Canada`s socio-economy, one needs a macroscope to examine the "rules of operation and structures of institutions for the system as a whole rather than ... the decision rules of individuals within the system" (Adelman 1973).

Such a macroscope would attempt to identify the main forces which appear to explain the drift in the Canadian socio-economic process in order to understand the role of certain key institutions, and to make sense of crises tendencies within it.

Drift in the Canadian socio-economic process

Over the last century, a confluence of internal and external forces, through many rounds of adaptation/adoption, has contributed to getting the economy/society/polity of Canada instituted quite differently from what it used to be, and to its acquiring significantly different characteristics: the economic/social/political partitionings have evolved, the valences of the actors (old and new) have changed, and the information systems binding segments of the Canadian system and the whole have been transformed. (Dubuc 1966)

One might usefully underline a few overall characteristics of the Canadian system which have not always been as fully appreciated as would be required to understand the strains put on our system of governance:
 - the shift from the *Nouveau Régime* to a *Régime Contemporain*
 - the dematerialization of economy activity
 - the growth of regulation in a world of "limited identities"

i.   The century that preceded Confederation had seen the replacement of relations of coercion and reciprocity by relations of exchange and commerce as the central piece of the new instituted process of the economies of the western world.

At the time of Confederation, the full impact of Polanyi's "Great Transformation" had been felt in Canada: the *Ancien Régime* instituted for the minimization of collective risks, subject to an adequate income-generating constraint, had come to be replaced by a different institutional environment – the *Nouveau Régime* – instituted to "maximize (more or less) the overall social value-added subject to a maximum risk constraint" (Adelman 1973). The country's constitution was drafted within an era dominated by this ideology of growth. It was only with the acceleration of economic development (and the concomitant processes of industrialization and urbanization which ensued over the last century) that the "creative destruction" of laissez-faire arrangements became apparent, and that "the hope of a self-regulating world of persons" (Vickers 1970) began to disappear.

The heightened degree of relevant uncertainty and turbulence which accompanied this acceleration of change, and the growing complexity of the urban/industrial socio-economy, led to more and more demands for and instances of deliberate regulation, of information supplied in the form of edicts or explicit incentives by state institutions as a complement and/or a substitute to "institutional information" supplied by the market. This in turn led to the emergence of a new institutional environment – le *Régime Contemporain* – instituted to reduce risk of societal and individual disasters subject to a minimum value-adding being maintained (Paquet 1977).

ii.   An important change in the world economic process in the thirty years after World War II also had important reverberations in the Canadian economy, although with some unevenness: a dematerialization of economic activity, i.e., a shift of employment toward the tertiary sector, and in particular toward information-processing and knowledge-intensive activity (Perroux 1970).

Some have even announced the arrival of the information economy. In Perroux' words, "le bien économique n'est pas une structure physique, c'est une combinaison de services: il est conçu comme tel par celui qui le fabrique et le vend et par celui qui l'achète".

The emergence of such an information economy has had some important reverberations in the economic process. One has progressively witnessed a deterritorialization of economic activities, to the extent that many aspects of the economic process have become less dependent on the presence of immobile or not easily movable physical resources. The economic process has become more footloose. This has triggered important reorganizations in the manner in which the economy is instituted: a shift from enterprises built around a product to enterprises defined by the control of a process, and more recently, with the increased importance of information processes, to the large firm as a flexible organization, based on gains from information transfers.

The massive economies of scale in information processes underlie the oligopolization process which has been noted over recent years, but also the new international division of labour, embodied in the multinational enterprise and the transformation of the labour process (Schon 1971, Langdon/Paquet 1976). To the extent that the organization of economic activities became less dependent on geo-technical constraints, it became also more susceptible to interventions by regulators.

iii.   The emergence of the Régime Contemporain in response to the heightened environmental turbulence, and the concurrent de-materialization of economic activity increased both the need and the will to regulate. However, not only the amount of regulation, but also the type of regulation changed. Individual actors and organizations, even the very large ones, could not adapt successfully simply through their direct interactions: the state became omnipresent, and regulation in the different sectors became a "differentiated, responsive, continually changing but connected reaction" in the light of what could only be termed a loose and unwritten plan (Lowi 1975). "Regulation became an instituted learning system: a network of negotiators and facilitators rather than enforcers" (Paquet in Doern 1978).

This growth and omnipresence of the public sector had important effects on the Canadian scene, where planning and regulation were not functions over which any one level of government had control. Intergovernmental competition over regulation, in conjunction with and in response to changes in the Canadian economic process, led to a strengthening of provincial consciousness and regional identities. (Dubuc 1966, Careless 1969). Regions, classes and cultures had only "limited identities" to begin with; the net impact of this growth of regulation was to strengthen and confirm these limited and regional identities, and to confirm "the articulation of regional patterns in a transcontinental state" not really unification or consolidation (Careless 1969).

The growing importance of coordination failures and systemic instability led to stronger statements about the responsibility of the different regions for regulatory purposes, about the lack of an underlying social ethos necessary for the operation of a Canadian system, and about the limits of the regulable for Canada as a whole.

This thumbnail sketch has focused on the informational/institutional dimensions of the Canadian economic process, considered as a non-zero sum game. It has examined the way in which a system evolves through an adaptation/adoption dynamic and, in a macroscopic way, some of the drifts in the overall Canadian socio-economic process since Confederation.

This sketch has inevitably drawn attention to the paramount importance of communicative competence and to the pragmatic institutional requisites (formal and tacit) for a socio-économy to have the ability to concert the activities of the players in a socially useful and efficient way. In this connection, we have been particularly insistent not only on the organizational form of the instituted process, but equally on the underlying ethos -- the sum of characteristic usages, ideas, standards, and codes by which a group is differentiated and individualized in character from other groups (Banfield 1958) – for an understanding of the socio-economic game. As we shall see, these dimensions may hold much of the explanation for the Canadians' ability and inability to concert.

Federalism as social technology

Any federal arrangement is difficult, for it is by nature a compromise and also in certain ways, an expedient, based on the belief that there is some machinery which can get around the difficulty of reconciling majority will and minority rights, centralization and decentralization, etc. Federalism is, therefore, an attempt to fragment sovereignty and, by definition, to create a social oligopoly. Any particular set of rules arrived at, at a given moment, is tantamount to an allocation of power and rights which must of necessity be influenced by the socio-economic conditions of the time: it amounts to a "deal", to an allocation of claims to resources among the groups in a "group of groups".

However, any system of governance for a society is designed not only to serve the purposes of the day, i.e., 1867 ("the political institution necessary for the pursuit of an economic project"— Dubuc 1966), but it also embodies governing relations which are meant to serve as a stewarding mechanism to guide the system over time. But since nobody can say what goals the next generation will wish to pursue, the utopian objective of the framers of any constitution must be to combine *maximum dynamic efficiency* with *maximum flexibility* in goal pursuit. (Carson and Paquet 1971).

The major claims of federalism as a social technology is that it provides a significant portion of the "outer framework of society" – part of the external institutions in the sense of Lachmann 1971 – which satisfies Ashby's law of requisite variety (Beer 1974). Given the variety of limited identities present at the outset, only variety in the system of governance could accommodate it.

The constitution defines some fundamental external institutions (allocating enormous responsibilities for economic development to the federal government) allowing internal institutions to "evolve gradually as a result of market processes and other forms of spontaneous individual action" (Lachmann 1971), albeit often as unintended consequences.

The primacy of functioning

Only the more immutable and entrenched norms and rules are protected from the ignominy of settlements, between quarrelling individuals and maneuvering organizations, through processes of convenience ministered through the courts or the bureaucracies. This does not mean, however, that even these entrenched norms and rules of the game are effectively protected from change for ever, or that they should be. At no time should a bit of technology like a constitution become sacred. There are dangers in turning a constitution into a "sacred piece of parchment above politics and beyond the reach of men" – as has been demonstrated in the U.S.. A more mature example of the belief that "no machinery is sacred" has come from Switzerland. (Steinberg 1976). In fact, as time passes, the environment and the socio-economic process change, and the requisite system of governance is modified more or less in keeping with them through the continuing modification of internal institutions.

This is often sufficient to make irrelevant any reference to the constitution. Indeed, it may be said that in Canada, until very recent times, the Constitution has not been a serious reference point: the Constitution has been simply a "basis for bargaining" (Lederman in Scott 1976).

Federalism as a system of governance has therefore changed according to the times and needs without much necessity to refer to the Constitution; it has oscillated between centralization and decentralization and has witnessed the widening, drifting, developing and evolving of institutions over the last century. (Lamontagne 1954) The "innards" and the functioning of the federal state as a regulatory system (operating through the complex machinery of federal-provincial and inter-provincial relations) have proved much more important than the outer structure of the system, as embodied in the Constitution.

This is not to say that Canadian federalism as a social technology has always evolved smoothly or that it satisfies everybody, but it has evolved as a working institution and has not been really limited by the constitutional shackle.

Executive federalism

The expansion of the public sector in response to what were perceived as coordination failures in the economy led to a penetration of the state into areas where either jurisdictional dominium was unclear, or where cooperative action was required. As a result, the burden of adjustment was left to an executive composed of senior politicians and bureaucrats at both federal and provincial levels. The complex machinery of consultation and coordination has led to a continuous multilogue between experts, with the bureaucrats taking an ever larger role as the issues became more complex, and as public administration became less tied to party patronage. Citizens more and more became silent partners in this "executive federalism". (Smiley 1976) One of the key features of executive federalism and of the democracy English-style which has inspired our political traditions is a great distrust of the people: one need not be reminded that in the old debate between Jefferson and Madison, Jefferson lost.

In Canada, we do not have a democracy in the sense of the Swiss where the people have a say on virtually everything, rather (and to paraphrase Steinberg) the government we have has not necessarily been the one we deserve, but what the senior civil service and the front bench of the governing party thought we should have. (Steinberg 1976). These functionaries of executive federalism have put the emphasis on stability and a form of procedural or administrative rationality – "une rationalité de fonctionnement" – in the management of the socio-economy. This management style was referred to as "functional politics", and was rhapsodized in manifestos of the new middle class. This was said to constitute, very much like the pursuit of self-interest through the market, a third way, "exempt from both the destructiveness of passion and the ineffectuality of reason", (to borrow the apt phrase of Hirschman 1977).

However, it has turned out that the stewarding mechanism entailed by executive federalism proved increasingly ineffective in designing adequate policies in the face of the new turbulent environment. As long as the senior federal oligarchy was allowed to define the broad parameters of national policies, and to enlist provincial authorities to effect and implement these policies within the guidelines, the semblance of procedural rationality was preserved.

Even by the 1920s grumblings were heard from the provinces, and it was only because of the impact of the Depression and the War that the federal oligarchs could maintain their dominium. Indeed, it may be said that this pattern persisted until the 1960s: executive federalism was highly centralized, and the effective "institutional information" came down from Ottawa. But the size and complexity of the provincial bureaucracies, the great rigidity with which the federal imperium came to be implemented by the federal bureaucracy, the growing recognition of the failures of certain national policies to provide the desired provincial goods, and in general, a rather unimpressive performance in the turbulent times, led to a serious alienation of citizens in all regions. Federalism came to be seen as a cumbersome instrument which prevented effective policy-making in a complex and turbulent environment. A growing capacity by the provinces to challenge the federal imperium, combined with a rather arrogant federal style displaying little taste for anything but functional politics and procedural rationality as a guide, led to many deadlocks in the ruling oligarchy, to the shifting to the provincial level of many debates for which the federal government had traditionally defined the broad parameters, and a strong disaffection for the "feds" by a citizenry which neither saw nor heard the federal government much, except when it chose to re-assert its "leadership" in a way which was often seen to be in opposition to the aspirations of the provincial communities. (P. Fortin, G. Paquet, Y. Rabeau 1978)

Exit and voice

In the face of deteriorating organizational effectiveness, two solutions are available to actors or parts: exit or voice. (Hirschman 1970) The first option – exit – is very much in the spirit of the standard economic adjustment in the market: the dissatisfied customer simply leaves. This is the form of adaptation which French Canadians chose in the face of the first economic crisis of the federation, in the late 19th and early 20th century: over a million left for the U.S. (Lavoie 1972). This is an option still very much in the air, and one Prime Minister Trudeau was prone to suggest to dissatisfied Canadian citizens.

The second option – voice – is more information-rich for the government under strain, in that it conveys the nature of the disgruntled citizens' concerns, and an expression of their demand for reform.

In a mixed socio-economic process, less dominated by geo-technical constraints, and one where a range of institutional arrangements are viable, one would expect that voice would become relatively more important, and that adaptation would take a new form: a mixture of exit and voice processes. In this context, loyalty might be measured by the extent to which one uses voice before deciding to exit. One may indeed find evidence of a more extensive use of mixes of voice and exit in modern economies, but there would appear to be no stable or optimal mix for a given instituted process. Moreover, the wide array of alternatives opened up by the possibility of strategic uses of such mixes and/or deceitful or mischievous uses of the voice option cannot be ignored.

For instance, it has been said that Quebec's threat to exit is a loyalist threat, and a way to sound a warning that if the functioning of federalism is not amended, she may have to exit. Others have seen Quebec's move (1976 election) as an irreversible decision to exit. Still others have insisted that Quebec's politico-bureaucratic oligarchy and Quebec's citizens do not speak with the same voice on these matters. The strategic definition of the optimal voice/exit mix is also central within the federation for many other groups: British Columbians, English-speaking minorities in Quebec, large metropolitan masses, amorphous groups of state clients, etc. Despite the expectation that the voice option would come to play a greater role in modern economies, it is also true, as Hirschrnan aptly puts it, that "voice often loses out, not necessarily because it is less effective than exit, but because its effectiveness depends on the discovery of the new ways of exerting influence and pressure." This is particularly true of the "underarticulate mass" for whom exit often turns out to be the only defense. However, even if in Canada the discovery of these new ways is a major challenge in the face of failing communicative competence, an ever more fragmented information system, and a rather insensitive and somewhat deaf executive federalism, it may also be that the solution is not to be sought only at the level of such technical devices.

Such devices are not unimportant, for they constitute an integral part of a refurbished social technology. But it would be a mistake to focus exclusively on the creation of formal channels of communication without recognizing that the reason for the low communicative competence may be more than simply the lack of channels. One might have to delve into the underground of the socio-economic game (that is, in the socio-cultural ethos) to understand fully the reasons for the failing of the voice option.

In the socio-cultural underground

One of the central tenets of recent analyses of the socio-economic process as a game has been that "the interdependence of individuals in a tightly-packed urban society itself produces a set of new and major problems that cannot be solved by conventional economic and administrative methods". (Preface to Schelling 1971) Neither market nor usual non-market mechanisms work, and there may be a breakdown of the game.

The ecology of micromotives and the process of adaptation/adoption (in a complex and interdependent world fraught with unintended consequences) create macro problems that would appear insoluble either by exit or voice as adjustment processes. The only way out is in some form of *collaborative action*, very much like in the textbook case of the prisoner's dilemma. And yet one cannot explain many forms of cooperation and participation (like the decision to vote) simply as a function of individual objectives without referring to group processes, and without referring to the socio-cultural underground of the economic game.

Building on a proposition put forward by Adam Smith, to the effect that men "could safely be trusted to pursue their own self-interest without undue harm to the community not only because of the restrictions imposed by the law, but also because they were subject to build-in restraint derived from morals, religion, custom and education"(A. Smith in *The Theory of Moral Sentiments*), Hirsch (1976) has argued that "truth, trust, acceptance, restraint, obligation - these are among the social virtues ... which are also seen to play a central role in the functioning of an individualistic, contractual economy".

In other words, market relationships depend on non-market norms. It has been a central theme of Hirsch's book that "the absence of explicit moral justification and/or of specified moral obligations within the system is now seen as weakening its operating efficiency in the previously neglected problem of securing the necessary public goods and socially functional individual norms. Yet dependence on these grows rather than lessens as economies become more interdependent and complex".

These dimensions are central to the understanding of the functioning of modem complex economies, and central to a critical discussion of functional federalism as a technology for the provision of public goods. Hirsch argues that "where mutual interdependence is strong, the group is more efficient as a decision-making body than individuals acting in isolation", and that in cases where collective action is the efficient way to satisfy preferences, "individuals can attain their self-interested objectives only if they behave as if they were altruistic".

This might require some guiding by "human convention, or instinct or attitude" or by changes therein, or by other forms of guidance.

The responsibility for failing communicative competence and therefore for the failure to make the voice option more effective may be ascribed to the failings of this socio-cultural underground or ethos, and of the social conventions, to provide the supporting social morality for the social technology. Indeed, Hirsh has made a rather persuasive argument linking this lack of an effective set of social conventions to the social limits to growth and finds this deficiency at the roots of the "distributional compulsion" and of the "reluctant collectivism" that has ensued in modern Western economies. This does not lead one to an instant solution to the endemic crisis in Canadian federalism, but it opens up for discussion a whole new dimension of the socio-economic process, and one which can be said to acquire an increasing importance in complex economies.

This vindicates the position of economic historians like Albert Faucher who reminded us for years that "l'action économique procède de l'intime même des cultures" and that "les investissements sont la manifestation d'aspirations culturelles ... expriment un ensemble de propensions qui, précisément, s'élaborent au sein même d'une culture". (Faucher in Wade 1960). It also underlines the fact that the best way to investigate and study the Canadian problem or the Quebec question is not in isolation from the broader changes in modern socio-économies. This focus on the socio-cultural underground might help to put into perspective much of the undercurrents in the ongoing national debates, for as Joan Robinson reminds us, "from the standpoint of evolution, it seems plausible to say that ideology is a substitute for instinct" (quoted by Hirsch).

A shifting crisis

Our view of the importance of the socio-cultural underground as *terrain des operations* is further corroborated by some work done on the macrodynamics of advanced capitalistic societies by Jurgen Habermas (1973). He sketches a theory of two-stage crisis displacement in advanced capitalistic economies which traces the ways in which the stresses and strains of the economy, as coordination failures became more important, led to massive offsetting and corrective interventions by the state at both the macro and micro economic levels.

This omnipresence of the state and public administration trying to correct the malefits of the free market generated an expansion of interventionist and regulatory activities into all sorts of areas of community and personal life, as a result of the actualization of a whole array of social rights – rights to material things and income, but also the right to be heard, the right not to be excluded, etc ... (Macpherson 1977).

An overload on the state ensued and the state became pressed to legitimize not only what it would do, but also what it would not do, in the face of rising expectations by groups (old and new) making never ending demands. The economic crisis had become a state crisis. The Canadian case closely follows the pattern described by Habermas, with the added twist that the global overload of the state was coupled with chaos in federal-provincial coordination. The growth and actualization of these new social rights proceeded differently in different parts of the country, but much of the post-war period may be said to correspond to a broad shift of this sort.

The 1970s showed the Canadian government (like many others)

running short on its capacity to legitimize its activities. In the face of legitimation deficits, and a withering of the mass loyalty it needed, and of the motivations necessary to the system, the state, according to Habermas, has begun to indulge in conscious manipulation. In the words of a commentator (Wiley 1977), the state, "by a kind of methodological or epistemological coup, needs to be empowered to do anything required by the technical logic of systems theory, and to be able to convince people that the technical has replaced the moral, and that the state is thereby self-legitimizing. In other words, to get back to the question of displacement, the state wants to export its crisis into the culture by diminishing the autonomous power of morality and by gaining strength for itself at the expense of what can only be called the natural and normal consciousness of human beings".

The instrumental rationality of functional politics has already permeated our governments to such an extent that it has begun to shift the state crisis into a cultural crisis.

The 1970s have left Canadian executive federalism rather vulnerable because of its incapacity to legitimize its interventions and unsuccesses. The federal government has probably more than the provincial governments attempted to obtain a "blank cheque". Opposition to federal policies or views are regarded as 'immature' or as 'sabotage' and one detects a form of cognitive despotism which attempts to substitute a certain scientism that is self-legitimating to replace the intellectual resources by which people grant or withhold legitimation. The provincial governments have also indulged in such activities to a greater or lesser degree: they do not shy away from fast and loose use of statistics and technical analyses. They have, however, resorted to a greater extent to systems of symbols and ideological devices to appeal to the "normal" consciousness of their communities, especially in Quebec. This has tended both to develop a resistance to the federal government's efforts, and to nurture the development of competing "scientisms", at least in certain areas of the country.

Coda and futuribles

Over the last century, the functioning of Canadian federalism has registered oscillations between these two tendencies as the need arose over the last century, but of late the tension between these conflictive rationalities has been heightened. We have argued that an important factor in this heightening of tension has been the strengthening of a centralized executive federalism, promoting functional politics and procedural rationality as the alternative seen by the federal government to destructive passions or ineffectual planning – both being regarded as leading to inferior political orders.

This federal move has changed the game: the previous situation had witnessed a state of *conflictive equilibrium* between the different levels of government, each with a portion of the sovereignty, but quite well aware that it would not rid the system of the other, and that a compromise with the other would be necessary to reach its own objectives (Crozier 1970). Informal bargains could be arranged, and compromises arrived at, on the basis of such mutual understanding and some trust between the parties. In that sense, the federal/provincial game could be regarded as a microcosm of the larger socio-economic game, and the tensions it revealed were a fair measure of the incongruence between the socio-economic games at the bottom.

Some aspects of the strategic activities called for in the context of such a game have been analyzed in Canada (Simeon 1972), but such analyses have not fully taken into account the important changes which affected Canada's political economy over the last few decades. These changes, that some analysts have traced back to earlier developments (Paltiel 1966), considerably modified the *rapports de force* between the federal and provincial levels. The unsuccess of the functioning of federalism therefore generated a much more sharply felt concern, and alienation loomed large.

However, the new game embodied a much stronger cleavage between the parties. This stemmed from a growing incongruence between the federal society and the federal political system (Stein 1977), and from the failing of the voice option – a failing which appeared to relegate Canadians to the role of spectators in the debate about the governance of their own affairs and about the sharing of power between the two "féodalités administratives" (Crozier 1970). The reasons for the growing incongruence and the voice failing are to be sought, we argued, not so much in the structural features of the federation, embodied in the Constitution, or in other external institutions, but in a growing communicative incompetence rooted in the weakening of the social conventions needed to support and enhance the dynamic efficiency of the federal social technology, and in forms of emergent "cognitive despotism" at the different levels of the federal structure.

The rhetoric and the "scientisms" which have come to plague the debate "*par bureaucraties interposées*", without the benefit of limits imposed on the situation by the citizenry, would appear to allow the most aberrant solutions to become possible. There is no determinate solution in oligopoly situations. Indeed, the game may break down altogether.

SCHEMING VIRTUOUSLY: THE ROAD TO COLLABORATIVE GOVERNANCE

We have been led by this analysis to point the way to what appear to be dead ends, and to indicate some steps that might be taken to improve the communicative competence of Canadians, and thereby to help the citizenry to impose limits on the situation.

On the negative front, we suggest that one should not search for "solutions" to this country's problems, either in some technical legal reconstruction of the Constitution, or in some technical reassignment of functions between levels of governments, or through a renewed quest for inter-governmental coordination, which (as Smiley, quoting Seidman in Scott 1976 puts it) "is in many respects the twentieth century equivalent of the philosopher's stone". The primary answer lies elsewhere.

On the positive front, our analysis emphasizes the paramount importance of communications and participation in the regulation of modern complex systems. This does not lead one to attempt to preserve at all costs the moral and social conventions which enabled the citizens to cooperate in the past, but rather to suggest that these conventions are most important, and that we have to ensure that those basic elements for effective participation which used to be nested in the socio-cultural underground, and in the realm of morality, are brought to the foreground and made the subject of negotiation. Only at this price can we hope to develop new modes of participation by the citizenry, which will be neither a fraud nor a sentimental return to Illyria. (Crozier 1970)

Such an investment in communicative competence and in the institutional support it requires should not, however, lead us to presume that we will like what we are going to hear and witness. It may well be that the citizenry of Canada, when allowed to communicate effectively, will reveal that it prefers to opt for separate facilities, for a socio-economic process instituted differently in different parts of the country.

This in turn may well reveal the possible separability of the socio-economic game into sub-games, and the strong preference of at least some portion of the citizenry for such an effective restructuring of the economic organization. (Bessières 1969) In the same spirit, communicative competence and participation may well reveal the unreality of a "federal society", and the limitations of a federal political system. (Migué 1971) The form that such an action can take is varied almost to the extreme, for what is involved is the elimination of systematically distorted communications, and an attempt to give a voice to those who have none, or who have lost it. But what is called for is more than just a condescending ear: it is the generation of better institutional information, in a world where the economic process is more malleable and therefore more easily influenced by all.

136

This commitment to participation and institutional information of higher quality requires a revolution in the mind: the list of specific ways in which this might be done could fill a book. A few instances more or less picked at random might help to illustrate the process.

1. Fundamentally, what is involved is the most significant public good that the state can produce in a democracy: an actualization of the right of people to have a say. It might be worth exploring the practical use of referenda and plebiscites. In the longer run, such devices, by providing some incentive for the citizenry to obtain information, and to invest in exploring specific issues, might very well develop a stronger taste for the citizenry having a say.

2. Another outreach operation would consist in decentralizing and deconcentrating the federal administration. This would reduce the distance between the federal government and the citizenry, and would tend to better perform this integration function of the different communication networks, and the different regional games which are a central role of the federal government. A zero-growth for the Ottawa-based civil service could, over the next twenty years, shift a significant portion of the federal civil service to the regions. In the same manner, non-administrative activities, like the operations of the National Research Council, could be deconcentrated by dispersing the largely Ottawa-based research personnel into a large number of government-funded research laboratories attached to different Canadian universities, thereby helping to create a national scientific communication network.

3. We have also argued that dynamic stewarding is likely to be more effective in an information economy. It could be argued from our discussion that the lack of loci for collaborative and co-participatory planning in Canada has acted as a social limit to growth and development. Since the Economic Council of Canada (after becoming more and more a crusader without a crusade) was put to death, could it be re-created in the form of an agency, deliberately designed not to be restricted to economic matters. Equipped with a broader mandate and a refurbished composition – imaginatively chosen to provide a voice for major segments of the collectivity which have been denied the opportunity to be heard (large metropolitan areas, for instance) – it could improve the quantity and quality of institutional information.

In the same spirit, a refurbishment of the Senate in order to make it into a Council of Social Values providing a forum for discussion by individuals, groups, and technical experts on certain crucial issue domains would provide a sounder basis for collaborative governance (Paquet 1968). There are hundreds of ways in which Canadian federalism as a social technology can be made less rigid, and its functioning better attuned to the wishes and wants of Canadians. But this can only be done if the citizenry renegotiates a certain basis of mutual understanding and trust. The "féodalités administratives" have no taste for such mutual understanding in the development of their strategies, and it is to them that we owe our fouled nest. The temptation at the moment is to transform our problem into a puzzle, and to search in visionary reconstructions or scenarios for the solution. As David Nowlan put it, "puzzles have solutions, problems don't; problems have responses."

References

I. Adelman, "Social and Economic Development at the Micro Level" in E.B. Ayal (ed) *Micro Aspects of Development*, New York 1973

G. Akerlof, "The Market for Lemons" *Quarterly Journal of Economics* 1970

A.A. Alchian, "Uncertainty, Evolution, and Economic Theory" *Journal of Political Economy* 1950

E.C. Banfield, *The Moral Basis of a Backward Society*, New York 1958

S. Beer, *Designing Freedom*, Toronto 1974

C. Berger, *The Writing of Canadian History*, Toronto 1976

F. Bessières, "The Concept of Separability and the Optimization of Economic Organization" *European Economic Review*, Fall 1969

J.M.S. Careless, "Limited Identities in Canada" *Canadian Historical Review* 1969

R.L. Carson, G. Paquet, "Elements for a Theory of Systemic Change" Mimeo 1971

M. Crozier, *La société bloquée*, Paris 1970

L.E. Davis, D.C. North, *Institutional Change and American Economic Growth*, Cambridge 1971

A. Dubuc, "The Decline of Confederation and The New Nationalism" in P. Russell (ed) *Nationalism in Canada*, Toronto 1966

P. Fortin, G. Paquet, Y. Rabeau, "Quebec in the Canadian Federation: A Provisional Evaluative Framework", *Canadian Public Administration*, 21(4), 1978, 558-578.

J. Habermas, *Legitimation Crisis*, Boston 1973

F. Hirsch, *Social Limits to Growth*, Cambridge 1976

A.O. Hirschman, *Development Projects Observed*. Washington 1967

A.O. Hirschman, *Exit, Voice and Loyalty*, Cambridge 1970

A.O. Hisrchman, *The Passions and the Interests*, Princeton 1977

L.M. Lachmann, *The Legacy of Max Weber*, Berkeley 1971

M. Lamontagne, *Le fédéralisme canadien*, Québec 1954

S.W. Langdon, G. Paquet, *The Multinational Enterprise and the Labour Process* O.E.C.D./Paris Mimeo 1976

Y. Lavoie, *L'émigration des Canadiens aux Etats-Unis avant 1930*, Montreal 1972

B.J. Loasby, *Choice, Complexity and Ignorance*, Cambridge 1976

T.J. Lowi, "Towards a Politics of Economics: The State of Permanent Receivership" in L.N. Lindberg & al (eds) *Stress and Contradiction in Modem Capitalism*, Toronto 1975

C.B. Macpherson "Human Rights as Property Rights" *Dissent* 1977

J. Marchak, "Economic Planning and the Cost of Thinking" *Social Research* 1966

J.L. Migué, "L'industrialisation et la participation des Québécois au progrès économique" in *Le Québec d'aujourd'hui*, Montréal 1971

R.F. Neill, "Harold Adams Innis: Canadian Economics" *Journal of Economic Issues*, 1969

G. Newman, "An Institutional Perspective on Information" *International Social Science Journal* 1976

K.Z. Paltiel, "Federalism and Party Finance" in *Studies in Canadian Party Finance*, Ottawa 1966

G. Paquet, "L'économie non-marchande dans l'économie de marchés" *Revue d'économie politique*, 1977

G. Paquet, "The Economic Council as Phoenix" in Lloyd and McLeod (eds) *Agenda 1970*, Toronto 1968

G. Paquet, "The Regulatory Process and Economic Performance" in G.B. Doern (ed) *The Regulatory Process in Canada*, Toronto 1978

F. Perroux, *Industrie et création collective* - Vol. II, Paris 1970

K. Polanyi, *Primitive, Archaic and Modem Economies*, New York 1966

T.C. Schelling, "On the Ecology of Micromotives" *Public Interest* 1971

D.A. Schön, *Beyond the Stable State*, New York 1971

A. Scott (ed) *Natural Resources Revenue - A Test of Federalism*, Vancouver 1976

D. Seckler, *Thorstein Veblen and the Institutionalists*, London 1975

R. Simeon, *Federal-Provincial Diplomacy*, Toronto 1972

D.V. Smiley, *Canada in Question*, Toronto 1976

M. Stein, "Québec and Canada": The Changing Equilibrium Between "Federal Society" and "Federal Political System" *Journal of Canadian Studies* July 1977

J. Steinberg, *Why Switzerland?* Cambridge 1976

G. Vickers, *Freedom in a Rocking Boat*, London 1970

M. Wade (ed) *Canadian Dualism*, Toronto 1960

N. Wiley, Review of Habermas' Legitimation Crisis *Contemporary Sociology* 1977

Chapter 7

An informational view of the regulatory process

"the economic organization problem degenerates into the problem of choosing the optimal information system"

– Jacob Marschak

Introduction

The problem of gauging performance under regulation, or the differential effects of particular forms of regulatory processes, has been one of the most troublesome on the agenda of industrial economists and investigative commissions for very many years. The blatant lack of success of all interested parties in grappling with this issue led Richard Caves to suggest in 1964 that "the right questions [had] not been asked about the effects of regulation nor the right tests performed" and to call for an expanded frame of reference and for a new tool-box better adapted to the task at hand.[1]

The growth in the regulation of private economic activity over the last decades, and the consequent increase in the attention given to regulatory experiments have contributed to enriching somewhat the documentary base pertaining to the phenomenon, but the analysis has not progressed much beyond the reiteration of a few clichés meant to condition all observers to accept the diagnosis of a "regulatory crisis" (whatever that is supposed to mean). Much of the conventional wisdom may be summarized in a few lines: "regulation, in many instances, is unnecessary and, as currently practised, is inept," and the "lawyers who have dominated the regulatory field must bear the brunt of the blame for the current regulatory crisis." [2]

It may be that "the machinery for deliberate regulation is unequal to the demands on it"[3] and that the dominant legal framework has contributed to exacerbating the problem. However, a review of the economic literature would confirm that the sort of questions raised and tests performed by economists over the last decades – with and without the help of econometric pyrotechnics – have neither produced especially illuminating results, nor succeeded in overcoming the difficulties identified by Caves in 1964.

Our understanding of the role of regulation in the socio-economic process, and of the impact of particular forms of regulation on economic performance, remains rather unsatisfactory, and industrial organization – the specialized sub-field of economics interested in regulatory problems at the micro and mezzo levels[4] – "has grown rather narrow and technocratic, with certain orthodox concepts and a mandarin prose".[5]

Our presumption is that to deal with the question at hand one requires a refurbished view of the socio-economic process and of the nature and limits of the regulable within it. The traditional image of the economic process derives from the use of a method that tends to reduce market phenomena to individual choices, and all economic activities to market activities. This underpins the search for "monopoly explanations" for all business practices that are suspected of generating waste or inefficiency, and the unhelpful focusing of the analysis of the regulatory process on a few institutional devices or rules designed to control monopoly power.[6]

What is called for is a broader political economy framework and a richer notion of the human economy in the study of the organization of economic activity. In the next section, we sketch briefly the contours of a broader framework that we have found useful in analysing the interactions between the socio-economic process and the regulatory process.[7] It is in this context that we then analyse the impact of the regulatory process on economic performance. This analysis suggests a dynamic which we attempt to document and illustrate in a preliminary manner by reference to some Canadian experiences.

A frame of reference

Analytical frameworks constitute the first stage of the investigative process, and the perspectives they generate "may be looked upon as toolboxes from which we can fashion theories to explain events". This first stage would appear to be well-suited to the ill-defined problem at hand, and to hold the promise of a preliminary "vision" (in Schumpeter's sense) of the problem, on which one might construct robust theories and models.[8]

Our analytical framework has a cybernetic and Vickersian flavour: it puts forward an image of the socio-technical reality as a going concern defined and characterized by a net of ongoing relationships between persons, organizations, and their environments.[9] We therefore present human economies as essentially *relational*, as systems of ongoing relations between persons, groups, and environment defining a process with a characteristic generating function (in the sense that statisticians use the term). Such a framework thus puts the emphasis much less on the monads or "globules of desire" (Veblen) than on the co-ordinating mechanisms between them, and as a consequence on the informational nature of the social process. By contrast, the standard reductionist framework provided by neo-classical economics is rooted in a sort of *fundamental monadism* and radical individualism. In this choice-theoretic framework, human economies are dissolved into choices and marginal adjustments by rational independent monads with stable objectives operating within well-defined constraints.'[10]

As will become apparent in the rest of the paper, these contrasting images of the economic process with their different emphases lead to diverging views of the structure and functioning of human economies, and of the norms to be used in gauging their performance. They also point to different dynamics for the relationship between the regulatory process and the socio-economic process, and to different directions for the evolvement of this interface.[11]

The human economy as instituted process

The pattern of relationships defining a human economy as a going concern is rather complex, and may be structured according to different principles. Such a pattern is the product of different processes, and becomes crystallized into structures, institutions, instrumentalities, and rules which are subject to change, but are recognizable through time. Following Polanyi, we define the human economy as "an instituted process of interaction between man and his environment, which results in a continuous supply of want-satisfying material means".[12] The crucial aspect of this definition is the "transcending importance of the institutional aspect of the economy": the organization of economic activity according to different principles (exchange, redistribution, reciprocity – in the parlance of Polanyi), or a mix of them as means of co-ordination of the actions of the large number of actors.

A number of economists have adopted similar schemata, though using slightly different labels, in their attempts to suggest a theoretical framework that would explain the different patterns of processes and institutions in human economies.[13] Yet such a general theory remains in its infancy, and any reasonable diagnosis would have to conclude that economists have failed, up to now, to construct a coherent account of the manner in which activities of economic agents are co-ordinated in modern monetary economies.[14] At best, some preliminary analyses of specific relations and patterns have been attempted over the last decade or so, but the results have been promising enough for some to see in them the harbingers of a move toward a *new institutional economics*.[15]

This literature has emphasized the importance of institutional arrangements as the very fabric of the human economy, and has proposed new perspectives on the genesis of certain patterns of interactions and arrangements used to co-ordinate and to organize economic activities. It has also examined the reasons why these arrangements change from time to time and from place to place.

While one can go part of the way by introducing costs of transaction and friction into the standard neo-classical framework, a more fruitful analysis has stylized the economic system as an *information system*, i.e., as a signalling system in which the nature and pattern of the messages between actors acquires a relative autonomy or at least can be analysed separately both in itself and in its impact on the network of actors and their valences (defined by bundles of property rights).[16] Indeed, some like Marschak have gone so far as to state that the problem of economic organization degenerates into a "problem of choosing the optimal information system".[17]

It is essential to underline how the nature and structure of messages are integrally related to the nature and structure of the institutions that embody or transmit them. A process of intercreation is at work here.[18] This dialectic process through which information-flows shape institutions, and institutions shape information-flows, does not rely exclusively on the characterization of institutions for the system as a whole, or the transmission of these rules through the imperatives of some genotypic code. In fact, the dynamics it suggests appear to be the result of a composition of the forces of adaptation by the parts, and of adoption by the whole, in a manner which would condemn any effort to construct explanations exclusively on one or the other set of forces to generating nothing but incomplete theories of the human economy as instituted process.[19]

The regulatory process in Canada

The adaptation-adoption dynamics

The human economy changes through time and its dynamics may be understood as the result of the interaction between the adaptation of the parts to the whole, and the *adoption* of certain parts by the whole. This process has been sketched rather persuasively by Alchian, and shown to be enlightening for the understanding of the evolution of economies in a world of uncertainty.[20]

The process of adaptation is rather well-known, and constitutes the basis for much of traditional micro and mezzo economics. It is assumed that in the face of certain constraints the economic actors will modify their programs of consumption and production to bring them in line with environmental constraints in the name of self-interest, and that their messages are modified accordingly. The process of adoption is less well understood and not really discussed in the literature. It corresponds to a process of economic natural selection which depends on environmental adoption, on the causal texture of the environment, and on the structure and rules of operations of the system as a whole. These rules of operations bestow differential probability of survival to different parts given their particular characteristics.[21]

In the experience of a human economy, there are obviously very many rounds of adaptation and adoption, and these rounds of interaction generate changes in the instituted process. Through the confluence of unintended consequences and unforeseen short-circuiting, the environment acquires new traits by a process of sedimentation, with the result that a different adoption process and different adaptive behaviours are triggered.[22]

The informational texture of this interaction is rather interesting: individuals or parts send messages which are aggregated (including all the direct and indirect effects, foreseen or not) and mediated by institutional structures, but this gives rise to "institutional information" (Newman), i.e., information supplied by the institutional structures and the whole to the component parts.[23]

In fact, the adaptation-adoption dynamics might be regarded as a dialogue between parts and whole (in the simple two-level case) or a multilogue between parts and between parts and the whole (in a more complex case), which generates through a multiple number of rounds the contours of the organization form.[24] This particular stylization of the human economy provides not only a closer integration of the economic process, but shows the economic system to be akin to a non-zero-sum game.[25]

Governing relations

The human economy has a structure that contains feedback couplings that act as steering controls. Much work has been done on the nature and working of these self-equilibrating, self-steering, and self-organizing mechanisms at work in human economies[26], but it is not entirely clear what the *governing relations* are that set and maintain the course of human economies.

Lange has argued that the process of development of economic systems is ergodic (i.e., with time, the process becomes independent of its initial state, and disturbances which affect the process disappear) but that "the ergodicity of the process may be bounded in duration, that the speed with which disturbances disappear and the magnitude of the disturbances to which the system is resistant may vary, too."[27] The governing relations are this hard core of robust and resistant sub-processes: the net of other relations (external and internal, metabolic and functional) becoming adjusted to this more resistant core and evolving a pattern that composes the governing relations with the imperatives of the environment. In the words of Lange, "their self-steering is efficient in the conditions of a given environment."[28]

In turbulent environments, this hard core of governing relations has been eroded, self-steering forces have been weakened, and co-ordination failures and organization failures have become more prevalent. This is the world of *corridor phenomena* (in the parlance of Leijohnhufvud), i.e., one in which "sustained and serious co-ordination failures. . . would temporarily eliminate from the economy homeostats that are essential for effective co-ordination of the notional economic plans of individual agents".[29] The economy moves then outside a corridor where the governing relations have full strength into a penumbra where the gyroscope of the economy no longer functions.

This has been regarded as evidence that regulation is called for, either to maintain the course of affairs, i.e., to institute a replacement for the gyroscope and to maintain the economy on the same path that it would have followed if the governing relations had prevailed, or to modify the governing relations artificially, when they would not appear to evolve naturally in line with the logic of the situation, or would appear to evolve too slowly.[30]

Regulation

In the normal functioning of human economies, self-regulation is nothing more than the maintenance of governing relations through time. The matter of what relations are to be maintained, and within what level of reliability, is resolved by the system and embodied in its appreciative setting, its own "jurisprudence". The system distills its own standards and its own way to reconcile the inconsistent demands that it experiences. The governing relations may change as a result of pressures brought onto it but also as a result of the accumulation of experiences, very much in the way that legal norms are distilled by the accumulated jurisprudence.[31]

The degree of resiliency of certain sub-processes defines the direction of the evolution of the system, but this does not correspond ordinarily to the willed purposes of any one part: indeed, there is no such thing as the purposes of the system *stricto sensu* in this context. The rationality of the whole, if one may be allowed to use such a term, is a "*rationalité du fonctionnement et de l'évolution du système*" (in Godelier's terms)[32] and it is not captured by the psychological mould of the rationality of the parts—maximizing some objective function subject to constraints. While the *microrationality of the parts* is cast in a psychological mould and is largely outcome-oriented, the *macrorationality of the system* can be understood only at the logical level and is process-oriented.[33]

Neo-classical economics has attempted to gauge the functioning of the whole by reference to the evaluation of the parts on the assumption that the individual is the best and probably the sole judge of his/her own well-being, and that the welfare of the community depends exclusively on the welfare of its members. This reduction of the n-person-game situation to a series of independent and individual games against nature has led some to suggest that profit maximization underpins all governing relations, and that market economies are rational and efficient.[34] These statements are usually followed by an enumeration of instances of market failures calling for specific interventions in cases where the benefits of regulation (i.e., the waste eliminated) are greater than the costs of regulating (including the waste it generates).

The difficulty with this method of gauging the performance of the economic system is that, as McAuley stresses, it breaks down in game situations: as soon as interdependencies, ignorance, complexity, and uncertainty are introduced, it is no longer possible to generate a reliable gauge of performance for the human economy from the microrationalities of individual parts.[35]

Consequently, in the absence of an economic magistrature which would elicit the governing relations of the economic process, and therefore contribute to defining the underpinnings of the macrorationality of the system, *and* in the absence of a firm foundation for gauging the performance of the whole in the microrationalities of individual parts, purposive regulation will inevitably be anchored in the *macrorationale of the state*, in the coherent pursuit of certain goals which are in the "plan". This plan, as Lowi puts it in a discussion of contemporary advanced industrial societies, is "not entirely conscious or systematic and . . . it is not written, published, debated, revised and so on", but it exists and it may or may not approximate what the macrorationality of the system would call for. Lowi has suggested some interesting features of its functioning which might hold the key to the rationale that guides the state in its regulatory function.[36]

The governing relations defined in this loose and unwritten plan are those that the state wishes either to maintain or to bring to "some level *more acceptable to those concerned* than the inherent logic of the situation would otherwise have provided".[37] However, the state experiences important limitations in its efforts to regulate the human economy. These limitations stem both from the limits of our knowledge of the economic process, and from the limits to the regulable, both points being obviously closely connected. Both Solo and Loasby have emphasized our lack of an economic theory of processes, and Vickers has underlined the conditions to make regulation possible.[38]

Performance under regulation

The conceptual framework sketched in the last section has drawn attention to certain features of human economies: their fundamental relational/informational nature, their evolutionary character, and the central import of the governing relations in the economic process. It also contrasted the self-regulation of the process with the purposive regulation anchored in the macrorationale of the state.

Purposive regulation has been introduced for a variety of reasons and it has taken a multitude of forms. It makes no sense to seek definitive general propositions about performance under regulation, for environments change, regulatory processes evolve, and human economies adapt/adopt continually.

The advantages of a broader framework like the one we have used is that one is less likely to assume the problem away, and to miss what Caves has perceptively referred to as the "important side-effects on performance".[39] Regulation is characterized within this framework as a dynamic process of intervention within a dynamic differential game.

Uncertainty, complexity, ignorance, and strategic behaviour are an integral part of the "multi-loop non-linear feedback systems" we use as simulacra for human economies, and the behaviour of such systems is often counter-intuitive.[40] The analyses relying on the derivation of the "net effects of regulation from its virtual impact" (Caves) are therefore rather unsatisfactory, and any unambiguous evaluation of the regulatory process remains rather problematic since "unintended and indirect consequences may have more economic significance than the desired direct ones".[41]

In the rest of this section, we examine first the drift in the regulatory process over the recent past, and we then take a cursory look at some alternative ways of looking at performance, in an attempt to gauge the impact of the regulatory process on the economic process.

The drift in the regulatory process

The State's use of purposive regulation to organize economic activities is not new. Many human economies have been instituted according to principles of coercion and centrally regulated at different times. The best known example may well have been *medieval regulationism*, "a system of regulations, so marvellously adapted to its purpose that it may be considered a masterpiece of its kind. . . . The city economy was worthy of the Gothic architecture with which it was contemporaneous."[42] This form of economic organization, and the motif of its socio-economic architecture were to change dramatically with the triumphant rise of the market and the Great Transformation, which may be regarded as the political and economic origins of our time, in the parlance of Polanyi.[43]

From the origins of commercial capitalism to the first quarter of the twentieth century, the State receded to a less prominent role: it performed what Solo refers to as the *household function*: "protecting liberty . . . providing a rag bag of residual services that the market did not make available . . . divvying up whatever surpluses might appear in the public domain . . . [and] . . . keeping the market competitive."[44] The public authority was "not outside the market system" and the market relation was the criterion of value and the governing relation.

In the second quarter of the twentieth century, public authorities, in the face of major stresses to the social system, took on an additional economic role, an *offsetting function* (Solo) : the intent was to correct market failures, dislocations, co-ordination failures, by measures designed to affect the aggregate level of spending or to change the legal framework for economic decision-making. Out of this came a set of rules of administration meant to create "structures around the economy—floors, ceilings, frameworks, forward pricing, etc. ...within

149

which economic activity would operate"[45], and designed to keep the economy or sectors of the economy within the corridor.

The third quarter of the twentieth century has witnessed a transubstantiation of the economic process and led to a new form of regulation, *a system of co-participatory planning* (Solo). This *"second XXe siècle"*, as Perroux calls it, witnessed a "loss of the stable state" (Schon), a passage from "placid clustered" to "disturbed-reactive" and "turbulent" environments.[46] This increased complexity and interdependence in the environment meant a heightened level of relevant uncertainty and a substantial increase in the likelihood of organizational failures. Moreover, during the same period, the human economy experienced a dematerialization of economic activity, and a shift from energy intensity to information intensity.[47] These changes in the environment and in the economic process reinforced each other in generating yet more relevant uncertainty and organizational precariousness.

Standard attempts to correct these failures by edicts and rules from the centre in the offsetting mode became more and more inefficient: in the differential game played in turbulent fields "individual organizations, however large, cannot adapt successfully simply through their direct interactions" and "the deepening interdependence between the economic and the other facets of the society" led economic organizations to being in "increasingly enmeshed in legislation and public regulation".[48] Regulation, however, was to take a new form: "The need is for differentiated, responsive, continually changing but *connected* reaction" and not for a simple emitter of edicts and rules. Regulation became an instituted learning system, a network of negotiators and facilitators rather than enforcers.[49]

The failures of centre-periphery regulation, based on the enforcement of administrative rules more likely to be obsolete by the time they come into force, or ill-adjusted to different and rapidly changing environments, led to the development of forms of regulation where facilitators and negotiators were asked to take decisions "on the merits" of the case, and in the light of the loose and unwritten "plan" Lowi talked about. What became important was less the regulatory instrument than the "manner of use".[50] Regulatory tribunals had become negotiating tribunals.

With the changes in the structures and the growth in the discretion of the facilitators, the concerns of regulators have drifted from *market efficiency* to fairness within the socio-economy, from rate of return/price/entry considerations very clearly pertaining to an industry or a firm to aspects of production and sales which cut across many industries, from governing relations rooted in the sphere of exchange to governing relations anchored in "organizational stability" in the broadest sense.[51]

The logic of this development is to adapt the regulatory process to the features of the differential game. This has already led to other new forms of intervention: governments have now realized that even such negotiated quasi-contracts arrived at by the new regulatory bodies may lack sufficient flexibility in some cases. Consequently, the public authorities have begun to experiment, where it seemed useful, with "government firms in oligopoly industries" and Crown corporations.[52]

Instruments of this sort institute elements of the "plan" in the objective function of the government firm, and allow these elements to have an impact on the game: this is regulation from within the industry, so to speak. While offsetting regulation had often used mechanical devices to correct failures, at this phase one is operating almost in a biological mode in the body economic. Even though these forms of intervention are relatively recent and constitute only a minute fraction of existing regulatory activities, and even though their role may appear on the face of it to be limited to intervention in one industry – an erroneous view in my opinion, for such interventions in well-selected key industries might have reverberations on the whole economic process – they constitute harbingers of the regulation of tomorrow.

Judging economic performance

Economists are really in a quandary when they are forced to judge economic performance. As Herendeen puts it, "in the absence of the competitive model of welfare economics, there are no clear-cut criteria for judging economic performance" and yet "the competitive model no longer offers us adequate criteria for judging economic performance" in the present environment.[53]

This has led to the development of three different strands of argument in dealing with economic performance.

Group I has simply decided to act "as if" the human economy was satisfactorily depicted by the competitive model on the whole, and has proceeded to gauge the performance of specific sectors and/or of economies by reference to the canons of welfare economics and to the *competitive ideal*. The case for efficiency became the case for competition, since in this stylized world competitive markets are the most efficient way to organize economic activity.[54]

Group II, recognizing the difficulties in using the competitive ideal as a norm in the context of the "*second XXe siècle*", attempted to develop criteria of *workable competition* and standards of workability of the human economy.[55] As could be expected, this shift toward a more realistic image of economic reality has meant that clear-cut criteria were replaced by a multitude of dimensions of performance which then had to be composed into an aggregate judgment which could not be completely devoid of subjectivity.[56]

Group III completely abandoned the hope to work from the competitive model and addressed the problem of performance by a decision to "select *a set of targets or objectives for the economy* and then analyse the performance of particular sectors of the economy in terms of whether or not this performance aids or impedes the achievement of these overall goals."[57]

In a fundamental way these three approaches correspond roughly to definitions of performance rooted in the microrationalities of individuals, in the macrorationality of the system, and in the macrorationale of the state, respectively. The governing relations which are regarded as the basis for judgment are consequently quite different.

While these different approaches to performance have evolved in quite different directions, a number of clusters of performance indicators have crystallized over the years, subsumed under the general headings of efficiency, stability, distribution/equity, and progressiveness à la Perroux (i.e. capacity to transform), and have come to be referred to – albeit with different intensity and valences – in most discussions of economic performance. Of these, efficiency is clearly the dominant criterion. This is due to the great importance of the neoclassical program which has considerably played down reference to other criteria. Consequently, the literature is replete with definitions and attempts at measurement of *allocative* and *organizational* efficiency, between firms and households and within organizations, in the *short* or the *long* run, at the *micro, mezzo*, and *macro* levels, and in a *dynamic* or *static* context. Moreover, for each of these cases, a variety of specific measurements and estimates have been proposed. Progressiveness has been regarded by many as a synonym for full dynamic efficiency (Schumpeter).

Stability and distribution/equity refer to characteristics of the functioning and of the structure of the system, respectively. For Group I, there is an optimal amount of instability and inequity; this is the one that makes the human economy as efficient as possible in the broadest sense. However, members of Group III have argued for a greater valence for stability and equity as overall goals, and have been led to reduce the relative importance of efficiency as a gauge for economic performance. In certain cases, the pursuit of stability and equity (or for that matter growth or the construction of a particular economic structure) has completely overridden the concern for efficiency.

Members of Group II have sought to extract an always uneasy picture of what are the resistant features of a workable economic process given the environment, and have usually either defended a compromise which did not create unanimity or made a reference to an instrumental or "higher rationality" which was beyond the realm of the verifiable.[58]

Little or no attention is paid in the judging of performance to *interaction between the human economy and the "rules of operation and structure of institutions for the system as a whole*" (Adelman), i.e., the "institutional and socio-cultural setting within which individuals and sub-groups in the system exercise their choice", and/or to the information system as *instrumentality per se*. Yet these dimensions are essential for the deepening of the Group II approach.

Regulation and the economic process

A full account of the impact of regulation on the economic process of advanced industrial countries would require an elaborate probing into the net observed benefits or malefits at the micro, mezzo, and macro levels, i.e., of the different forms of regulatory activities imposed on different sectors for different reasons under different circumstances. Moreover, such an impact would have to be gauged by reference to some benchmarks reflecting the performance of the human economy according to some agreed-upon governing relations, and we have seen that there are sharp differences of opinion about what those should be. Such a task is beyond the scope of this paper.

All we can hope to present are some general and provisional observations on the impact of regulation on economic performance both *in the small* and *in the large*. This separation of perspectives flows naturally from the framework we have sketched earlier, and it underlines very sharply, as we shall see, the partial nature of many "ideas in good currency" on the subject.

Through the microscope

The documentary evidence purporting to demonstrate the ineptitude and wasteful nature of regulation has been constructed almost entirely *in a microscopic mode* and on the basis of two techniques: the derivation of the virtual impact of regulation within the context of a theoretical model, with the inference that such a virtual impact is bound to materialize, *and* the cross-sectional comparison between regulated and non-regulated firms or sectors. The evidence on both counts is not really robust, as Caves has demonstrated, but it is massive and extensive enough – ranging from rent control, minimum wage legislation, rate-of-return regulation of public utilities, transportation and communications laws, safety standards, tariffs, etc. – that it has to be addressed.[59]

Most of the evidence is based on models attempting to gauge the static inefficiency of regulation by reference to the competitive norm. These studies are cast in a context which is often based on most unrealistic assumptions and too narrow a concern for efficiency to the exclusion of all other concerns, and are too clearly rigged to generate the expected conclusion.[60]

As soon as the models are relaxed to allow for uncertainty, complexity of goals, or interchange with the broader environment, most of these unambiguous conclusions become open to question. Even the famous Averch-Johnson effect, probably the clearest and most discussed distortion effect of rate-of-return regulation on the capital-labour ratio, becomes open to question (even *a priori*) in a context of uncertainty.[61] Work on the effect of regulation on progressiveness in the sense of Perroux (i.e., capacity to transform) is inconclusive: in some sectors, regulation distorted or slowed technological change; in others it speeded it up.[62]

Even if inefficiency is virtually or *de facto* induced by regulation (and as we mentioned the evidence is often inconclusive) it is not clear what one can infer from these microscopic perspectives. Inefficiency *in the small* is not really a mortal sin: a tariff may induce inefficiency and stimulate economic growth (and with it technical change) with the result that the benefits outweigh the efficiency costs. In fact, most of the serious studies of regulatory activities, focusing (as a consequence of the nature of their searchlight) on efficiency norms only, conclude that regulation is not costless and that it should be subjected, like any other good, to cost-benefit considerations.[63]

The position to which this line of reasoning, based on the ideal competitive model, leads is rather paradoxical: regulation is said to generate inefficiency since it interferes with the workings of the market on the one hand, but on the other hand regulation is regarded as a good like any other good supplied by the State and demanded by interest groups; therefore, the amount of regulation resulting from this market should be optimal. One can understand why some nihilism ensues.

If the evaluation of the impact of regulation on economic performance – via the micro-rationality route and the competitive ideal – has led to inconclusiveness and the reiteration of the need to subject regulation to cost-benefit considerations, the statements made by regulatory agencies on the basis of some exegesis of their terms of reference and some anamorphosis of reality, does not throw much light on the question either. The vaporous nature of the "plan", and the lack of precision of the desiderata embodied in the macro-rationale of the State, together with a greatly simplified image of economic reality and the normal self-interested mediation of the politicians and bureaucrats, would appear to have led to some political illusion on the part of regulators that there exists a political and administrative solution for everything, and that there are no limits to the regulable.[64]

The lack of strict and open accountability has allowed the regulators to use their control of the information, together with the general fuzziness of the objectives explicitly imposed on them, to avoid any real scrutiny or analysis by outside evaluators. This, together with the primitiveness of the analytics available for the economic study of politics and bureaucracies, has made this particular angle of vision rather less helpful than it might have been. Most certainly, no thorough internal analysis has yet provided an unambiguous view of the net effect of regulation on economic performance. In any case, since the "unintended and indirect consequences may have more economic significance than the desired direct ones" (Caves), it may be that this particular route will never prove very helpful.

Through the macroscope

One can also look into the impact of the regulatory process on economic performance, *in the large*, i.e., on the workability and instrumentality of the human economy, and on the way it fits with the rest of the social process.

From the heyday of *laissez-faire* to the present, regulation has provided a continuous and connected reaction to the failings of the market, but more importantly, maybe, the emerging regulation institutions were throwing some light on "the nature of institutional learning".[65] At first, offsetting organizational failures helped maintain the workability of market economies; in the more turbulent period of the "*second XXe siècle*", regulation evolved to permit change without too much disruption and intolerable organizational instability.

These different forms of regulation were often brought about at different times and on a piecemeal basis as a result of circumstances and/or political bureaucratic expediency, and because of the rigidity built into the earlier regulation systems, the permanence of certain practices has demonstrably been detrimental to the good functioning of human economies. However, on balance, the workability of the human economies of the advanced industrial countries has been smoothed by regulation: the role of regulation has been to steer the human economy between "*le probable et le souhaitable*".[66] Not all these experimentations have been equally successful, and there is a need to improve the capacity for collective decision on these matters, but the relatively limited incidence of malefits from *corridor phenomena* provides a meaningful testimony to the effectiveness of the regulatory process.

Two broad inter-related shifts in the economic process are particularly worth noting, since one can link them largely to the growth of regulation, and since they have brought about a significant transformation in the economic process of advanced industrialized economies during this "*second XXe siècle*", shifting them from economies geared to produce a maximum surplus, subject to an acceptable level of collective risk to economies geared to the minimization of collective risk, subject to an acceptable level of surplus.[67]

The first is the process of socialization of risk through regulation noted by Lowi[68] and the second is the broadening of the notion of property rights noted by Macpherson.[69] Both these changes have been instituted in the human economies via regulation, and both have contributed to better integrating the considerations of efficiency, distribution/equity, and stability in the governing of the economy, and to maintaining a balance between change and order.

One of the major influences of regulation on the economic process has been, according to Lowi, the underwriting and the socialization of risk. Instead of spending public resources to perform those tasks which would remain undone in a market economy, the State manages "institutional information", and acts as facilitator between parties who otherwise might not come to terms. The advantages of this sort of policy are that it directly addresses the problem of the increased relevant uncertainty in the environment by changing the adoptive texture of the environment, but also that such underwriting activities do not cost much, are capable of subdivision and fine tuning according to changing standards or governing relations, and have, when carefully chosen, important effects on the whole economy.[70] The "organizational conservatism" (Lowi) revealed by this process may be interpreted as a defence of the *status quo*, but equally well as a reduction in the cost of overall adjustment, and an improvement in the dynamic organizational efficiency.

Another important contribution of regulation has been the process of change and broadening in the notion of property rights that it has instituted. As late as the seventeenth century[71] the notion of property was quite broad, but it went through a process of narrowing as a "result of the rise of the competitive capitalist market economy" to the point where it came to mean "an exclusive individual right to use and dispose of material things", a content well adjusted to the market system. The rise of the regulatory process has broadened the concept of property rights considerably: they are not only rights in marketable things but rights to income, not only exclusive and alienable rights, but also non-alienable rights not to be excluded, not only rights in things and revenue, but also property in life and liberty. These new or rather broader rights cannot be marketed, and they triggered a greater enmeshing of economy, society, and polity in the human economy.

We would conclude from this overview that the regulatory process has had a positive impact on the performance of the *"socio-économies"*, to use Fernand Braudel's label. This does not mean that all regulatory instruments in operation today are contributing to a greater instrumentality and workability of the economic process. In fact, there is a need for a refurbishing or the elimination of many "geological" layers of regulatory instruments inherited from yesteryears, which constitute impediments to the smooth functioning and adjusting of the economic process. Some portions of the regulatory process may also be havens of ineptitude or be entirely unnecessary and costly They should be exposed by the growing commando brigade of deregulators. However, on the whole, the most plausible hypothesis appears to be that the regulatory process has induced a greater *procedural rationality*[72] into the economic process, and thereby enhanced its performance.

Some vignettes

Our conjecture that, despite much inept, costly, and unnecessary regulatory activities, the regulatory process had induced a greater procedural rationality overall into the economic process, and improved the performance of the *"socio-économie"*, does not represent a consensus.

While some have called for more national planning and a greater degree of design and regulation in our type of socio-technical systems,[73] the mood of the day is rather to deregulation on principle – an understandable reaction to the "political illusion of many utopian regulators of the *"second XXe siècle"*.

And so, astute observers of the Canadian scene, like Douglas Hartle, have drawn attention with some concern to what they see as the emergence of a new medieval regulationism – "a new feudalism". The thrust of the argument is that we are now knee deep in regulations—regulations that impose enormous costs of compliance, that distort private decisions, and surreptitiously alter the distribution of income, usually in favour of those being regulated. With growing constraints on government expenditures and personnel, Hartle sees a likely pressure toward even greater reliance on regulation in the future.[74] Hartle only sounds a warning, but many studies and commentaries on the regulatory process appear to agree on the diagnosis, and to be quasi-unanimous in their call for and their faith in competition as an alternative to regulation.[75]

This dominant view insists that regulation is not costless, but it marshals arguments which rely almost entirely on short-run efficiency criteria, or assume away the complexities, uncertainties, and strategic dimensions of the real game that underpins the human economy. The gains from the regulation of the economic process are rarely examined. This makes it doubly important to underline some of these dimensions of the regulation of complex organized systems.[76] In this section, we wish to illustrate in a very preliminary fashion some of the ways in which the regulatory process has contributed to improving the performance of the human economy in Canada: some virtue in the large has evolved from the publicized vices in the small. Our vignettes draw attention to the improved economic process, as regulation makes it multistable and as intervention takes on a more strategic flavour.

Multistability by regulation

As mentioned earlier, the human economy of the "*second XXe siècle*" in Canada has experienced a shift from energy intensity to information intensity within a transnational environment of increasing complexity, connectedness, and turbulence These interacting forces have affected some "essential variables" (Ashby) of the existing system, and shifted major sectors of the economy outside the corridor of acceptable performance.[77]

This is largely as a result of the very nature of information and knowledge which are central features of the "new economy". Information and knowledge are not commodities, generate massive externalities, and cannot be handled effectively by the market. Moreover, information processes are likely to be subject to important economies of scale.[78] Consequently, both naturally and artificially, a large number of non-market mechanisms have emerged and become important within market economies.

Some of it has occurred naturally, through the functioning of the human economy as an ultrastable system[79] - a system with a dual feedback loop. *One* (in the small) links the environment with the reacting part within the constraints imposed by the existing institutions and accounts for the small changes in the environment and the responses it induces in the reacting part; the *other* (in the large) links the environment with the reacting part via changes in "essential variables", which bring the economy outside the corridor, and trigger a change in the institutional parameters. Such changes in the essential variables provide the reacting part with a modified performance program. Refurbished property rights and new non-market forms of organization have emerged naturally in response to the new situation.[80]

However, artificial forms of regulation have often proved necessary: the ultrastable system reacting too sluggishly or too imperfectly to the heightened level of relevant uncertainty, and in the increased information intensity, massive co-ordination failures might ensue without regulation.

The problem is dramatically illustrated by many examples mentioned in the literature on market signalling. Where "clear cut informational asymmetry and considerable buyer uncertainty" entail that no effective market signalling occurs, market transactions cannot occur.[81] As a result, the benefits from non-market institutions and organizations increase in both the private and the public sector: redefinition of property rights and a rich array of market-supplementary practices emerge.[82] The possibility of gains for entrepreneurs in social change leads to the introduction of artificial and new forms of regulation.[83] The possibility of effective planning is enhanced to the extent that the economic process becomes more malleable and the manipulation of institutional information easier.[84]

But whatever facilitating of the adjustment to this "information revolution" might be said to have been accomplished by regulation, the central contribution of purposive regulation has been to introduce some fragmentation into the texture of the human economic system, to set up partial ultrastable sub-systems, subject to slightly different rules and interacting incompletely, or only through the mediation of specific channels where a somewhat unified and richly joined system had existed before. Ashby refers to such a system as a *multistable system*[85]: one in which a greater ability to adapt is ensured through discontinuities between the sub-systems—an adjustment called for by a shift in some "essential variables" being delegated, so to speak, to a partial system enabling the overall process to adjust to important shocks in the environment in a manner which would have been either impossible or very time-consuming had the overall process been forced to adjust *in toto*. By transforming the human economy into a multistable system—or at least by contributing significantly to such a transformation—regulation has contributed to a smoother and faster adjustment to the "information revolution".

Much of this improvement in the adaptability of the human economy has come, it must be said, as a matter of unintended consequences. In a sense, regulation has played on the economic front much the same role that federalism has played on the political front: the fragmentation of the overall process led to some additional costs of transaction and friction, but the system's overall cost of adjustment has been lowered.

From Ruling to Gaming

Regulation has increased the economic system's capacity to transform by making it multistable, but this in turn has led to a change in the nature of the regulatory process as a result of the new systemic features of the economic process and of its environment. Complexity, uncertainty, turbulence, and greater information intensity, together with the new forms of interdependence and social colligation, have led to the emergence of a new brand of regulation commensurate with the environment (new functioning within old structures), but also the emergence of new types of structures, a shift from outcome-oriented activities to process-oriented activities by regulatory agencies, the abandonment of simple external rules imposed from the outside and a greater reliance on and involvement in the bargaining process from within the game.[86]

In the Canadian context, this transformation has been most notable, if not sufficiently noted by students of regulation: the regulatory activities have acquired a strategic flavour. In a changing environment, this represented for the regulator a natural counter-ploy to opportunism and strategic behaviour by the regulated, and a shift in this direction explicitly or subterraneously would be revealed by a serious study of the regulatory process. It has often represented a valuable middle of the road between the polar organizational forms represented by markets and hierarchies – both subject to well-known limits in turbulent environments.[87]

Indeed, the tendency for this view to become important on the Canadian scene, and the consequent "handing over to a technocracy (of economists?) within the government the authority to specify the terms on which the strategic economic decisions for the society would be made", has been noted and criticized in the Skeoch report.[88] While there may be many reasons to be concerned with this drift of the regulatory process into a negotiating/bargaining mode, the circumstantial evidence available on this process of change from ruling to gaming is very strong[89], and there are good reasons to believe that this shift has improved the workability of the economic system. The paragraphs below draw attention to a few cases which have exemplary value.

New functioning

It has been argued that there has been a drift in anti-combines administration in Canada in the 1970s, "from the adversary resolution of conflict provided *ex post* by the courts... towards *ex ante* harmonization of public and private interests through the guiding conciliation of bureaucrats".[90]

The drift has been clearly noted in the operation of the Bureau of Competition Policy where the professional staff doubled over the

1970–75 period while the investigative case-load (formal inquiries excluding misleading advertising) remained rather stable. This is the period during which informal instruments like the *program of compliance* –offering the possibility of informal consultation between industry officials and bureaucrats about the way to interpret combines legislation – would appear to have become more important, and to have experienced a transformation: from the *information function* it was performing on a small scale in the 1950s, and the *education function* it was conducting on a still relatively small scale until the mid-1960s, the program developed into an important *opinion-giving function*. Skinner has been able to show, from the limited evidence available on the program of compliance, how this has led to a new form of bargaining: industry officials seeking guidance from the bureaucrats about their planned activities, and making those who were to be the drafters of the new legislation aware of the needs of the private sector. The possibility of strategic manipulation of information in such a context is very clear.

The revised Competition Act, tabled in the Commons in early 1977, strengthened this general drift: the power to administer the competition laws became vested in a quasi-judicial board of legal and business experts, whose function it will be to judge cases on their merits, and it is empowered to approve mergers, rationalization or specialization agreements, and monopoly practices, if prospective gains in efficiency and increased ability to meet foreign competition justify it. This would appear to institutionalize the greater discretion given to experts and bureaucrats to assess cases on their merits and to eliminate the burden of rules which turn out to be difficult to apply in a rapidly changing modern economy. Flexibility, pragmatism, nothing but process objectives and the creation of a forum to confront alternative conjectures and to bargain—such would appear to be the thrust of the new Act.[91]

New structures

The great difficulty in operating from without, and on the basis of relatively rigid rules where speedy and strategic actions in a complex and changing environment are called for, and when an appreciation of the issue at hand within its particular circumstances is required, has led the public authorities to make use of Crown corporations and government firms more and more often; but there has also been a tendency to set up regulatory structures which have built-in features not unlike those of the competition policy.

Such structures are set up to deal with the problems which are unstructured or ill-structured and to use methods adapted to the nature of the problems.[92] Governing relations provide only a sense of direction and the groups of bureaucrats charged with the regulatory task are allowed to learn on the job, so to speak. Each case is judged on its merits by reference to this direction, with little or no requirement that the rationale for the decision be explained, or even stated clearly.

The Foreign Investment Review Act was the epitome of this new breed of legislation. The members of this regulatory agency were asked to review *ex ante* [beforehand] foreign takeovers of Canadian and foreign businesses in Canada, and also the establishment of new foreign-owned businesses in Phase II.

The governing principle guiding the regulators is whether or not such new takeovers or investments would bring "significant benefit to Canada". This provides extreme flexibility and discretion for the regulators in evaluating each case on its merits. Indeed, this is feature of the review process which has come under criticism in certain quarters because it embodies both "explicit flexibility" ("designed to accommodate differences between cases") and "discretionary flexibility" (depending on "how strict or liberal the authorities choose to be in interpreting non-specific clauses"). But these features would appear to us to constitute the very substance of the procedure which was meant to be embodied in these new structures. [93]

Can one demonstrate that the learning process triggered by such dynamic monitoring will lead to "better" results than those achievable by administrative rules of thumb? It has been argued that such is the case: such procedures accelerate the learning process of the system and facilitate adaptation by the economic process. [94] This does not deny the possibility that self-interested bureaucrats will pervert the process. Some evidence has been produced showing that this has indeed occurred. [95] However, such procedural defects might better be dealt with by procedural correctives, like better disclosure requirements and less administrative secrecy. This, in turn, should be made easier when it is better understood that these flexible structures have usefulness and legitimacy. [96]

Conclusion

This paper has attempted to sketch the contours of a framework to analyse the interactions between the regulatory process and the socio-economic process, has examined the drift in the regulatory process, and has explored alternative ways in which the impact of the regulatory process on economic performance could be gauged. It has evolved a view of regulation within a cybernetic paradigm [97], and has suggested that the regulatory process has induced procedural rationality in the economic process and consequently enhanced the performance of *socio-économies*. Some circumstantial evidence drawn from the Canadian context has been presented in support of this plausible hypothesis.

The analysis has identified some conceptual difficulties of the standard reductionist neo-classical framework in providing a satisfactory image of the economy as instituted process, and in gauging its performance. It has attempted to show the usefulness of a complementary macroscopic, evolutionary, and institutionalist perspective on the structure and functioning of human economies. The reader may be left with a sense that the two frameworks are consecrating a basic methodological dualism leading to contradictory and irreconcilable conclusions. This is not the case. It has been argued that these two perspectives were "on a path of convergence and that, in fact, much could be gained through a merger of these apparently antipodal schools".[98]

One must agree with Popper when he observes that "only a minority of social institutions are consciously designed while the vast majority have just 'grown', as the undesigned results of human actions", and that "social institutions may emerge as unintended consequences of rational actions". One must agree also with Hayek when he states that the basic problem facing the social sciences is the creation of a "composite theory of social phenomena" capable of explaining "how the independent actions of many men can produce coherent wholes, persistent structures of relationships which serve human purposes without having been designed for that end".[99]

Our contention is that the cybernetic paradigm provides a locus for the effective reconciliation of these different perspectives, and a basis for this "composite theory of social phenomena". Consequently, we are tempted to suggest to the specialists on regulation what Robert Campbell once suggested to the specialists on the Soviet economy: that they "should take mass leave, and study cybernetics together for a year".[100]

Endnotes

1   R. E. Caves, "Direct Regulation and Market Performance in the American Economy", *American Economic Review* (May 1964), 172, 181.

2   C. Donahue, Jr., "Lawyers, Economists and the Regulated Industries: Thoughts on Professional Roles Inspired by Some Recent Economic Literature", *Michigan Law Review*, LXX (1971), 198, 207.

3   Sir Geoffrey Vickers, *Freedom in a Rocking Boat* (Harmondsworth, 1970), p. 19.

4   While for some purposes, as for instance in gauging the demand for regulatory activities, it may not be of great help to separate micro- from macro-economic regulation (A. Breton, *The Regulation of Private Economic Activity* [Montreal, 1976], pp. 3—4), in other cases when the focus of interest is the impact of certain types of regulatory activities on sectors and enterprises, the distinction is crucial. We shall focus in this paper on the micro- and mezzo-economic aspects of the

social process and ignore the adjustment of broad aggregates for macro-economic stabilization and related purposes. Mezzo-economics is defined by Alec Nove as the branch of economics dealing with systems and industry-wide analysis and falling between the micro and macro perspectives. The emphasis is "on systems of interrelationships, institutional factors and multi-dimensionality, within which margins and marginal analysis do have their proper place, in the context of systems", A. Nove, *Efficiency Criteria for Nationalized Industries* (Toronto, 1973), pp. 134—35.

[5]   W. G. Shepherd, *The Treatment of Market Power* (New York, 1975), p. 1

[6]   A masterly indictment of current practices has been done by R. H. Coase in "Industrial Organization: A Proposal for Research", in V.R. Fuchs, ed., *Policy Issues and Research Opportunities in Industrial Organization* (New York, 1972), pp. 59—73.

[7]   There have been some attempts in the American literature to construct expanded frameworks. It may be useful to mention W. J. Samuels, "Public Utilities and the Theory of Power", in M. Russell, ed., *Perspectives in Public Regulation* (Carbondale, 1973). This paper has an institutionalist flavour; it is a rather ambitious effort to redefine the problem in terms of a paradigm of choice-cum-power. Shepherd (*Treatment of Market Power*) does not stray as far from the standard paradigm but provides a refurbished theory of market structure in the presence of market power.

[8]   For a full discussion of the differences between analytical framework, theory, and model, see H. Leibenstein, "What Can We Expect from a Theory of Development?", *Kyklos*, xix (1966), fasc. 1, 1-22.

[9]   While we have not attempted to present our framework in any formal way, we have adopted what Lange has called a form of cybernetic thinking—i.e., an approach which emphasizes the significance of certain particular aspects of reality (O. Lange, *Introduction to Economic Cybernetics* [Oxford, 1970]) . We owe much of the framework to Sir Geoffrey Vickers, whose many books have provided many elements and components of our framework; but more importantly it is the overall appreciative system proposed by Vickers—more than specific elements of definition (although we have borrowed freely there too)—which has branded our presentation here. The reader might refer to his *The Art of Judgment* (New York, 1965), *Value Systems and Social Process* (Harmondsworth 1970), and *Freedom in a Rocking Boat* (Harmondsworth, 1972).

[10]   On the central features of the neoclassical reductionist program, see A. Coddington, "Keynesian Economics: The Search for First Principles", *Journal of Economic Literature*, xiv, no. 4 (December 1976), Section I; on the central features of the alternative view of the economic process, see G. Paquet, "L'économie non-marchande dans l'économie de marchés: à la recherche d'un cadre de référence", *Revue d'économie politique*, LXXXVII, no. 4 (1977), 607—25.

[11]   We do not intend to suggest here a thorough critical appraisal of the standard reductionist neo-classical framework. This would require more space than is available. However, it is impossible not to suggest why the standard framework is not satisfactory and how it has led discussions about performance into a dead end. We shall attempt to underline some of these points by way of contrast as we develop the components of our own framework. It might be useful however to draw attention from the start to the fact that what is in question is the possibility of recreating the economic process or the collective game from the individual games (one-person games or games against nature). We claim that it is not possible and

that the very notions of rationality and efficiency built in the monadic approach break down outside the rarefied atmosphere of the competitive model. It becomes impossible, therefore, to make use of them to gauge the performance of segments of real economies, and different tools have to be forged. The simple addition of *ad hoc* frictions and costs of transaction does not change the fundamental nature of the difficulty. See N. Howard, *Paradoxes of Rationality* (Cambridge, 1971), *passim*, and J.B. Herendeen, *The Economics of the Corporate Economy* (New York, 1975), Chapter 13.

12   K. Polanyi, "The Economy as Instituted Process", in K. Polanyi, C. M. Arensberg, and H. W. Pearson, eds., *Trade and Market in the Early Empires* (New York, 1957), p. 248.

13   One might refer to F. Perroux, *Economie et société* (Paris, 1960), and K. E. Boulding, *A Primer on Social Dynamics* (New York, 1907). Whether one refers to échange/ contrainte/don or exchange/ threat/ integration, the triad of co-ordinating principles is fairly similar.

14   This is the diagnosis of R. Clower and A. Leijonhufvud, "The Coordination of Economic Activities: Keynesian Perspective", *American Economic Review* (May 1975).

15   Interesting examples of this sort of work which have the merit of providing good illustrations or a pro- visional synthesis of the state of the art might be J. Hirshleifer, "Exchange Theory: The Missing Chapter", *Western Economic Journal* (June 1973); A. A. Alchian and H. Demsetz, "The Property Right Paradigm", *Journal of Economic History* (March 1973); O. E. Williamson, *Markets and Hierarchies* (New York, 1975). Williamson is the one who has used the expression "new institutional economics".

16   L. Hurwicz has presented a rather interesting view of the economy as an information system ("Conditions for Economic Efficiency of Centralized and Decentralized Structures", in G. Grossman, ed., *Value and Plan* [California, 1960]). In this paper, a classification of messages according to their degree of anonymity and operationality is suggested: market-type economies are defined as those processing anonymous and operational messages while command economies are stylized as those processing messages which are neither anonymous nor operational. For a use of related concepts in the comparison of different economic systems, see R. Carson, *Comparative Economic Systems (New York, 1973.)*

17   J. Marschak, "Economic Planning and the Cost of Thinking", *Social Research*, xxxiii (Summer 1966), 151—59.

18   This process of interaction between institutions and information is a rather complex one which can be analyzed at many levels. For some preliminary perspectives, see G. Paquet, "The Structuration of a Planned Economy", *Canadian Slavonic Papers*, VIII (1966), 250—59. A more sophisticated and more ambitious framework has been developed by G. Newman, "An Institutional Perspective on Information", *International Social Science Journal*, III, (1976).

19   Some of the Marxian literature on the reproduction of social relations has this sort of flavour and one might also derive the same impression of one-sidedness from too cursory a reading of some of the holistic literature.

20   A. A. Alchian, "Uncertainty, Evolution and Economic Theory", *Journal of Political Economy*, LVIII, no. 3 (June 1950), 21 1-21.

21   For an interesting preliminary examination of the process of adoption both at the economic-process level and at the social-process level, see I. Adelman, "Social and

Economic Development at the Micro Level – A Tentative Hypothesis", in E. B. Ayal, ed., *Micro-Aspects of Development* (New York, 1973). Also F. E. Emery and E. L. Trist, *Toward a Social Ecology* (New York, 1973).

[22] Both A. O. Hirschman, *Development Projects Observed* (Washington 1967) and L. M. Lachmann, *The Legacy of Max Weber* (Berkeley, 1971), developed a conceptual framework along these lines to explain institutional change. Also B. Roberts and B. R. Holdren, *Theory of Social Process* (Iowa, 1972).

[23] With Newman ("An Institutional Perspective on Information", p. 488) it is important to distinguish "institutional information" from information supplied purposively by institutions. The best example of information of this first type is obviously the market price of a good, while a good example of the second type would be an edict by government.

[24] Paquet, "Structuration of a Planned Economy", Section II.

[25] This perspective has been suggested by K. Lancaster in "The Dynamic Inefficiency of Capitalism", *Journal of Political Economy* (September-October 1973). Lancaster suggests this paradigm of capitalism as a differential game and analyses a simple case to illustrate the possibilities of this line of inquiry. He shows that one can demonstrate the suboptimality of capitalism as a game and explain the social losses by the separation of consumption and investment decision in the simplified example he works with. Moreover, this co-ordination failure cannot be easily remedied: workers and capitalists face the same sort of dilemma faced by the prisoner in the famous game-theory example.

[26] For a discussion of these mechanisms with a cybernetic twist, see O. Lange, *Wholes and Parts* (Oxford, 1965); C. Gini, *Pathologie économique* (Paris, 1959); and A. Leijonhufvud, "Notes on the Theory of Markets", *Intermountain Economic Review*, I, no. 1 (Fall 1970), 1-13.

[27] Lange, *Wholes and Parts*, p. 71. The discussion in this paragraph draws heavily on the illuminating discussion of Lange's Chapter ix.

[28] Ibid p. 68

[29] Clower and Leijonhufvud, "The Co-ordination of Economic Activities", p. 187.

[30] Vickers, *The Art of Judgment*, Chapter 1.

[31] There is no accumulated written jurisprudence in economics and no economic magistrature charged with the task of confronting alternative rules against the facts of individual situations. This is indeed one of the fundamental weaknesses of the discipline, according to Benjamin Ward, *What's Wrong with Economics?* (New York, 1972).

[32] M. Godelier, *Rationalité et irrationalité en économie* (Paris, 1971), especially Tome I, pp. 180ff., and Tome II, pp. 192ff.

[33] For a critical examination of these different kinds of rationalities see G. Paquet, "The Multinational Firm and the Nation-State as Institutional Forms", in G. Paquet, ed., *The Multinational Firm and the Nation State* (Don Mills, 1972).

[34] While this may be regarded as an extreme position to hold, there is plenty of evidence that this is the prevalent perspective. It follows naturally from the limiting conceptual famework referred to in the introductory section. For a critical evaluation of this position, see A. N. D. McAuley, "Rationality and Central Planning", *Soviet Studies*, xviii (1967); also Vickers, *The Art of Judgment*, p. 29; and Howard, *Paradoxes of Rationality*, Chapter 2.

[35] Howard. *Paradoxes of Rationality* and B. J. Loasby, *Choice, Complexity and Ignorance* (Cambridge, 1976).

36 Theodore Lowi, "Toward a Politics of Economics: The State of Permanent Receivership", in L. N. Lindberg et al, eds., *Stress and Contradiction in Modern Capitalism* (Toronto, 1975); see also R. A. Solo, "The Economist and the Economic Roles of the Political Authority in Advanced Industrial Societies" in the same volume.

37 Vickers, *The Art of Judgment*, p. 29.

38 Solo, "The Economist and the Economic Roles"; Loasby, *Choice, Complexity and Ignorance*, Chapter 12; and Vickers, *Value Systems and Social Process*, pp. 95—96. The Vickers conditions read as follows: First, the regulator must be able to discriminate those variables that are involved in the relations it seeks to regulate and to predict—or control—their future course over a period at least as long as the time needed to make an effective response. Secondly, it must be able to preserve sufficient constancy among its standards and priorities to make a coherent response possible. Thirdly, it must have in its repertory or be able to discover some response which has a better than random chance of being successful. Fourthly, it must be able to give effect to this response within the time which the first and second conditions allow. Some would add a fifth condition—that the results of the response must be sufficiently distinguishable in the future course of affairs or prove or disprove its aptness and thus give the opportunity to learn by trial and error. I do not include this, because it seems to me that in important political decisions we often must and do get on without it.

39 Caves, "Direct Regulation and Market Performance in the American Economy", p. 181.

40 J. W. Forrester, "Counterintuitive Behavior of Social Systems", *Technology Review*, lxxv (January 1971).

41 Caves, "Direct Regulation and Market Performance", p. 175.

42 Quoted by K. Polanyi in *The Great Transformation* (Boston, 1957) , p. 279, from Pirenne's Medieval Cities.

43 In *The Great Transformation*, Polanyi examined the rise of the market economy in the nineteenth century and the emergence of the strains which led to the receding role of the market in social organization as the market society began to search for correctives for the hardships generated by the market.

44 Solo, "The Economist and the Economic Roles", p. 100.

45 Lowi, "Toward a Politics of Economics", p. 119.

46 D. A. Schon, *Beyond the Stable State* (New York, 1971); F. E. Emery and E. L. Trist, "The Causal Texture of Organizational Environments", *Human Relations*, XVIII, no. 1 (February 1965), 21—32.

47 F. Perroux, *Industrie et création collective* (Paris, 1970), pp. 61ff., and J. Attali, *La parole et l'outil* (Paris, 1975). For a discussion of the implication of this change in the economic process on national economies and the international division of labour, see S. Langdon and G. Paquet, *The Multinational Enterprise and the Labour Process: A Provisional Analytical Framework*, a report prepared for the Directorate of Social Affairs, Manpower, and Education of the OECD, 1976.

48 Emery and Trist, "The Causal Texture of Organizational Environments".

49 The argument is developed in some detail in Schon, *Beyond the Stable State*, Chapter 6.

50 The argument is made persuasively, if in a rather sketchy way, in Lowi, "Toward a Politics of Economics", pp. 116, 119-21. For a legal perspective on these developments and some views on "le droit négocié" and "les quasi-contrats", see A.

Jacquemin et G. Schrans, *Le Droit économique* (Paris, 1970), Chapter 3.

51 A scanning of Emery and Trist, Schon, and Lowi would help to document this broad shift. See also M. L. Weidenbaum, *Government-Mandated Price Increases* (Washington, 1975) for a look at the new wave of government regulation in the United States.

52 For an examination of these cases, see W. C. Merrill and N. Schneider, "Government Firms in Oligopoly Industries: A Short-Run Analysis", *Quarterly Journal of Economics*, LXXX, no. 3 (August 1966), 400—12. Also A. Breton, "Crown Corporation as an Alternative to Industrial Incentive Grants", in *The Challenge, Conference on Economic Development in Winnipeg*, Manitoba (25-26 October 1971).

53 Herendeen, *Economics of the Corporate Economy*, p. 229.

54 A fairly good overview of this approach together with the criticism which it generated is presented in F. M. Scherer, *Industrial Market Structure and Economic Performance* (Chicago, 1970), Chapter 2. This approach focuses almost exclusively on efficiency considerations in gauging performance.

55 Scherer presents sixteen norms and criteria used to bracket the notion of workable competition as a standard (*Industrial Market Structure and Economic Performance*, p. 37). This approach would appear to postulate a market economy (i.e., one where economic activities are reduced for all practical purposes to market activities) in some versions like the one proposed by J. Markham ("An Alternative Approach to the Concept of Workable Competition", *American Economic Review* [June 1950]) but this need not necessarily be the case.

56 This particular criticism of lack of operationality and of value biases is, however, far from being as lethal as might first appear. See Scherer, *Industrial Market Structure and Economic Performance*.

57 Herendeen, *Economics of the Corporate Economy*, p. 230. Also C. E. Ferguson, *A Macroeconomic Theory of Workable Competition* (Durham, NC., 1964), Chapter 3.

58 Any serious discussion of these issues would require a psychoanalysis of the concept of performance, probably the most difficult concept that economists have to deal with. We have had occasion in the previous section to define most of the terms used in the preceding two paragraphs. For a review of the different types of efficiency in the context of the enterprise see G. Paquet, "French Canadian Entrepreneurship: Quebec Must Design its own Brand", *The Business Quarterly* (Summer 1972); for the concept of "higher rationality" see H. Marcuse, *One-Dimensional Man* (London, 1964), Chapter 6. It should be clear, however, that the strategy of Group I, for all the impression of certainty and clarity it would appear to generate in some circles, may not be more meaningful than the strategy of the drunk who, having lost his watch in the dark back alley, was searching for it under the lamp-post because there was light there.

59 For an extensive review of the literature on both the principles and institutions of regulation, see A. B. Kahn, *The Economics of Regulation*, 2 vols. (New York, 1970/71). Both the *Journal of Law and Economics* and the *Bell Journal of Economics and Management Science* (now *Bell Journal of Economics*) have provided a rich documentation on these questions in recent years.

60 To the extent that a competitive market system is used as the norm and that efficiency considerations are regarded as the only relevant ones, any costly regulatory activity, except in the case of gross market failures, is bound to generate inefficiency.

61 S. Perrakis, "Rate of Return Regulation of a Monopoly Firm with Random De-

mand", *International Economic Review* (February 1976).

[62] W. M. Capron, ed., *Technological Change in Regulated Industries* (Washington, 1971).

[63] G. Bruce Doern et al., "The Structure and Behaviour of Canadian Regulatory Boards and Commissions: Multidisciplinary Perspectives", *Canadian Public Administration*, xviii, no. 2 (June 1975), 199ff.

[64] The problem has been exposed in passionate terms by J. Ellul, *The Political Illusion* (New York, 1967). For an examination of the state of the art on the economic analysis of political behaviour see *Journal of Law and Economics* (Special Issue, December 1975) and in particular the paper by W. A. Niskanen, "Bureaucrats and Politicians".

[65] Schon. *Beyond the Stable State*, p. 60.

[66] Commissariat au Plan, 1985—*La France face au choc du futur* (Paris, 1972), Chapter 3.

[67] This is a hypothesis suggested in Paquet, "L'économie non-marchande dans l'économie de marchés", Section 4.

[68] Lowi, "Toward a Politics of Economics".

[69] C. B. Macpherson, "Human Rights as Property Rights", *Dissent* (Winter 1977).

[70] Lowi, "Toward a Politics of Economics", pp. 119-20.

[71] This paragraph attempts to summarize Macpherson's argument

[72] The notion of procedural rationality has been introduced in a different context by H. A. Simon, "From Substantive to Procedural Rationality", in S. J. Latsis, ed., *Method and Appraisal in Economics* (Cambridge, 1976). It has a family resemblance to the notion of macro-rationality we have used earlier.

[73] For instance, Abraham Rotstein, "The 20th Century Prospect: Nationalism in a Technological Society". in P. Russell, ed., *Nationalism in Canada* (Toronto, 1966). On a more global scale, see E. Jantsch, *Design for Evolution* (New York, 1975).

[74] Douglas Hartle, "How to Cope with New Feudalism", *The Financial Post* (4 December 1976), p. 14. A Financial Post digest of a paper presented to the Canadian Tax Foundation.

[75] The Economic Council of Canada (ECC) has been a particularly eloquent defender of this option on the external and the internal scenes; for instance, Economic Council of Canada, *Looking Outward* (Ottawa, 1975), where a liberalization of international trade is proposed. The strength of the faith is indicated by the following sentences (p. 65) where, after having established the central importance of the development of knowledge-intensive industries in the next phase of Canada's development, the ECC concluded—"There is, of course, no guarantee that the liberalized trading environment would, of itself, lead to a concentration of knowledge-intensive endeavors. The point is that it would open up the inherent possibilities, enabling competition to do the rest." (Our emphasis.) One may also consult, on the internal scene, *ECC, Efficiency and Regulation* (Ottawa, 1976). This report examines the regulatory structure imposed on deposit institutions and is much less extreme. It suggests "ways to increase efficiency through competition and a more flexible regulatory framework" (p. 2). A recent paper has proposed guideposts to help in the decision to replace regulation by competition; see G. B. Reschenthaler, "Regulatory Failure and Competition", *Canadian Public Administration*, xix, no. 3 (Fall 1976), 466-86.

[76] M. Crozier and J. C. Thoenig. "The Regulation of Complex Organized Systems", *Administrative Science Quarterly* (December 1976). The authors examine the rela-

tionships between the "games which are played at the bottom of the system" and the "game which regulates the system".

77 Langdon and Paquet, *Multinational: Enterprise and the Labour Process*, Chapter 1. While these "essential variables" are not the same in all parts of the economic process, they all pertain to "governing relations". They are the variables which must remain within certain limits if the system is to function smoothly. When these variables are pushed beyond certain thresholds, a discontinuity is triggered (best illustrated by a move along a step-function) and the regime of the system is altered.

78 Economic Council of Canada, *Report on Intellectual and Industrial Property* (Ottawa, 197 1), Chapter 2; R. Wilson, "Informational Economies of Scale", *Bell Journal of Economics* (Spring 1975).

79 The notion of ultrastable systems was developed by W. R. Ashby, *Design for a Brain*, second ed., rev. (London, 1960), Chapter 7. The concept has been used in the study of the evolution of the organizational form of the economic process by O. E. Williamson, *Corporate Control and Business Behavior* (Englewood Cliffs, 1970), chapters 3, 8.

80 Langdon and G. Paquet, *Multinational Enterprise and the Labour Process*, where the growth of the multinational enterprise is shown to be the result of such a process.

81 For a discussion of the informational transfer underpinnings of markets, see A. M. Spence, *Market Signalling* (Cambridge, 1974). The example referred to here is drawn from Chapter 12, in which Spence analysed the problem raised by G. A. Akerlof, "The Market for 'Lemons': Qualitative Uncertainty and the Market Mechanism", *Quarterly Journal of Economics* (August 1970).

82 Spence enumerates a variety of practices engendered as a result of informational deficiency. R. McKean, Economics of Ethical and Behavioral Codes (St. Louis, 1976), has shown that voluntary practices may be effective.

83 For a look at institutional innovation see, L. E. Davis and D. C. North, *Institutional Change and American Economic Growth* (Cambridge, 1971), Part I.

84 Newman, "An Institutional Perspective on Information", has discussed this problem.

85 Ashby, *Design for a Brain*, Chapter 16.

86 Ibid., p. 210. Ashby has shown that this process was predictable for a multistable system: "Within a multistable system, sub-system adapts to sub-system in exactly the same way as animal adapts to 'environment'. Trial and error will appear to be used; and, when the process is completed, the activities of the two parts will show co-ordination to the common end of maintaining the essential variables of the double system within their proper limits."

87 Willliamson, *Markets and Hierarchies*, chapters 2, 7.

88 L. A. Skeoch, *Dynamic Change and Accountability in a Canadian Market Economy* (Ottawa, 1976), p. 15.

89 The drift of regulation into process-orientation and regulation as negotiation, on the one hand, and the emergence of a new social architecture of regulation impregnated with this sort of bias like FIRA and AIB, On the other, may be documented from the works of economic morticians on regulatory mishaps or from the all-too-rare institutional analysis of regulatory bodies. For a view of the manner in which the present environment forces the development of new forms of government-owned firms as a means of regulation in the resources sector see

Eric Kierans, *Report on Natural Resources Policy in Manitoba* (February 1973). The need to obtain crucial information about the extent of reserves, transfer pricing within multinational organizations, etc. (all necessary for regulation to be effective but only available from the regulated firms in the absence of active participation by a government-owned firm within the industry), shows the rationale for PetroCan or for the proposal by the Quebec government to buy one segment of the asbestos industry. The operations of a multiplicity of boards dealing with sectoral adjustments have also had to adjust to this gaming situation as more and more regulatory agencies have had to "negotiate on the basis of what is expected to happen, not only on what has happened" (C. Pestiau, *The Canadian Textile Policy* [Montreal, 1976], p. 20). The current debate on a formula to adjust rates automatically (FARA) proposed by the Canadian Transport Commission for federally regulated telecommunications firms like Bell Canada underlines the extent to which such a formula would make "the regulated firm more dependent on the Commission's judgment alone" but also the extent to which the regulation of Bell in the face of a lack of "performance evaluator" has become a debate over procedures (L. Courville and M. G. Dagenais, "On New Approaches to the Regulation of Bell Canada", *Canadian Public Policy* [Winter 1977]).

90 This proposition has been put forward and tested in a preliminary way by one of my students in his honours essay (W. R. Skinner, *Competition Policy in Canada – An Exploratory Essay in the Economics of Politics*, Carleton University (April 1976). Much of my discussion in this sub-section draws extensively on Section 4 of Chapter v of Skinner's work. The essay investigates the blend of democratic and bureaucratic forces which shaped the competition policy review over the last decade.

91 The great similarity between the context described by Skinner and formalized by the new proposed legislation and the "bargaining context" cannot be missed. See J. G. Cross, *The Economics of Bargaining* (New York, 1969).

92 For an examination of the relationship between the degree of structuration of the problem and the type of method appropriate to it, see H. I. Ansoff, "A Quasi-Analytic Method for Long-Range Planning", in C. W. Churchman and M. Verhulst, eds., *Management Sciences: Models and Techniques* (London, 1960).

93 T. Abdel-Malek and A. K. Sarkar, "An Analysis of the Effects of Phase II Guidelines of the Foreign Investment Review Act", *Canadian Public Policy* (Winter 1977).

94 G. Paquet, "Social Science Research as an Evaluative Instrument for Social Policy", in G. E. Nettler and K. J. Krotki, eds., *Social Science and Social Policy* (Edmonton, 1971); Vickers, *The Art of Judgment*; and Crozier and Thoenig, "Regulation of Complex Organized Systems".

95 A good example of this use of latitudes available to bureaucrats when discretionary action is possible is presented in K. Acheson and J. F. Chant, "Bureaucratic Theory and the Choice of Central Banks' Goals: The Case of the Bank of Canada", *Journal of Money, Credit and Banking* (December 1973).

96 D. C. Rowat, "How Much Administrative Secrecy?", *Canadian Journal of Economics and Political Science* (November 1965). Rowat shows that the degree of secrecy in Canada is especially important. It would be possible to repair many of the difficulties involved in the lack of accountability of bureaucrats by better disclosure procedures and some practical use of standing committees to which the agency might be asked to report annually.

[97] For an exposition of the basic features of the cybernetic paradigm, see 3. D. Stein-bruner, *The Cybernetic Theory of Decision* (Princeton, 1974), Chapter 3.

[98] D. Seckler, *Thorstein Veblen and the Institutionalists* (London, 1975), p. 79.

[99] K. R. Popper, *The Poverty of Historicism* (New York, 1964), p. 65 and F. A. Hayek, *The CounterRevolution of Science: Studies on the Abuse of Reason* (London, 1955). Both quotations are cited in Seckler, Veblen and the Institutionalists, p. 80.

[100] R. F. Campbell, "On the Theory of Economic Administration", in H. Rosovsky, ed., *Industrialization in Two Systems* (New York, 1966), p. 203.

Chapter 8

An agenda for change in the federal public service

*"It only becomes an issue when
you can do something about it"*

−Saul Alinsky

Like many other OECD countries, over the last few decades Canada
has not been able to effect changes rapidly enough to meet the
major challenges of the day. A century of relentless rule-making, regulation, and institution-building has produced an aging Canadian socio-
economy suffering from "institutional sclerosis."[1] Such inflexibilities
can be costly, so most advanced economies have tried to eliminate those
rules, structures, and institutions that prohibit needed adaptation. In
this process, there have been pressures to identify those major segments
of the socio-economy where reform might prove to be both easier to
implement and more likely to serve as a demonstration project. One
such sector is the federal public service.

Five major challenges

The federal public service was born with Confederation. At first,
it drew most of its personnel from the administration of Ontario and
Quebec and, as governments came and went, so came and went the
political appointees. It was not until 1908 that the Civil Service Commission (CSC) was created, after many commissions of inquiry, and in
response to a number of patronage scandals.[2] With the CSC began the
implementation of a personnel policy inspired by the ideology of scientific management: a centralized employment department, purporting

intended

173

to operate on the sole principle of merit, evolved as the cornerstone of the federal public service personnel policies.[3]

Blatant political patronage was eradicated but the need to regulate the competition between departments within the public service led to a "plethora of detailed controls split among the CSC, the Treasury Board, and the departments," which resulted in a system that the Glassco Commission characterized in 1962 as "disastrous for the civil service."

Efficiency and effectiveness are expected from and by departments; economy is demanded by Treasury Board; merit is what the Public Service Commission (PSC) – the new incarnation of the CSC after 1966 – insists upon; while the citizens require service. These competing claims have eroded the supremacy of the merit principle, while at the same time generating waste.[4]

Those growing internal difficulties had already reduced the capacity of the federal public service to deal effectively with the immense task of management in an advanced, sophisticated, and fragmented economy. But more recently, a number of new challenges, triggered by changes in the environment, have raised important questions about the capacity of the existing system to cope with the task devolved to it.

The first challenge has come from economic growth. The phenomenal growth of the Canadian socio-economy in the postwar period, and more especially for the public sector since the 1960s, as an echo effect of the demographic boom of the 1950-65, has created geometrically expanded personnel management problems. Staffing and personnel selection at all levels of the bureaucracy could no longer be handled centrally. Increasingly, senior departmental officials for all practical purposes came to control staffing appointments. As a result, while the legal responsibility and accountability for such staffing remained with the PSC, the effective decision ceased to be theirs.

The second challenge came from the shift from a resources economy to an information economy. No longer was it controlled by comparative advantages carved in stone, minerals, natural resources, or geographical proximity to sources of energy or to major markets. As the economy becomes less dependent on energy, raw materials, and natural resources, and more on design, technical knowledge, and the information revolution, it is being transformed into one where the market mechanism operates less effectively. Thus a growing need has developed over the last few decades for different forms of stewardship functions by government. In the past, governments had built their legitimacy largely on their roles as agents of protection, redistribution, and stabilization. These were mainly reactive functions. What governments have had to learn, in this new setting, is how to become agents of integration, coordination, and networking. They have had to learn to develop a more proactive stance.[5]

The third challenge has come from the public service unions. Employees were not satisfied with the protection given by the merit system, and have sought additional power by setting up organizations outside the PSC. The top-down management obligation to honor the merit principle as a moral commitment has been replaced by unions who demand their social rights to merit bargained with Treasury Board from the bottom up. This has further eroded the powers of the central staffing agency. A further challenge comes from the accelerated pace of socio-economic change, and from the consequent need to react more effectively to rapidly breaking situations. As a result, departmental managers have come more and more often to resort to certain stratagems to circumvent the appointments process of sifting and selecting suitable staff. A variety of schemes were invented: task forces, advisers, freelance persons hired on personal service contracts, contracts awarding certain departmental tasks outside the public service, all designed to operate outside the normal personnel channels. Finally, since the end of the 1960s, the public service has had to meet the challenge of affirmative action. Overall objectives in the personnel management arena were defined by politicians who superseded the established personnel policies. The policy on bilingualism is a case in point: it evolved for "superior reasons", and it came to be associated formally for a long time with the PSC (in other words, it was delivered by the PSC) even though it did not even fall under the routine scrutiny and evaluation procedures of the PSC. Action on the visible minorities front has been a more recent version of the same challenge.

A two-level strategy for change

These challenges and the responses they elicited exacerbated what was by 1962 already a difficult situation. The size and costs of the federal bureaucracy grew increasingly unwieldy, and citizens became critical of the quality of service, given the price tag. Two lines of attack have been suggested by reformers to meet these challenges.

Transforming the social architecture

There are many ways to deliver essential public services effectively, efficiently, and economically. The real challenges posed by societal changes, by the changes in the rules of the game, and by the demand for a more productive public service must translate into a modification of the array of public services, and the way in which they are provided.

Should the Canadian government be in the business of providing air transportation or in the postal service business at all? And if it is decided that government should be in such businesses, how should that responsibility be carried out? By delegating it to the provinces, or to private contractors, or to NGOs? Should it be done through a grant, the issuing of permits, with the aid of taxes and subsidies, via a voucher system or simply by decreeing that the citizens will have to secure it privately?[6]

Some guiding principles for the design of the new social architecture have been suggested by Michael Kirby. They cannot be applied to every aspect of the federal public service but, together with a determination to decentralize, in order to bring the points of service as close as possible to the ultimate consumer groups to serve them better, they suggest a clear agenda. They include:

- the principle of full costing of public services;
- the principle of revenue dependency for all units where the services have the potential of being marketed;
- the principle of encouraging direct private/public competition;
- and the principle that if a subsidy must be given, it should be given to the consumers.

As Kirby put it: "Such a system would make government managers subject to the strong economic incentives that now exist only in the competitive business world; and this would make at least part of government decision-making subject to the same kind of discipline which governs decision-making processes in the competitive private sector."[7] This philosophy would dramatically transform the contours of the federal public service. It may not be less government (although, one may venture the guess that it might) but at least it would be a different form of government.

Modifying the public service culture

Transforming the institutional architecture is not sufficient. One must also change the organizational ethos of the federal public service if the forces of dynamic conservatism are not to prevail. This can be done in two stages: first, by challenging the personnel managers' view of employees as "inert instruments" or simple programmable automata – an idea inherited from the heyday of Taylorist personnel management; second, by injecting into the organizational culture of the federal public service new values, new motivations, and new sources of vitality.

Nicole Côté has explored these problems within the Quebec public service. According to her analysis, what makes the public service personnel unproductive has to do with a mistaken appreciation of what really motivates public servants. She is very critical of the mechanical devices invented by personnel managers to energize their employees (executive development seminars, conceptual refurbishment seminars, institution-alized mobility, etc.) and she puts the blame for low productivity at the feet of personnel management.

By unloading onto personnel managers the job of maintaining uniform human resources management systems, public bureaucracies have freed agency/departmental line managers from the obligation of taking good care of their employees; this has severed the link between the employee and his/her organization. According to Côté, employees are not managed by their steward, but by collective agreements, directives, rules, and so on. It is not difficult to understand why they have become "irrespons-ables, i.e., incapables de répondre, car il n'y a personne à qui répondre."[8] Professionalism, collective pride, and the sense of civic responsibility have disappeared from the public service to a great extent. In its place, one finds anomie and alienation but little trace of any "goût du travail bien fait." Yet experiments have shown that corporate culture can be modified and become an instrument of revitalization of the workplace.[9]

In praise of shortcuts

Such a transformation of the architecture and the ethos of the federal public service may be long in coming. In the meantime, some mod-est changes might trigger important echo effects. The following few suggestions are not put forward as panaceas, but as modest proposals deserving more attention than they have received recently.

Intraprises/extraprises

There are ways to effect some decentralization/competition within the public service by creating *intraprises* or profit centres within large agencies or departments, much as the Japanese have done.[10] Breaking up the stiflingly large organization into smaller self-contained units has often made possible impressive increases in productivity and efficiency. Peter Kemball has extended the idea by exploring the possibility of exporting such clusters of activities outside the purview of the agency or department. Activities such as training and accounting services, for example, might be contracted out by the agency to groups of civil ser-vants who would offer to perform those services with a savings of fifty per cent of current internal costs. The idea is to transform civil servants into entrepreneurs by offering them long-term contracts to take care of certain well-defined tasks.

The *extraprise* would lead public servants to resign their bureaucratic position to obtain some sort of franchise to perform a certain task under a multi-year contract.[11] Through a judicious mix of intraprises and extraprises, one might be able not only to effect important cost reductions and cost containments, but also be able to modify the ethos of the public service and to help recreate a healthier concern for the client within and around public organizations.

Refurbishment at the Public Service Commission.

It would therefore seem appropriate to consider recasting the role of the PSC in the direction suggested by Glassco – in other words, restrict it to recruitment services at the lower level (where large numbers trigger economies of scale) and a role as an audit/certifying agent (or even only an appeal court) to ensure that proper procedures have been followed in the case of higher appointments.

The PSC would thus become a much leaner organization, and the departmental line managers would be better able to manage their human resources. The PSC scrutiny/audit function should suffice to buy effectiveness/efficiency/economy at not too high a price in terms of patronage. The rest of the responsibilities of the PSC might best be nested elsewhere, if a nest is indeed needed. This would create a new role for the PSC, more akin, on the personnel front, to that of the Auditor General on the financial front. By re-creating between employees and managers the missing link that is at the root of a more professional and effective public service, this institutional change might also lead to a more productive federal public service. [12]

In search of a new covenant

But such quick fixes are not enough. The very nature and ethos of the federal public service must also be transformed if it is to be able to react with speed, flexibility, and creativity to a topsy-turvy environment bubbling up with surprises.

Big firms, big government, and big social agencies have reacted to this sort of pressure in three ways: (1) they have attempted to become leaner; (2) they have deconstructed themselves into smaller and more non-centralized units (organizationally and locationally) in order to become more flexible, more attentive to citizens and clients, and more creative; and (3) in order to become more agile, they have begun to renegotiate with their partners the nexus of contracts and treaties they had forged with them.

The first two responses (downsizing, delayering, and dispersing power) have elicited much discussion in the specialized literature and have been critically appraised. Much less work has been done on the third front, especially as it pertains to the relationships between organizations and their employees.

While much has been written about new rapports with customers and suppliers, about outsourcing and sub-contracting, it has not always been realized that "a quieter revolution has taken place. It has redefined employees' roles, and in doing so, has rewritten the implicit contract they had with employers".[13] Employers require maximum nimbleness to survive in this new turbulent and fast-changing economy, so they cannot use employees effectively as passive instruments of production. They must come to regard their employees as *partners* whose knowledge and initiative they need on the front line. And yet, (*this is the core of the paradox*) at the very time when downsizing, the requirement to do more or different with less, and the need for maximum flexibility and creativity are leading employers to demand more from these employee-partners (including longer hours, more dedication and loyalty), they have also asked them to forgo much of the security that they used to have.

Employment contracts are never easy to rewrite and the process is even more difficult in the public sector where there is no bottom-line to coax parties into workable solutions. This is especially difficult for the whole Canadian public sector, at this time, because this rewriting is undertaken at a time when, throughout the socio-economy, a process of "dejobbing" -- the disappearance of the "steady job" -- is swamping the private, public, and social sectors.[14]

In order to be able to design an effective process of transformation of the federal public service, one must first examine the public service culture as it stands, and the recent questioning of its efficiency and effectiveness.

The Public Service Culture in Question

The principles associated with the traditional culture of a career public service in Canada are nowhere explicitly stated in a form that would be readily accepted by all stakeholders. They have evolved through time, and are embedded in a number of explicit and implicit, legal and psychological contracts. This evolving nexus of implicit contracts has been loosely recognized as *de facto* conventions by most stakeholders, and its existence has even been acknowledged by the courts.[15]

This culture has been synthesized very well by Kenneth Kernaghan "in a pure and idealized form": public servants as permanent employees appointed on the basis of merit, a job-description, generous fringe benefits, job-security and a career-path, expectations of anonymity, impartiality, and accountability to ministers.[16] Kernaghan has emphasized that four

179

principles "have been - and continue to be - closely linked with the concept and practice of career public service" (554):

- appointments made with a view to preserving political neutrality;
- appointments based on merit of the best qualified candidate;
- appointments from within the public service as far as possible;
- assistance for public servants in selecting career goals and pursuing them.

While it is readily admitted that (1) there may have been differences of opinion as to the exact content of such a covenant among stakeholders, (2) the daily practice may have been at odds with these principles, and (3) these principles may have been applied or interpreted quite differently from department to department, there is also a general agreement that this culture corresponded roughly and generally to the existing public service culture, circa the 1980s.

In the 1990s, this traditional culture has been challenged in two quite different ways. First, there were questions raised in a modest way by *a new vision from within*: Public Service 2000.[17] Then the traditional culture was hit by *a strong pressure from without*: the harsh new financial and economic realities that forced the Directors of Personnel, Treasury Board and the Public Service Commission to question the existing arrangements.[18]

The first challenge, through PS 2000, recognized the need for public service employees

(1) to attend better to the needs of the citizenry and to provide better services to their clients,

(2) to make the highest and best use of their creativity in this work; but also the need for the employer

(3) to improve training and development of their human resources and to put greater emphasis on career planning and

(4) to develop a new focus for accountability as responsibilities are devolved to managers so they can manage.

This challenge did not shake the traditional culture. Few if any of the actions initiated in the PS 2000 era really questioned neutrality or merit (with the possible exception of the new concerns for equity and representativeness) and the emphasis on career planning was not really challenged; the merit principle might appear to have been relaxed some-what through the new arrangement, allowing lateral transfers not to be regarded as appointments under the Public Service Employment Act, and therefore being exempted from the merit principle. But this loosening up did not have a profound impact on the public service culture.

The second challenge has been much more significant. It was the result of the state's fiscal crisis. While it is difficult to establish clearly the moment the crisis hit the system – because its seriousness was acknowledged at different moments in Alberta, in New Brunswick and in Ottawa – one can reasonably suggest that it emerged as a result of the realization by the different governments that the conventional rules of the game would not be able to deal effectively with the deficit and debt problems.

While Alberta led the parade of provinces in the attack on deficit and debt in the early 1990s, and Quebec was the last to join the parade in 1996, it could be said that the federal Liberal government bit the bullet in the Fall of 1994.

The message was clear in the Purple Book and in the Grey Book tabled by Paul Martin, and the full implications of this message for career public service were first presented in the Directors of Personnel discussion paper, in the Fall of 1994. This document puts forward a perspective inspired explicitly by David Noer's *Healing the Wounds*[19] and sets out to "define the steps required to achieve a new public service model for Canada" (p.2).

Noer's message is simple and basically twofold: first, for organizations to face the new realities and acquire the requisite flexibility and nimbleness, the old employment contract guaranteeing much security to the employee must be abrogated; secondly, the traditional employment terms of reference might not have been very healthy in any case (for both the employees and their organizations) because they fostered an undesirable sort of co-dependency between employees and their organization.

The attack on a career public service by the Directors of Personnel is stark: they diagnose it as "unrealistic", "not necessary or affordable" and "an unhealthy expectation" (p.5). Their document suggests the termination of the current policy of conversion from term to indeterminate employment after 5 years; it puts forward a framework where "employees, not the employer, are responsible for their own employment options, but the employer would provide support to enable the continued employability of staff" (p.17). One is clearly faced with a new "moral framework" (p.9) that would have to be renegotiated, and in which the key parameters would have to be clarified and amended in consultation with labour.

Even though this plea for a "new Public Service model" does not refer explicitly to the general debate about the future of work ("dejobbing")[20], and avoids confronting head-on the meaning of the new arrangement for some perennial values (accountability), the inescapable conclusion is that the current questioning of the traditional culture necessarily entails the redefinition of many of the fundamental principles on which the career public service had been built throughout Canada.

Strategically, the Directors of Personnel could not and did not come forward with the details of a new model, since the new framework would have to be negotiated with other stakeholders. Yet the document generates a sense of urgency: parameters have to be clarified very quickly for events are running ahead of plans at this time, and there is a danger that a de facto "new model" will emerge that might leave all parties worse off.

There is no consensus on what the "new model" should be, nor on the manner in which the new model will be implemented. However, there are signs that at least two broad options are considered.

In the first case, the debate has begun on the tentative features of the workable model that may be the outcome of this transformation, and officials have speculated in public about the nature of the new public service. In a May 1995 interview, the President of the Public Service Commission, Ruth Hubbard, sketched a three-tiered system with a small "core of permanent and highly skilled knowledge workers, supported by a pool of short-term employees who work in government for stints of several months or years and move on"...(plus) a "parapublic service that could emerge as various levels of government cooperate on delivering services and as private-public partnerships take over services that were once provided by government".[21] While this remains vague on specifics, the strategic direction hinted at is congruent with the ruminations contained in the Directors of Personnel document.

In the second case, the debate has focused on the implementation process, the final outcome being allowed to emerge from the process. This model has been favored in Quebec, where an agreement has been signed between the government and a host of public sector unions that sets up both joint ministerial and joint sectoral committees, charged with the responsibility of rethinking the organization of work to reduce public expenditures, while keeping in mind both the welfare of the citizens and of the public employees. This emphasis on process allows all issues like sub-contracting, the hierarchical structure, job classifications, etc., to be debated by these committees, and the collective agreements to be modified according to the consensus reached at this level.[22] In this case, it is not clear that any one particular pattern will prevail in the new framework, nor which ones are likely to.

The Context for the transformation of the public service[23]

The context within which this transformation is occurring is bound to have an impact, not only on the methods used to reach this new covenant, but also on its final contours. In this section, we discuss four clusters of forces that will both constrain and shape the nature of this new public service model: the limitations imposed and the opportunities raised (1) by the *new governance*; (2) by the *new sociality* necessary for a mobilization of the team players in the new dispersed and distributed governance system; (3) by the likelihood that *new basic moral contracts* will prove tractable and agreeable to all stakeholders in the near future; and (4) by the nature of the *socio-economic conjuncture* in the next few years.

New governance, more implicit contracting

rapid, quick

In order to ensure the flexibility and nimbleness required by the turbulent environment of the late 20th century, a new distributed governance system is emerging. Participants have "a rough sense as to general principles with which unforeseen contingencies will be met", and "corporate culture plays a role here by establishing general principles that should be applied (in the hope that application of that principle will lead to relatively high level of coordination)".[24]

In this context, much coordination has to be handled by the unwritten or implicit portion of the employment contract, because rule-writing has become more difficult. Indeed, new principles have begun to surface: everyone's employment is contingent on the results of the organization, there is no clear job description, employees shift from project to project, they must manage their self-development and their own career as if they were in business for themselves, and the only commitment of benefits by the employer is to help the employee maintain his/her employability.[25]

In such market-type employment contracts, explicit provisions allow the employer to modify duties and responsibilities in a major way. There are also easy provisions for severance. Employees may be allowed to choose among various arrangements for severance: from agreement about notice periods to non-compete covenants or other restrictions linked to longer notice periods and higher severance packages for core personnel.

Some observers, like Murray Axsmith, believe that the new governance system need not entail more in the form of implicit contract. The Axsmith model suggests that, as employees become free agents and entrepreneurial suppliers, more and more elaborate, flexible fixed-term written contracts will emerge; these contracts may typically be for terms of three years for core staff, with possibility of renewal; compensation would be made up of a modest base salary, limited benefits, and substantial incentive rewards tied to performance. For shorter-term staff, ranging from one month to two years, compensation would again be a modest base salary, with substantial bonuses linked to performance. Axsmith suggests that these employment contracts may contain "soft" clauses pertaining to expectations for staff, organizational values and the fiduciary duties and responsibilities of employees, but these clauses have no legal clout; they might at best serve to clarify expectations, and need not be more important than in the past.[26]

While there is much to be said in favour of this shift from bureaucratic to market principles, market ligatures *stricto sensu*, backed and constrained only by explicit written contracts à la Axsmith, are unlikely to ensure the requisite coordination in the public service, any more than they can be expected to be satisfactory in the case of partnerships.[27]

We believe this sort of arrangement is flawed in three fundamental ways:

First, however flexible the contract may be, it remains an employee's contract with all the trappings of top-down supervision. This cannot be adequate in a turbulent environment where the organization needs to secure the engagement of the employee as partner on the front line.

Second, this sort of arrangement leaves too little room for the social cohesion and civic commitment required in the governance system. In the market-type employment scenario, "the commitment is to the quality of the work being done. The employee's reputation and future marketability will depend on this".[28] Yet one of the major points that is made in Steven Rosell's *Changing Maps*, based on the important work of James Coleman and Robert Putnam, is the primary importance of building *social capital* (embodied horizontal and transversal networks of civic engagement, trust, norms, and standards) to enhance the performance of a group.[29]

The main challenge of the information age is to construct such social capital, shared values and perspectives in a world where diversity and pluralism are daunting. Market employment contracts will not foster the requisite accumulation of "social capital".

Third, the new market employment contract cannot deal adequately with the problems of accountability and loyalty. In the new governance system, the loyalty of public servants cannot be only to the quality of the work done. It must also take into account and balance many transversal and horizontal loyalties: toward one's own "community of practice"[30].

184

For it is from this network that the support flows for the sequence of contracts that will keep one employed will flow) and toward the citizen or customer that one is serving (value for money is the basis of performance evaluation). And these more horizontal loyalties may conflict with the fundamental vertical accountability to the Minister as representative of the democratically elected government. Accountability and loyalty must therefore be balanced among the citizen, one's "community of practice" and the Minister. This cannot be resolved by a collection of market-type contracts.

Consequently, one must find ways to enrich the implicit content of the employment contract, in order to ensure that the burden of risk-sharing and the responsibility-sharing is not simply shifted completely from the employer to the employee. This sort of drastic switch from minimal to maximal responsibilities for employees may not ensure that the employee's creativity can be mobilized as fully as it needs to be. A middle-of-the road solution between dependency and market-type employment contract must be found if such a sharing of risk must be renegotiated.

Such a middle-of-the-road solution is unlikely to be negotiated as part of the explicit employment contract. The employer must face too many varied contingencies, and attend to too many idiosyncratic needs on the part of different employees, to be able to attend to those personal needs formally (i.e., through the explicit portion of the employment contract): employers would be in danger of generating a new minimal right for all employees whenever they attempt to provide tailor-made assistance. Therefore, one may expect the development of the requisite foundations for a middle-of-the-road solution in the implicit portion of the employment contract.

Multiple loyalties, new sociality

Every partner in the new governance system is partially connected with many others, via all sorts of networks. Coordination requires ways to *integrate those overlapping networks* transversally, in order to allow the individual to balance adjustments in these different dimensions. These loyalties are not equally meaningful and significant, and there are differences of opinion about their relative importance, according to time and place.

For instance, the different value systems in good currency in different countries generate very different trade-offs among loyalties[31]. What has to be found in the case of Canada is the particular balancing act (among the loyalties to self, network, community, society, and the accountability to citizen, peers, superior, or Minister) that will meet with

185

the entrenched beliefs in our value system and provide the basis for an effective performance.

Multiple limited identities in an individualistic society entail weak ties. Such ties cannot recreate the traditional community. The construction of a *new sociality* is required.[32]

The belief that weak ties (and therefore limited loyalties) can indeed prove to be a valid foundation for a strong community of the new type is rooted in the observation of Mark Granovetter that weak ties are often more important than strong ties in understanding certain network-based phenomena. Strong ties tend to bond participants that are *similar* to each other, and information obtained through such a network is often redundant. A weak tie often represents a "local bridge" between parts of the systems that would otherwise be disconnected, and therefore provides much new information from disparate sections of the system. In Granovetter's world, no tie or extremely weak ties are of little consequence; weak ties have maximum impact, and strong ties have diminished impacts.[33]

If our information age, organization is nothing but "an ensemble of interconnected communities of practice", and "learning is the process of becoming member of a community of practice"[34], the challenge proposed by Steven Rosell's *Changing Maps* is to construct a learning network of communities of practice in the Canadian governance system, while keeping in mind that Canadians are more individualist than communitarian, and closer to the American psyche than to the Japanese psyche.

This means constructing new forms of social cohesion on the basis of weak ties with others. In this complex and fluid informational environment, effective coordination can occur neither by threat nor coercion *stricto sensu* (i.e., via power systems) nor by the operations of the market exchanges *stricto sensu* (i.e., via transaction systems). One has to count a great deal on consensus, on voluntary adherence to norms, and on inducement-oriented arrangements. These are at the core of membership and of shared stewardship.[35]

This form of sharing is central in the definition of the implicit content of the new employment contract. While there were costs attached to the old implicit contract generating dependency, it cannot be presumed that the optimal amount of protection for the employee is zero, if one wishes to promote learning and creativity. The new sociality must provide some form of basic 'security zone' that is necessary for the entrepreneurial spirit to thrive. The former implicit contract was hierarchical and paternalistic; the new implicit contract is a jointly negotiated risk-sharing agreement on the minimal security zone necessary for creativity to flow.[36]

New moral contracts

A number of years ago, I examined the malaise of Canadian public servants in the late 1980s and their loss of drive and initiative.[37] Invidiously, the employment contract had begun to shift, but the contours of the new work arrangements had not yet crystallized. We suggested, at the time, that a possible way out of this quandary was through the renegotiation of two moral contracts, in addition to whatever changes might be required in the explicit employment contract. These moral contracts were meant (1) to enrich the implicit context of the employment contract; (2) to embed better the explicit employment contract in the corporate culture; and (3) to provide guidance in balancing the two basic ingredients necessary for an intelligent organization (freedom of choice and the responsibilities vis-à-vis different communities or the whole of society).[38]

We argued that the addition of these two moral contracts would generate a proactive, entrepreneurial, and responsible public service capable of balancing loyalties and accountabilities in a creative way.

The two moral contracts were:

Moral Contract I - the *ethics moral contract* - called for a redefinition of mutual responsibilities and obligations between the citizenry and the bureaucracy, and

Moral Contract II - the *professionalism moral contract* - called for a rethinking of the mutual obligation, trust requirement, and esprit de corps between the politicians and very senior bureaucrats on the one hand, and the junior public servants on the other.

The situation has continued to evolve since the early 1990s, and it would now appear that a further enrichment of the implicit employment contract is necessary.

First, some action is needed to minimize the negative impacts of the politicians' centralized mindset, the arrogant logic of internal administration, and the unrealistic expectations of the citizenry. This calls (a) for a re-affirmation of the fundamental responsibilities of individuals for their own affair; (b) for a re-confirmation that the state is to intervene modestly, as a reserve army, only when its action is necessary to help the citizens take care of their specific needs, and not on the basis of entitlements ordained from above; and (c) for the reminder that if and when the state must intervene, it should always be at a level as close to the citizen as possible, where the help can be provided efficiently. In this context, the task of any higher-order governance unit (i.e., regional, provincial, federal, etc.) is to assist the more localized units in carrying out their tasks, and to manage only those functions that cannot be effectively delivered within these forums.[39]

From these new circumstances emerges the need for *Moral Contract III* (among the citizens, the bureaucrats at all levels, and the politicians at all levels) - *the axiom of individual responsibility and subsidiarity in the governance process* - which calls for an explicit re-affirmation of the fundamental responsibility of the citizens for their own affairs, and of the crucial *devoir de prudence et de réserve* of politicians and bureaucrats at the time of intervening in the life of the citizenry, on the basis of needs, and not entitlements.

Second, it has become necessary to re-affirm that the debates leading to the development of a new moral framework demand that dialogue and deliberations be civil, free from coercion or any form of organizational violence. A democratic society is built on dialogue and deliberation. The difficult task of framing a just society, taking into account the growing plurality of interests in Canada, is to ensure that the conversation goes on.

The condition for the dialogue to continue is a *Moral Contract IV* (among the citizens, the bureaucrats at all levels and the politicians at all levels) based on *tact* and *civility*, and on *trust* that there is a capacity to suspend judgment until one's own and the other person's assumptions have been explored.

For Mark Kingwell, "if citizens are to talk to one another, they must refrain from saying all the things they have it in mind to say; they must likewise open themselves up the possibility that a claim made by someone else has merit".[40] We take this to mean not that people should refrain from expressing their views but that they should do so in a way respectful of other points of view. This is a bare minimum, but only with the assurance of at least that much, can we hope to build an organization where *personal meaning* and *mutually beneficial dreams* will serve as an anchor at the time of making these difficult balancing acts.[41]

Moral Contract IV - dialogue based on the primacy of tact and civility - reaffirms simply the importance of the moral climate for organizational effectiveness and social learning. While this last requirement may appear trite, one should not underestimate the difficulty of overcoming the existing degree of cognitive dissonance about the existence of *organizational violence* in the rapports among and between politicians, bureaucrats and citizens, and the breakdown of trust which obviously ensues. Until this reality is squarely confronted, and individuals accept that they cannot change anything unless they are willing to change themselves, it may be difficult to obtain an agreement on *Moral Contract*

IV either because it is wrongly assumed that it is a non-problem, that civility prevails already, that everyone that has anything to say is heard, or because, equally wrongly, it may be presumed that the content of such a norm is trivial and inconsequential.

These *four moral contracts* constitute the necessary conditions for the creation of a new corporate culture capable of ensuring a deliberative and participative governance. They are required if a new workable implicit employment contract of the new public service is to be negotiated. The central question is: how likely are we to be able to count on such moral contracts emerging as new norms in the near future?

* * *

Summarizing the last section in the reverse order in which the issues were brought up, we can say:

- first, that much will depend on the sort of wind that will be blowing over Canada and that a reasonable forecast is that those changes will be carried out in a world of slow economic growth and strong socio-political resistance to change;
- secondly, that while much progress has been made in emphasizing the central importance of the new moral contracts as new partnerships develop to provide the requisite flexibility and nimbleness, and in allowing them to be discussed openly, the stakeholders are still very far from being persuaded that such conventions and norms are necessary, and not very well equipped when it comes to guidelines in the process of arriving at workable conventions;
- thirdly, that the very recognition of the existence of multiple loyalties and of the need for a new sociality is neither recognized nor even acknowledged: the rigid top-down Westminster model of governance is still regarded by a fair majority of the stakeholders as the only acceptable model. Therefore, it is unlikely that the notions of accountability and loyalty will be redefined completely in the next quinquennium, even though, informally, it is recognized as necessary by a large number of observers;
- finally, and this is an echo effect of our third point, even though market employment mechanisms may appear flawed to most, the view in good currency is that they represent the only workable way. The Axsmith model is therefore proposed as the workable protocol to deal with alternative delivery mechanisms, while the upstream policy development continues to be regarded as a natural preserve of the traditional public service. While models such as those developed in New Zealand would appear to question the existence of

any obvious border between the policy development domain and the delivery mechanism domain and while social learning would appear to require an integration of the two domains for an effective evolutionary policy-making, the putative boundaries between the two domains remains in good currency.[42]

From Here to the New Covenant in Six Difficult Steps

Strategic action to catalyze the transformation process of the Canadian public service culture can be examined under two general rubrics: (1) there is the action required to develop a new philosophy of governance so as to ensure that the Canadian socio-economy will modify its guidance system to ensure goodness of fit with the new realities; and (2) there is the action required to develop a new philosophy of stewardship so as to ensure that the whole process through which we choose, evaluate, and help executives do their work will be modified to make it congruent with the requirements of the new governance. In the case of each rubric, we proceed in two steps: first, we state for the record what would appear to be the new requirements on the governance and on the stewardship fronts, and then, secondly, we put forward some very precise pre-conditions for a coherent strategy to emerge.

Before we proceed, it may, however, be useful to minimize the possibility of misunderstanding by introducing a number of clarifications.

First, these issues need to be addressed at all levels of the public service, as well as by politicians, unions, and other stakeholders, but the requisite dialogue would be only a whimsical fantasy unless debates on these issues are legitimized and built into the daily practice of the federal central agencies. Otherwise, the sort of bottom-up process of social learning that is essential would soon die out.

Secondly, and this danger is the exact obverse of the first, it is essential that all the stakeholders take part in the renegotiation of the new covenant right from the start, and that the central agencies not be allowed to appear to hijack the process. Otherwise, again the bottom-up dynamics would soon die out. Consequently, we suggest that the process be designed in such a way as to allow maximum input from below, right from the beginning.

Thirdly, it should be clear that our modest proposals are not definitive, but rather a set of preliminary ideas that might deserve attention at a time when the dialogue is beginning on what a new public service model might look like.

A new philosophy of governance

i. General principles[43]

At first, when organizations were relatively small, governance had a fiefdom-quality. The dialogue was very informal, and strongly focused on the leader. This has often been the governance system of small entrepreneurial firms and of small public sector agencies. But as the size of the socio-economy grew, and the problems it has to face grew more complex, organizations had to develop more elaborate structures and more formal rules to orchestrate collective action; from this emerged more or less standardized bureaucratic forms of organization. Large private and public bureaucracies played an important role between the 1940s and the 1970s.

As long as the environment remained relatively stable, bureaucracies thrived: their rules remained valid and effective. However, as the pace of change accelerated, problems became less structured and ever changing, and the bureaucratic system, with its slow capacity to transform its rules, began to show signs of dysfunction. This led to efforts to partition private and public bureaucracies into smaller self-contained and more flexible units. In the private sector, large companies created a multiplicity of more or less independent profit-centred organizations, more attentive to the changing needs of the clients and more adaptable to evolving circumstances. With a lag, public bureaucracies have gone the same route with, for instance, the creation of executive agencies in the United Kingdom, or special operating agencies in Canada. Organizations came to be governed to a much greater extent than before by the invisible hand of the market forces.

But the price-driven steering mechanism often proved less than perfect. For instance, it proved insensitive to third-party effects and external economies, and very poorly equipped to appreciate and foster synergies. As a result, an effort was made to re-introduce the requisite amount of cooperation in the governance of organizations through the development of a variety of informal links - *liens moraux* - based on shared values, i.e., the corporate culture. The private sector developed these new informal clan-type organizations very quickly. Public organizations proceeded at a much slower pace. The Public Service 2000 exercise was one of the first occasions drawing attention to the centrality of organizational culture, but for all sorts of reasons we cannot analyze here, it never succeeded in modifying the traditional culture.

Such a modern bottom-up clan-type governance system cannot be engineered top-down by the leader: the organization can only govern itself by becoming capable of learning both its goals, and the means to reach them *as it proceeds*. This sort of governance system is fundamentally built on intelligence and innovation: a capacity to tap the knowledge and information held by active citizens, and by active public servants at all levels, and to get them to invent ways out of the predicaments the organization experiences. Stewarding in this new context must be able to ensure that the institutional setting is capable of promoting and ensuring the highest degree of *social/organizational learning*. This, in turn, requires that all stakeholders become part of the learning and the change process, and are led to effect and support change without hesitation because the institutional setting ensures fair risk-sharing.

ii.   Modest proposals

Our three modest proposals are in line with this new philosophy of governance. They pertain to three aspects of governance that need to be taken in for repairs.

The first one has to do with efforts to give a second life to the Program Review exercise, or to the equivalent or similar exercises that have developed in parallel at the provincial and local levels. We have argued elsewhere[44] that initially a philosophy of subsidiarity was underpinning the Program Review, but that the 1994 Program Review exercise was transformed into a simple cost-cutting process as a result of the pressures generated by the fiscal imperative. However, there may be a window of opportunity for a refurbishment of the Program Review process as a result of the continued fiscal imbalance between the three levels of government and the need to rationalize public expenditures when the economy experiences bad times.[45]

What is most important in the next round of Program Review, and in the parallel exercises conducted at the provincial and local levels is

(1) that it be fully geared to answering the six basic questions raised in round one, but especially the first four; it should generate an important degree of re-responsabilization of the citizen, and a massive devolution of responsibilities to the private and social sectors and to lower-order governments;

(2) that the required analysis and consultation involve in a meaningful way the citizenry on whom public services are bestowed, but also the private and social sectors, and the lower-order governments.[46]

While this may appear to be very far from concerns related to the renegotiation of the implicit employment contract, it is a pre-requisite to any real rethinking of the way in which the public service will be redesigned. Unless one knows as clearly as possible what the responsibilities devolved to the federal government in the new governance system will be, and also what will fall into the bailiwicks of the provinces, the municipalities, the social sector and the private sector, it is difficult to

192

gauge the nature of the transformation of the public service that is required and, what new public service model is called for.

The second proposal pertains to the adoption of new principles to reflect the multiple loyalties required for the success of the new governance system. As it stands now, the principles of the Westminster model are inadequate to meet the needs of the new governance. New guidelines (inspired by the moral contracts mentioned above, but by others as well perhaps) are required to help select, guide, inspire, develop, evaluate, and reward public servants in a manner that would recognize these multiple loyalties. Such principles, however, can be operative only if they are the result of a process of organizational learning involving all levels of the public service and all the stakeholders, with central agencies perhaps acting as facilitators.

At a minimum, the Privy Council Office, the Treasury Board Secretariat, and the Public Service Commission must give a clear signal that they are extremely open and presumptively favorable to a process of social learning leading to new principles. These should reflect the emerging multiple loyalties being actively developed to redefine the process of hiring, evaluation, remuneration of public servants but also the workable degree of risk-sharing that can be reasonably demanded from public servants to ensure maximum learning. This, of course, will require a reframing of the outlook of those agencies from that of order-giver and rule-setter to that of facilitator and *animateur*.[47]

The third proposal deals with the process of social learning which underpins the new governance. It calls for an explicit recognition that public administration deals with wicked problems where goals are multiple, ambiguous and uncertain, and means-ends relationships volatile and changing. This in turn requires that the governance system abandons its demands for infallible, universal, and mechanical methods of problem solving. Yet public administration has been prone to demand such infallibility in the past.[48] Such a view is dangerous, for it instills an undue optimism into the practice of public administration and such "optimism restricts anticipation of error, minimizes its probability, and leads to the concealment of both its occurrence and the severity of its effects".[49]

This state of affairs would appear to fit the Canadian scene very well. In a recent debate, Donald Savoie stated clearly the nature of the malaise, even though he did it without seemingly finding anything wrong with it: "in government, it does not much matter if you get it right 90 per cent of the time because the focus will be on the 10 percent of the time you get it wrong". In this context, it is hardly surprising that errors and mistakes are denied with such vehemence, and success-fixation revered in a manner that can only lead to a rejection of managerial techniques built on error-correction.

A more reasonable philosophy of governance would not be built on success-fixation. It would recognize that the greater the nimbleness and agility of an organization, the greater the probability of error. This in turn calls for the development of technologies, structures, and incentive reward systems, but also for an overall understanding of what the organization is legitimately about, that would take into account these sorts of constraints in designing the new governance.[50]

This requires that the new public sector governance system (1) be designed to incorporate technologies to detect error quickly, for artificial systems like organizations cannot necessarily restore themselves; (2) be structured in such a way that the requisite "security zones" and "empowerment levers" are in place so that the learners have both a firm ground on which to stand and the tools necessary to take the sort of action called for as a result of learning, and it is our view that this can only happen if some negotiated risk-sharing arrangement among the stakeholders has been arrived at; (3) be designed to ensure that the process of learning from errors and of "progressive reduction of error" are explicitly legitimized.

The emphasis must be clearly put on the *dynamic* cognitive efficiency and effectiveness of organizations: this tends to dedramatize error and to promote "progressive reduction of error" as a modest objective worth pursuing in the new modest state. This is what being a learning organization is all about.

Some have argued that the sole pressure of the threat generated by market competition suffices to drive employees to maximum performance. This is based on an unduly restrictive and reductive view of human beings, and one that is mostly wrong. Human beings have a broad range of sensitivities and needs: they demand both support and stimulation. Ignoring these sensitivities is bound to force the system to operate much below capacity.

The implicit part of the new employment contract must deal with both the *support side* (the "security zones" that even entrepreneurs need in order to be creative and the "risk-sharing" that will provide the maximum incentive to embrace change and to disseminate new knowledge) and the *stimulation side*, (i.e., the motivation of employees, by recognizing that it is not driven only by coercion and threat, but even more by the commitment to the pursuit of novelty).[51]

Indeed, the substance of the new covenant has to be very much determined by the negotiation of both the required additional stimulation from below and from above: the nature of the security required for the employee to perform the task creatively, and the nature of the entice-ment to pursue novelty and to go beyond one's limits that is required for the full creative capacity of the employee to be tapped.

A new philosophy of stewardship

i.   General principles

The critical challenge facing the public service is a direct consequence of the complexities and intricacies of the new kind of work required by the new governance. The inter-relationships among all levels of govern-ment, departments, stakeholders, and citizens, as well as among jobs and functions within the public service, are bound to be more complex and quite unspecified. The job is to ensure that the new governance system works well. Stewardship is about breathing life into structures. But it is crucial to recognize that "it is fruitless to be a leader in an organization that is poorly designed": stewardship entails, therefore, some concern for design and continuous interaction with the construction of the governance system.[52]

Even though we may refer to persons in positions of authority, it should be clear that stewardship is not the preserve of executives, sen-ior managers, and supervisors. Stewardship is a process (neither a task nor a position) in which persons at all levels of the organization must partake. By focusing on those who are expected to effect change, we wish to emphasize two main points: (1) that those in authority may, because of their authority, make or break the new governance; and (2) that those who wish to institute change cannot do it at arms' length and be themselves untouched by the change. Stewardship is not about manipulating an object outside of and independent of the leader: "sen-ior managers who labor under this misconception don't learn to play their complementary part and therefore unconsciously undermine the reorganizations or cultural change they initiate".[53]

For stewardship is about cultural change. And to modify a culture three main ingredients are necessary: a capability for meaning-making, a capacity for community-building, and much honesty and an ability to inspire trust and confidence.

First, the new governance system requires making sense of people's experience by putting it into a larger context, thereby providing a sense of purpose, a story of why people do what they do, and a way to shape the organization by building a shared vision with the many stakehold-ers. Meaning-making is about reflecting meanings that existed in the

195

partners, and connecting them to one another in new ways appropriate to the demands of the new situation.[54]

Second, community-building is about establishing, developing, maintaining, sustaining, and nourishing relationships within and between organizations. It is all about skilfully working interfaces where dilemmas, inconsistencies, contradictions, and paradoxes are omnipresent. This requires the mastery of dialogue, the capacity to suspend judgment, and to question one's assumptions.

Hervé Sérieyx describes the leader as community builder very well: "Le véritable acteur de l'entreprise en réseau est un accoucheur (il sait faire émerger une innovation), un fécondateur (il sait enrichir ses découvertes de celles des autres), un facilitateur (il met l'innovation en oeuvre sans déstabiliser l'organisation quotidienne), un guetteur (il apporte des idées venues d'ailleurs); c'est un peu un concierge le 'doorkeeper' qui fait circuler l'information entre des parties relativement séparées de l'entreprise), un intégrateur (il met en relation des acteurs complémentaires), un connecteur (il branche ensemble réseaux et autres 'susciteurs de vie', 'entreteneurs d'influx')".[55]

Thirdly, stewardship cannot emerge unless one can promote "adaptive capacities rather than inappropriate expectations of authority", for it entails "influencing the community to face its problems". This cannot be accomplished without some sort of "social contract" between the leader and the community: "leadership as influence promotes influence as an orienting value, perpetuating a confusion between means and ends".[56]

The heart of the matter is not goal-seeking and control, but intelligence and innovation: the definition of standards and norms, and the negotiation of a moral, intellectual, and emotional norm-holding pact, built on a multi-level dialogue. The whole institutional process becomes itself the learning process and the source of the redefinition of norms and standards as a result of experience.[57]

ii.   Modest proposals

Bringing about the kind of stewardship necessary for the new governance system to take hold requires a thorough renewal of our way of selecting, evaluating, and coaching executives.

The first proposal has to do with the selection, promotion, and deployment of executives. It calls for revisions in the current practices to ensure (1) that the selection be done according to criteria that echo the profile of the new *animateur*; and (2) that the selection is made through a process involving various stakeholders.

While this requires no change in legislation or policy, it would call for a significant modification in practice: the definition of the profile of the executive position and the choice of the incumbent would be made not only by the supervisor and the Public Service Commission, but also by representatives of the different stakeholders (employees, peers, major client groups, etc.) under the guidance of the PSC to ensure due process and impartiality. While current practices already encourage the composition of interview boards comprised of the stakeholders, our proposal goes much further: it calls for the stakeholders to be involved in defining the selection profile (which for the moment is left entirely to the supervisor, with possible suggestions from the Senior Personnel Advisory Committee), in arriving at a short list, checking references, etc.– with employees being present at each step of the process.[58]

The inclusion of the stakeholders would force dialogue among them, which can only help anchor the process of organizational learning. Critics will argue that this would require time and dilute management's authority to deploy personnel as it seems fit. That is precisely the point. Meaning-making, shared vision, community building, and organizational learning cannot occur without dialogue. Dialogue takes time and is costly. But poor selection, based on a very partial identification of needs and leading to demotivated employees, can only translate into organizational sclerosis or in-fighting, reduced productivity, low creativity and innovation, and dissatisfied clients. This is much more costly.

Our second proposal deals with how, once appointed, managers are supported, coached, mentored and developed. At the risk of generalizing, the current model is one of "sink or swim". Executives are expected to be quick studies, and to possess almost instantly all the knowledge and skills of their new positions. Some managers at all levels are known to boast not only that they expect instant high performance, but expect such performances instantly under the most extreme and demanding conditions. This sort of situation has led to organizational disaster, and would, if anything, be exacerbated by a shift to the market employment model.

This proposal calls for personal development to be regarded as a planned process of learning, through feedback, coaching, and mentoring, as well as other self-directed activities. Personal development becomes part of a contract where responsibilities are not shovelled onto the employee entirely, but shared by employer and employee. It would require a paradigm shift: from the boss knows, to the steward learns. It would also require that managers develop a new appreciation for all the phases of the learning cycle – questioning, finding possible answers, testing to see if they work, and reflecting on the lessons learned.[59]

Our third proposal calls for a new process of evaluation for executives, and a rethinking of the whole incentive-reward system for this category of personnel. Just as the stakeholders must be involved in selecting executives, so they must also be involved in evaluating them. The 360 degree appraisal must become the norm, and as a result of it a process of dialogue and values clarification must be instituted.[60]

Deputies and central agencies will be expected to reward both formally and informally those persons who meet all aspects of the new leadership profile and to avoid celebrating those who excel in certain areas only to the detriment of others. If one may use the Jack Welch approach as a template, it would suggest a system where several key dimensions are evaluated, and where even if an executive has had a very positive impact on the bottom-line, he or she will be released if their treatment of employees does not reflect the values espoused by the corporation. This is called "walking the talk", and our experience with hundreds of executives in the classrooms of the Canadian Centre for Management Development tells us that such an approach would be supported by most executives, who feel that several key factors are ignored when the time comes to reward and promote individuals.

This third proposal is the kingpin of the transformation process. No change will occur if employees continue to perceive that rewards go mostly to those whose policy skills and political savvy are geared entirely to serving mindlessly the whims of their superiors, irrespective of their capability for meaning-making, their capacity for community-building and their ability to inspire trust and confidence, and to deal with people at all levels.

As Hervé Sérieyx would put it: "demander à des fonctionnaires de travailler autrement sans prévoir de distinguer ceux qui acceptent d'accomplir cette mutation et ceux qui s'y refusent, sans transformer les systèmes de notation, de promotion, de rémunération, d'intéressement, c'est réduire le renouveau du service public à un sympathique encouragement du type 'Allez-y les petits gars'. Cette 'boy-scoutisation' des stratégies de changement est souvent perçue par les acteurs les plus dynamiques du renouveau du service public comme sa pire limite et, à moyen terme, comme son plus sûr germe d'échec"[61].

Conclusion

One may reasonably ask why we have felt we had to roam over such a vast territory in our reflections on the search for a new covenant for the public service. The main reason is that we believe that the traditional employment framework cannot simply be replaced by a nexus of market employment contracts, and we had to provide some basis for the development of the new "moral framework" that will be required as an essential complement to the market contracts.

The contours of this new moral framework are currently being debated, but nowhere is it presented very clearly. The recent Hubbard interview may have revealed the general shape of the public service of tomorrow, but it has not revealed the soul of this new model. It is not our role to determine what this new moral framework should be, but we have felt that it might be useful to sketch the process that might get us there.

This process depends first on the recognition that a nexus of market employment contracts will not suffice. This is a point we have made forcefully and, we hope, persuasively. As to the content of the required complementary moral framework, we have argued that it would have to provide (1) ways of dealing with multiple loyalties by public servants in the modern age; and (2) ways of effecting the moral contracts for the new moral framework to coalesce. We also emphasized the point that the task would be more difficult that had been anticipated, because of the likely period of slow economic growth and the high degree of social rigidity that would appear inevitable in the years ahead.

To forge the new moral framework, we have suggested that one must proceed in six steps. Each of these steps will be very difficult, because each calls for a genuine revolution in the mind, a *nouvelle manière de voir*.

On the governance front, we feel that wide-ranging consultations can lead (1) to a reconfiguration of the new federal public service (Program Review Phase II); and (2) to the replacement of the Westminster model by a more modern version taking fully into account the multiple loyalties of public servants; we also suggested that (3) a major redirection in the guiding principles of public administration toward a social learning process is absolutely necessary.

On the stewardship front, we feel that there is need to rethink profoundly the notion of leadership in the new non-centralized, distributed governance system. We have sketched the general features of the new stewardship, and we have suggested some dramatic modifications in the machineries that govern (1) the entry and promotion of executives in the federal public service; (2) the nature of the support and training they get in the process; and (3) the process of evaluation and the whole incentive-reward system for executives.

These changes point the way to a new moral framework that would appear to fall half-way between the old model and the nexus of market employment relations that has been suggested by some as the only workable alternative. This new moral framework will be based on a looser series of ties among a larger number of stakeholders. It will not easily accommodate dependency, but will emphasize the central importance of the *avventura comune* as the binding factor, or at the very least what Aristotle identifies as *concord* ("a relationship between people who ... are not strangers, between whom goodwill is possible, but not friendship ... a relationship based on respect for ... differences".[61])

This may provide for the federal public service what has been provided by successful private sector enterprises for their employees: not a naked market-based employment contract, but a two-tier contract, with a tacit unwritten but centrally important component to ensure a reasonable degree of risk-sharing between employers and employees. The full burden of risk will not be shouldered entirely by the employer, as in the old moral contract, nor by the employee, as in the market-type employment contract, but will be shared after extensive negotiations involving not only those two parties but many of the stakeholders who have such an interest in these negotiations that they will no longer permit that negotiations be carried on without them.

Endnotes

[1] OECD *Interfuturs. Rapport final : Face au futur: pour une maîtrise du vraisemblable et une gestion de l'imprévisible* (Paris, 1979).

[2] J.E. Hodgetts, W. McCloskey, R. Whitaker and V.S. Wilson, The *Biography of an Institution — The Civil Service Commission of Canada*, 1908-1967 (Montreal, 1972).

[3] V.S. Wilson, "The Relationship Between Scientific Management and Personnel Policy in North American Administrative Systems," *Canadian Public Administration* (Summer 1973), pp. 193—205.

[4] Hodgetts et al., *Biography of an Institution*, pp. 287ff.

[5] A number of books have documented persuasively this dramatic dematerialization of the socio-economy. See, for example, M.U. Porat, *The Information Economy* (Washington, 1977);
P. Hawken, *The Next Economy* (New York, 1983); C.C. Gotlieb, ed., *The Information Economy: Its Implications for Canada's Industrial Strategy* (Ottawa: The Royal Society of Canada, 1984).

[6] M.J. Kirby, "Reflections on the Management of Government in the 1980's," Alan B. Plaunt Memorial Lecture, 1980, Carleton University, Part II.

[7] Ibid., pp.54—55.

[8] N. Côté, "Pour revaloriser la fonction publique," *L'Analyste*, 8 (hiver 1984—85), pp. 21—24.

[9] La qualité des services ... faut s'en parler, Actes d'un colloque tenu à Québec les 2—4 mai 1984, Ministère de la Main d'Oeuvre et de la Sécurité du Revenu, Québec, 1984. See in particular the papers by A. Fournier and by M. Pellerin, pp. 113-37.

[10] This is a combination of ideas developed in N. Macrae, "Intrapreneurial Now," *The Economist*, April 17, 1982, pp. 67—72; G. Pinchot III, *Intrapreneuring* (New York, 1985); P. Kemball, "A Scalpel for Government," *Policy Options*, 3, no. 6 (November 1984),pp. 15—18.

11   Both Macrae/Pinchot and Kemball provide a wide array of illustrations of the sectors to which intraprises and extraprises would apply. They range from secretarial services, to employment offices, mail services, airport management, training and consulting activities. Experiments show that stenographers working through Typist Intrapreneurial (an experiment quoted by Macrae) have shown productivity increases of 500 per cent by comparison with the standards established as acceptable by auditors in the previous bureaucracy. Kemball sketches in a few paragraphs how a bidding system for extraprises could be developed, the criteria to be used to choose the winning bid, and some procedures for implementation for his scheme.

12   This point of view would also appear to be shared by J.J. Carson, former chairman of the PSC and former project director of personnel management for the Glassco Commission. In the early 1980s, Carson made the following diagnosis of the present situation: "Such a system (enshrined as it is in legislation) surely must absolve, and even deny, the line manager of any real sense of personnel management responsibility, particularly in the field of human resource planning and development. Indeed the present legislation might well be designed to make eunuchs of public service managers rather than to hold them to account in any meaningful way." J.J. Carson, "Is There Any Merit in the Merit System Today?" *Optimum*, 12, no. 1 (1981), p. 76.

13   Christopher A. Bartlett and Sumantra Ghoshal, "Changing the Role of Top Management: Beyond Systems and People" *Harvard Business Review* 73, 3 (1995) pp.132-142. See also Robert H. Waterman, Judith A. Waterman and Betsy A. Collard, "Toward a Career-resilient Workforce" *Harvard Business Review* 72, 4 (1994) pp.87-95.

14   W. Bridges, *JobShift* (Reading, Mass.: Addison-Wesley, 1994); Jeremy Rifkin *The End of Work: The Decline of the Global Labor Force and the Dawn of the Post-Market Era* (New York: Putnam, 1995).

15   See Fraser v. PSSRB [1985] 2 S.C.R. 455 and PSC v. Millar et al. [1991] 2 S.C.R. 69.

16   K. Kernaghan, "Career Public Service 2000: Road to Renewal or Impractical Vision?" *Canadian Public Administration*, 34, 4, (1991) pp. 551-572.

17   B. Mulroney, *Public Service 2000: The Renewal of the Public Service of Canada* (Ottawa: Supply and Services, December 1990); P.M. Tellier, *Public Service 2000: A Report on Progress* (Ottawa: Supply and Services, June 1992).

18   For a statement of the new vision, see The Way Ahead for the Public Service (Discussion Paper for the Directors of Personnel Conference, Cornwall, October 4-6, 1994). There are ongoing reflections on this issue in both Treasury Board and the Public Service Commission, and it is regarded as work of the highest strategic priority.

19   D.M. Noer, *Healing the Wounds* (San Francisco: Jossey-Bass, 1993).

20   A sample of the papers raising these issues in the popular press might be R.J. Barnet, "The End of Jobs" *Harper's Magazine*, September 1993; W. Bridges, "The End of the Job" *Fortune*, September 19, 1994; "Rethinking Work" *Business Week*, October 17, 1994; "Redefining Work" (A Dossier) *Challenges*, Fall 1994.

21   "A Vision of the Future" *The Ottawa Citizen*, May 14, 1995, A2.

22   Entente sur l'organisation du travail dans la fonction publique intervenue entre le Gouvernement du Québec et les organisations syndicales signataires, Québec 15 février 1995.

23   This section draws freely from G. Paquet and L. Pigeon, "Toward a Transformation of the Public Service" *Optimum* 26, 1 (1995) pp. 47-55.

24   David M. Kreps, "Corporate Culture and Economic Theory" in James E. Alt and

Kenneth A. Shepsle (Editors) *Perspectives on Positive Political Economy* (Cambridge: Cambridge University Press, 1990) pp. 90-143.

25   William Bridges, *JobShift* (Reading, Mass.: Addison-Wesley, 1994). See also Richard J. Barnet, "The End of Jobs" *Harper's Magazine* (September 1993) pp. 47-52.

26   Many academics and practitioners have developed similar ideas but few have been as influential as Murray Axsmith on the Ottawa scene. One may refer to Murray Axsmith, "Contracts to become flexible" *Canadian H.R. Reporter* (14 February 1994) pp. 14-15; Murray Axsmith, "The Work Force: How It Will Change" *Career Options*, 7 (1993/94) pp. 5-7.

27   Gilles Paquet "Paradigms of Governance" in M. Cottrell-Boyd (Ed.) *Rethinking Government*, The Dewar Series: Perspectives on Public Management - Exploration II (Ottawa: Canadian Centre for Management Development, 1994) pp. 29-42. In the case of partnerships, see S. D. Phillips, "How Ottawa Blends: Shifting Government Relationships with Interest Groups" in F. Abele (Ed.) *How Ottawa Spends, 1991-92: The Politics of Fragmentation* (Ottawa: Carleton University Press 1991) pp. 183-227; J.L. Armstrong, Innovation in Public Management: Toward Partnerships" Optimum, 23, 1 (1991) pp. 17-26; K. Kernaghan, "Partnership and Public Administration: Conceptual and Practical Considerations" *Canadian Public Administration*, 36, 1 (1993) pp. 57-76.

28   Murray Axsmith, "The Emerging Employment Contract" *Transitions*, vol.4, No. 3.0.

29   Steven A. Rosell et al. *Changing Maps: Governing in A World of Rapid Change* (Ottawa: Carleton University Press, 1995); James S. Coleman, "Social Capital and the Creation of Human Capital" *American Journal of Sociology*, 94, Supplement (1988) pp. 95-120; Robert D. Putnam, Making Democracy Work (Princeton: Princeton University Press, 1993).

30   Tom Peters, op.cit. pp. 174-175.

31   Charles Hampden-Turner and Alfons Trompenaars, *The Seven Cultures of Capitalism* (New York: Currency Doubleday, 1993).

32   Frederic Schick *Having Reasons: An Essay on Rationality and Sociality* (Princeton: Princeton University Press, 1984).

33   Mark Granovetter, "The Strength of Weak Ties" *American Sociological Review*, 78 (1973) pp. 1360-1380.

34   Tom Peters *The Tom Peters Seminar: Crazy Times Call for Crazy Organizations* (New York: Vintage Books, 1994).

35   Shumpei Kumon, "Japan as a Network Society" in S. Kumon and H. Rosovsky (Eds) *The Political Economy of Japan*, Vol. 3 (Stanford: Stanford University Press, 1992) pp. 109-141.

36   W.T. Easterbrook has examined the pre-condition of "entrepreneurship" in bureaucracies and enterprises. While the enterprise form is characterized with a greater dispersion of power, it requires nonetheless some 'security' to thrive. Easterbrook identifies four types of security necessary for enterprise (economic, social, ethical and political). These are the fundamental components that need to be provided by the negotiated implicit contracts. See "The Climate of Enterprise" American Economic Review 39 (1949), pp.322-335; "Political Economy and Enterprise" *Canadian Journal of Economics and Political Science* 15 (1949) pp. 322-333; "Uncertainty and Economic Change" *Journal of Economic History* 14 (1954) pp. 346-360.

37   Gilles Paquet, "Betting on Moral Contracts" *Optimum*, 22, 3 (1991-92) pp. 45-53. A moral contract is nothing more than a convention or a moral code in the relationship between or among partners. For a detailed examination of the way moral contracts and conventions have been analyzed quite differently in the American

and the European literature as mechanisms of coordination, see P.Y. Gomez, *Qualité et théorie des conventions* (Paris: Economica, 1994).

38   Gifford and Elizabeth Pinchot, *The End of Bureaucracy and the Rise of the Intelligent Organization* (San Francisco: Berrett-Koeler Publishers, 1993).

39   Gilles Paquet "Reinventing Governance" *Opinion Canada* 2, 2 (1994) pp. 1-5.

40   Mark Kingwell, "Interpretation, Dialogue and the Just Citizen" *Philosophy and Social Criticism*, 19, 2 (1993) pp. 115-144; Mark Kingwell, "The Polite Citizen; Or, Justice as Civil Discourse" *The Philosophical Forum*, 25, 3 (1994) pp. 241-266. For a more elaborate presentation of the argument, see Mark Kingwell *A Civil Tongue* (University Park, Penn.: The Pennsylvania State University Press, 1995).

41   Nicole Aubert, "Organizations as Existential Creations: Restoring Personal Meaning While Staying Competitive" in Thierry C. Pauchant (Ed.) *Search of Meaning: Managing for the Health of our Organizations* (San Francisco: Jossey-Bass, 1995) pp. 151-172.

42   P. Aucoin, *The New Public Management: Canada in Comparative Perspective* (Montréal: Institute for Research on Public Policy, 1995).

43   This section draws freely from Gilles Paquet "Paradigms of Governance" *op.cit.*

44   Gilles Paquet "Le fruit dont l'ignorance est la saveur" in A. Armit et J. Bourgault (Eds) *Hard Choices, No Choices : Assessing Program Review* (Toronto: Institute of Public Administration of Canada/ Canadian Plains Research Center, 1996) pp. 47-58.

45   G. Paquet and R. Shepherd, "The Program Review Process: A Deconstruction" in G. Swimmer (Ed.) *How Ottawa Spends 1996-97 - Life After The Cuts: Doing Less with Less* (Ottawa: Carleton University Press, 1996, 39-72.

46   The Program Review was announced in the February 22, 1994 budget and the basic philosophy and guidelines underpinning this review of government operations were spelled out in the form of six tests that departments were asked to apply in the review and assessment of their activities:

Public Interest Test -	Do the program areas or activity continue to serve a public interest?
Role of Government Test -	Is there a legitimate and necessary role for government in this program area or activity?
Federalism Test -	Is the current role of the federal government appropriate, or is the program a candidate for realignment with the provinces?
Partnership Test -	What activities or programs should or could be transferred in whole or in part to the private voluntary sector?
Efficiency Test -	If the program or activity continues, how could its efficiency be improved?
Affordability Test -	Is the resultant package of programs and activities affordable within the fiscal restraint? If not, what programs or activities would be abandoned?

47   While we do not know exactly the content of the report prepared in the early 1990s by Robert René de Cotret and a blue-ribbon panel of experts to suggest ways of restructuring the federal government apparatus, it has been reported widely that much of their recommendations purported to effect major changes in the role of central agencies, very much in line with what is suggested here.

48   Martin Landau and Russell Stout "To Manage is Not to Control: Or the Folly of Type II Errors" *Public Administration Review* (March-April 1979).

49   Martin Landau and Donald Chisholm "Success Oriented vs Failure Avoidance

Management in Public Administration: A Reconsideration" (Institut de Management Public, Paris: Palais des Congrès, mars 1992, mimeo 36p.) p.6

50   For a glaring illustration of the deplorable state of affairs in Canadian public administration, see the exchanges between Donald J. Savoie and Sandford Borins in *Canadian Public Administration* 38, 1, (1995) pp. 112-138. The ethos of Canadian public administration as described by Donald Savoie is one (by contrast with the private sector) with an extraordinarily low tolerance for mistakes. This fixation on success is attributed to "a political environment that is always on the lookout for 'errors'". Savoie's Manichean view of the world suggests, very much like Jane Jacobs' *Systems of Survival* (New York: Random House, 1992) that there is such incommensurability between the private and public sector that any attempt to reform the latter by using experiences from the former is bound to fail at best, or at worst to generate "monstrous hybrids". Savoie defends the status quo and holds the politicians and the political institutions responsible for what may be imperfect in the present system. Instead of focusing on the failings of bureaucrats and the public service, we should focus on "fixing" our political institutions and then laws of Parliament. Borins' belief that "by emphasizing clear objectives and written performance contracts, the new public management should increase rather than diminish the accountability of public servants to ministers and of ministers to Parliament" may be equally simplistic given the "wicked" nature of so many problems faced by public servants, and the impossibility of ever writing complete and all-comprehensive contracts in a turbulent world. Consequently, much will depend on "moral contracts" or implicit arrangements and conventions and these are not always given their due by the new public management literature. For instance, and this is a point suggested by Savoie's paper, though not raised explicitly by him, there may be a need for new moral contracts between the government and the opposition and the government and the media before one can escape the trappings of success-fixation. What would appear to emerge from this debate is that neither the status quo nor narrow-minded managerialism will do. The "wickedness" of management problems (which is not only a feature of public sector issues) demands that a third way be explored between the pure Savoie and the pure Borins positions. Indeed, this is exactly what we have tried to develop.

51   Tibor Scitovsky *The Joyless Economy* (New York: Oxford University Press, 1976).

52   Peter Senge, *The Fifth Discipline* (New York: Doubleday, 1990).

53   Robert E. Kaplan, Wilfred H. Drath and Joan Kofodimos, *Beyond Ambition: How Driven Managers Can Lead Better and Live Better* (San Francisco: Jossey-Bass, 1991).

54   Wilfred H. Drath and Charles J. Palus *Making Common Sense - Leadership as Meaning-Making in a Community of Practice* (Greenboro, N.C.: Centre for Creative Leadership, 1994).

55   Hervé Sérieyx *Le big bang des organisations* (Paris: Calmann-Lévy, 1993).

56   Ronald A. Heifetz *Leadership Without Easy Answers* (Cambridge: Harvard University Press, 1994). J. O'Toole *Leading Change* (San Francisco: Jossey-Bass Publishers, 1995).

57   Abraham Zaleznik "L'absence de leadership et la mystique managériale" *Gestion*, 16, 3, (1991) pp. 15-26.

58   While for the moment, (1) the Public Service Commission chairs the process, approves and appoints; (2) the supervisor defines the profile and is usually the "most listened to" in the appointment process; (3) some stakeholders are members of the selection board (but never employees), the new process would aim at getting most stakeholders (including employees) involved in the profile definition and selection

processes.

59 Charles Handy *The Age of Unreason* (Boston: Harvard Business School, 1989).
60 Robert Hoffman "Ten Reasons You Should be Using 360-Degree Feedback" *HR Magazine* 40, 4 (1995) pp. 82-85.
61 H. Sérieyx, op.cit. Adrian Oldfield *Citizenship and Community* (London: Routledge, 1990).

Part IV

Informational and learning perspectives

As was mentioned earlier, organizations may be defined as information systems: networks of relationships (what organizations are) analyzed as networks of information flows.

This is an approach that was proposed some fifty years ago. Leonid Hurwicz (who recently received the 2007 Nobel Memorial Prize in Economic Sciences) had, by 1960, already begun to classify economic systems in terms of degree of centralization, on the basis of the nature of the messages exchanged (Hurwicz 1960, 1969), and in the 1960s, this approach was already being used routinely in the study of comparative economic systems (Paquet 1967, 1968). It was meant to be the neo-classical economics response to the challenge of Hayek to professional economists in 1945 – when he suggested that economic theory should address, as a matter of priority, organizations and institutions as serving the essential function of collating and communicating widely dispersed information (Hayek 1945).

However useful this approach might have in other ways – and it has been – it did not manage to provide an answer to Hayek's challenge. While markets handle commodities well, they do not process non-commodities as effectively. Consequently, the neo-classical definition of information as a quasi-commodity was an escape mechanism. This is not unlike the trick perpetrated to domesticate uncertainty in the Arrow-Debreu world: by pretending to enumerate all the contingent states of nature, and allowing for trade-offs between them to be established, one abolishes uncertainty. But this stratagem does not provide any meaningful basis for taking uncertainty into account in governance strategy. In the same manner, reducing the communication process to "information bits" is a double denial of information as relationship and process.

Information and knowledge cannot be reduced to the status of quasi-commodity any more than management or entrepreneurship can be regarded as just another factor of production. In both cases, we are referring to *enabling resources* that inform, shape, and catalyze other resources, and any understanding of the dynamics of communication and learning requires forays into emerging new fields like cognitive economics and evolutionary economics (McCain 1992; Nelson/Winter 1984).

At the core of this nexus of forces is the notion of reflexivity that captures the full complexity of the informational underpinnings of the governing task in complex modern societies. Reflexive governance is governance that is conscious of its limitations, of the broader forces interfering with its steering activities, and of the unintended consequences of these activities as a result of our limited information and rationality, and that has ensured that it takes these factors into account in its operations. Reflexive governance amounts to actively designing mechanisms capable of mobilizing diffracted and dispersed information, and of generating new knowledge and learning through recursive feedback relations among the distributed steering activities. This reflexivity entails a process of self-correction and of self-reconfiguration of the very steering purposes and mechanisms along the way (Voβ et al 2006).

Don Lamberton deserves praise as an unorthodox and somewhat prudent pioneer on this front. In a spirit of accommodation, he first attempted to build a new informational approach to socio-economic realities with the traditional toolbox of conventional economics by postulating that that much of information and knowledge is "a commodity to only a limited extent". This 'limited extent' concession turned out to be too much of a concession. His later work has been more radical, and pioneered some of the heterodox approaches to the new evolutionary cognitive and learning economy.

This section reports on some work at this important new frontier. First, it looks critically at the seminal work of Don Lamberton (Chapter 9). Second, it sketches the contours of a provisional framework for evolutionary cognitive economics (Chapter10).

References

F.A. Hayek, "The Use of Knowledge in Society" *American Economic Review*, 35, 1945, 519-530.

L. Hurwicz "Conditions for Economic Efficiency of Centralized and Decentralized Structures" in G. Grossman (Ed.) *Value and Plan*. Berkeley: The University of California Press, 1960, 162-183.

L. Hurwicz, "On the Concept and Possibility of Informational Decentralization" *American Economic Review*, 89 (2), 1969, 513-524.

R.A. McCain, *A Framework for Cognitive Economics*, New York: Praeger, 1992.

R.R. Nelson, S.G. Winter, *An Evolutionary Theory of Economic Change*, Harvard University Press, 1984.

G. Paquet "The Structuration of a Planned Economy", *Canadian Slavonic Papers*, (8), 1966, 250-259.

G. Paquet "Anatomy of Recent Economic Development in the Communist World" *Culture*, 29 (11), 1968, 18-34.

J.P. Voß, D. Bauknecht, R. Kemp (eds) *Reflexive Governance for Sustainable Development*. Cheltenham: Edward Elgar, 2006.

Chapter 9

Lamberton's road to the information and learning economy

".... the existence of learning processes and likely variation in policy criteria in a business organization imply that the decision-making unit is undergoing continual change."

–D.M. Lamberton (1965:74)

Introduction

If a motto had to be chosen to epitomize Don Lamberton's research program, I would suggest a line from an old jazz tune by Bill Russell – "the difficult I'll do right now, the impossible may take a little while". Very early in his career, Don Lamberton developed a strong taste for tackling wicked policy problems, i.e., problems where the ends are ambiguous and ill-defined, and where the means-ends relationships are unstable and uncertain. His doctoral dissertation on the theory of profit was an omen of much that was to come. But he has always tackled these Himalayan tasks with a particularly conciliatory attitude. His research strategy has always favored a strategy of small steps, aimed at preserving much of the traditional heritage of conventional economics, in trying to deal with the vexing problems seemingly lying just beyond the boundaries of the conventional terrain.

This accommodation strategy has had two major consequences. On the one hand, over the last forty years, Lamberton has been able to carry out his research program in peace in the margins of the economics pro-

213

fession. He has never launched an all-out attack on canonical works, and has not really been attacked frontally, because his deliberately oblique approach to the world of new ideas never made him a major obstacle on the road of orthodoxy. On the other hand, through this strategy of little steps, he has not succeeded in truly forcing onto the agenda of the economics profession the paradigm shift that has underpinned much of his work during that period.

But Lamberton's crusade has had an impact. For example, information economics is now a formal category in the formal classification of canonical sub-topics in the *Journal of Economic Literature*. But Lamberton's impact has been diffused, a multitude of sharps and flats on the larger score, without his *problématique* being fully recognized, as it should have, as an original and heuristically powerful alternative *manière de voir*.

It is the aim of this paper to pull together from Lamberton's works a template of his perspective. This sort of endeavor is fraught with danger: first, the danger of trivializing Lamberton's perspective by unduly simplifying it, in sharp contrast to his determined effort to express it largely in shades of pastel; second, the danger of caricaturing his subtle and situation-sensitive approach, and trying to fit it into a formula; and thirdly, the danger of inventing a Lamberton that never was, in an effort to explicate his thought process. I have tried to avoid these pitfalls, and I hope that this reconstruction (however inadequate) will illuminate an *oeuvre* that deserves much more attention than it has received.

In the beginning

From the very beginning of his career, Don Lamberton worked in a British economic tradition derived from Alfred Marshall – a tradition that has always given much importance to knowledge and organization. It is a tradition, brilliantly illustrated by other important scholars like G.L.S. Shackle, G.B. Richardson, B.J. Loasby, et al. For Marshall, "knowledge is our most powerful engine of production", and for all those economists who have remained faithful to the teachings of Marshall, business decisions have been a central feature of the economist's vision of the world and of the process theory of the firm that ensues.

In the first pages of his book on the theory of profit, Lamberton puts his finger on the central question that will guide his research program in the following decades. It appears to him quite inadequate to presume that the prices of all goods could be deduced if we knew in sufficient detail (1) what each person likes; and (2) what each person possesses. One has to ask "a third question", he says: what does the person know?

what does the person believe? (Lamberton 1965:5). This third question would engage Lamberton for the next thirty years.

As early as 1965, Lamberton was highly critical of those who have tried to bury this third question in the first two, (a) by presuming that if rational behaviour is postulated and preferences are given and stable, the knowledge and belief question is unnecessary; and (b) by treating "knowledge and belief, the capacity to add to the store of information, the whole complex organization of the firm" as possessions. For Lamberton, these assumptions are unhelpful. But, instead of focusing directly on the analysis of the process underlying the generation of knowledge and belief, Lamberton has been attracted by an alternative strategy: the possibility of dealing with information and organization as inputs.

It is not that he is unaware of the relative importance of learning processes. Rather, Lamberton is attempting, through his knowledge-as-input strategy, to escape from the quicksand of the pure process orientation à la Shackle – a perspective in which the very nature of the decision-making unit is undergoing continual change, and therefore becomes ontologically elusive.

The source of that choice of research strategy, as a first concession to neo-classical economics, is most certainly ascribable to the influence of Lamberton's thesis supervisor, John Hicks. This is the sort of accommodation that Lamberton would occasionally make to the mandarins of neoclassical economics in the hope that, by moving ever so slightly into their terrain, he might persuade them to pay more attention to phenomena generally occluded from their perspectives. This accommodation strategy has succeeded to a certain extent, but has not paid off as handsomely as was expected.

Lamberton has made too many concessions along the way, and this will both weaken his arguments and fail to sway his opponents. More importantly, it has prevented him from fully exploiting the important insights about the centrality of learning processes that he developed in 1965, and that he has continued to refine in the years since.

Lamberton's accommodation philosophy also explains why he has failed to take advantage of the important contributions of the contributions of the Austrians school of economics and of the work of Friedrich Hayek in his endeavour, and why he has chosen not to use these in his efforts to incite economists to give more attention to information and knowledge.

Hayek and the Austrians offer a radical alternative to neo-classical economics formalist equilibrium models in dealing with information, with their focus on disequilibrium within the market process. They also emphasize the dispersal of information that makes it inaccessible except under special circumstances. By ignoring Hayek, Lamberton missed an extraordinary opportunity to make full use of a research program focused on the best way to make use of dispersed knowledge, and on the search for the best institutional arrangements for learning. But he could not invoke Hayek and the Austrians because of the fact that they were loathed by the neo-classical mandarins who were wedded to the notion of equilibrium (Boettke 1997). It is only in the very recent past that Lamberton has begun to refer explicitly to Hayek, and to make gestures to formally integrate Hayek`s work into his canon (Lamberton 1996).

Finally, Lamberton has remained very Marshallian in his definition of information and organization as important "agents" of production, and as forming a great part of what is broadly referred to as "capital". But he has developed, especially in his earlier works, a somewhat more reified notion of capital than the one used by Marshall. He has probably felt that it might be easier to get the neo-classical economists to agree to deal with the new realities of information and organization if they could be presented in a familiar language. Even the less reified notion of organizational capital that Lamberton has used in his more recent works is presented in such a way as to persuade neo-classical economists to integrate organizations as embodied information systems into their analysis as simply another form of capital.

Information and knowledge as significant inputs are a trademark of Don Lamberton. In his 1965 book, he made the point clearly, but, in 1992, in the preface to a special issue of *Human Systems Management*, he reiterates his commitment to knowledge as a separate factor of production. However, while Marshall was quite insistent on the coordinating role of this new sort of capital, Lamberton's notion of capital would appear to be used mainly in order to provide some tangibility to the notions of information and knowledge.

The choice of this research strategy would turn out to be consequential. By focusing on information as a quasi-commodity, and on organization as technology, Lamberton makes major concessions. This shift from learning to information, and from the Marshallian organization as aid to the growth of knowledge (i.e., learning) to something more akin to technology, prevents him from explicitly developing a more direct and idiosyncratic answer to the third question.

Lamberton would become conscious of the importance of these early decisions as they began to affect his work considerably in the following decades. He has spent a great deal of time trying to disentangle himself from the predicaments entailed by these early commitments.

216

Indeed, at times, Lamberton flirts with the process of cognition. But it never becomes the prime lever in his analyses. In his papers, he deals obliquely with this question, and mainly in some excursuses. Yet, despite the often serendipitous nature of this parallel development in his writings, many of the elements in the analyses he has woven over the years suggest that there is a Lamberton approach to cognitive economics that, while not well developed, appears very promising.

The knowledge-information nexus as commodification trap

The purpose here is not to review in detail the large number of papers that Don Lamberton has produced on the economics of information and knowledge. I only wish to benchmark very roughly the evolution of his thinking. So I have chosen to sample his work at some key moments over the last decades. At these junctures, I have attempted to identify the main pillars on which he has built his argument. The first main occasion was his Penguin reader in 1971, and a chapter published in 1972 in a book in honour of G. L. S. Shackle; the second observation points are two chapters in edited books in 1982 and 1984; and the third reading is in two chapters of edited books in 1994 and 1996 (Lamberton 1971,1972, 1982, 1984, 1994, 1996).

In 1971, Lamberton was uncharacteristically blunt: he situated himself squarely in the Marshall-Shackle tradition and asked the "third question" – what does the economic actor know? what does he believe? Equilibrium neo-classical economics is summarily dismissed. Even though some works by Hicks, Arrow, Debreu, and Radner are mentioned, the sympathy of the author is clearly with Shackle, and the focus of his queries on the challenges posed by the mysteries of business decisions as investigated by industrial economists like P.W. S. Andrews. The 1971 point of view flows naturally from the 1965 book and was re-affirmed in 1972 in the book of essays in honour of G.L.S. Shackle.

If the central concern was uncertainty and profit in 1965, in 1971 it had shifted to information and organization. Lamberton was somewhat taken by Frank Knight's characterization of information as "one of the principal commodities" supplied by the economic organization (Knight 1921:261). His focus of interest remained the pursuit of profit (which, for Shackle, has "become the pursuit of knowledge"), but the commodification worm is in the apple (Lamberton 1972:191).

As soon as the focus of attention became information and organization, Lamberton fell into the reification trap set by Knight, and the whole underlying process of the pursuit of knowledge (i.e., cognition and learning) was somewhat sidestepped. This is quite clear in the two papers of the early 1980s. One senses in these papers the influence of Machlup (1962) and Porat (1977) and their effort to measure the "information sector". Lamberton is clearly dissatisfied with the information sector approach; he says that to consider information as "just another commodity" will not do; but he did not provide the basis for a viable alternative approach in 1982. The same can be said about the 1984 paper. Again, the information sector approach is criticized, and alternative strategies were mentioned as having emerged along the road ,(emphasis on organizations, procedural rationality, etc.), but one is left with nothing more than the hope that it will soon be possible to avoid the trap of treating information as "just one more commodity" (Lamberton 1984:15).

In the two papers sampled from the 1990s, Lamberton's *problématique* had leaped forward.

The 1994 paper goes quite a distance toward reframing the debate, and appears to posit (in the first couple of pages) that "economic activity is a *process*, its participants having both histories and contexts", and that "progress lies in *learning*" (our emphasis). Yet Lamberton does not feel bound by these limiting premises in the rest of the paper: instead of focusing on the analysis of these dimensions, he allows himself to be dragged onto the terrain of the different authors whose work he is surveying. Since he is so intent on lending an attentive and generous ear to all, he does not have time and space to go beyond complaining about the fact that more fundamental dimensions may not have been satisfactorily explored.

The synthetic effort of the first section of the 1994 paper has a somewhat amphibological quality. Lamberton clearly documents the failures of traditional economics in analyzing the information economy (and he even underlines the high degree of cognitive dissonance that mars that literature), but he also appears to remain undeterred by these inadequacies, and seems confident that the confluence of new work in the diverse traditions he surveys will lead to a "less aggregative, less ambitious theory" that will prove both insightful and operational.

In the second section, Lamberton cobbles together some of the elements that should (in his view) be at the center of the new synthesis. This work is presented modestly as a preliminary collage of taxonomies and not as an alternative paradigm. Lamberton has chosen a deliberate strategy: to retain as the most effective/helpful language, the "language of problem solution" in good currency in neo-classical economics. This is a self-imposed constraint that endows the paper with a useful role as a bridge between mainstream economists and "information economists", but it also considerably limits the scope of analysis to the extent that

Lamberton operates strictly within a paradigm that, by his own admission, is ill-suited for the task at hand.

In 1994, Lamberton again re-asserted his basic gamble on continuity in economic thought. His paper documents the extent to which progress has been slower than anticipated, and he argues that one of the main reasons for this is that the original texture of communication links (and the process of learning it underpins) has often been swept aside by neo-classical economics, in its efforts to capture the central features of the information and knowledge-based economy in a commodity form.

In the neo-classical framework, information (à la Frank Knight) remains one of the principal *commodities* supplied by economic organization; information is costly, and is the result of earlier investment in search. Lamberton acknowledges that much of information and knowledge is "a commodity to only a limited extent", but he appears to concede (reluctantly) that it is a commodity nonetheless, and that markets and hierarchies may be efficient contraptions to process such an information-commodity. Neo-classical analysis therefore appears salvageable.

As to the possibility that a new framework might be capable of re-integrating the full life of communication and learning into the analyses of the information economy, and that it might emerge through the convergence of the different (more or less tradition-bound) research programs referred to in Lamberton's survey, it would appear to be low. The current exploration of the interfaces between management strategy and economics has shown that the latter is more likely to cannibalize the former without producing much help for those interested in practical knowledge. A true convergence may exist, but it has not been shown to exist; and, if it ever materializes, it might turn out to be a day late.

In a subsection of the 1994 paper (pp. 16ff) Lamberton opened a very important door: he explicitly introduced a discussion of learning and cognition. Making use of the work of Malerba (1992), Lamberton attempted to refocus the debate on the third question, and on the process through which a person comes to know what he/she knows, i.e., learning and cognition. But again, he is hesitant to jump right in, and clings to the old paradigm by probing not the process of learning, but the resulting "embodiment of a form of organizational capital" in the learning manager (p. 17). In the same manner, after having explicitly emphasized the distinction between perception and cognition, Lamberton veers immediately toward the notion of "capability" – very similar to the notion of organizational capital – to avoid being dragged into the analysis of the process of learning and cognition.

Lamberton was not temerarious. He would, however, create a clear break in his 1996 paper.

He did not opt out of the crusade to salvage the neo-classical paradigm (xvi),but, he now explicitly envisaged the need to "modify and extend economics", as well as the need for the creation of a *new interdisciplinary paradigm* that might hold the key to a fuller and more effective handling of learning. This shift was explained in a very cursory way, but was designed to help Lamberton to deal much more directly with the central process of pursuit of knowledge and learning that had been lingering in his work since the 1960s.

Flirting with the process of cognition

These latter papers provided ample material for a new paradigm, but it was only with the 1996 paper that the unconditional crusade to defend the neo-classical framework as the only vehicle capable of effectively dealing (some day) with the pursuit of knowledge was finally, if reluctantly abandoned. A reading of the 1971 collection of readings, and then of the 1996 reader, will give an indication of the reframing of perspective that Lamberton has effected.

In the 1996 introduction to the new reader, and, even more in Lamberton (1997), Lamberton goes further than he has ever gone before: he flirts with the process of cognition. He makes references to the new terrains – *cognitive economics* and *evolutionary economics* (McCain 1992; Nelson and Winter 1982) – and even anthologizes Hayek. The Trojan horse through which Lamberton would be brought into these new perspectives was a recasting of his concern for organizational capital and tacit knowledge. These drew him to the study of capabilities, but perhaps more importantly, to the manner in which they are developed and nurtured in a learning economy.

This shift toward a *learning economy framework* (though Lamberton never uses these words) is not one of degree but of kind. The new economy, under this label, is defined as innovation-mediated and innovation-driven. Individuals' and organizations' learning capabilities are the source of wealth creation. But most importantly, the learning economy is rooted in a social or collective mobilization of knowledge: learning harnesses the collective intelligence of the team as a source of continuous improvement (Florida and Kenney 1993). This in turn commands a degree of collaboration to take advantage of positive externalities, economies of scale and scope, and strong cumulative experience learning processes (Jacquemin 1995).

Since knowledge is traditionally *segregated* into institutionally-imposed sub-divisions, and much of it is *tacit* (i.e., heuristic, subject-ive, embodied knowledge not easy to articulate) and *dispersed* widely among agents, what are required are new techno-organizational forms endowed with a capacity to aggregate, tap, and harness all these ca-pabilities (Minkler 1993; Senker 1995). This is essential if learning is to proceed. These new ways of creating value are forcing an integration of mental and manual labour into *self-managing work teams* that bear little resemblance to the traditional division of labour: "teams are used to develop links to and connections across the innovation-production spectrum" (Florida 1991:571). It is far from the Taylorian system where this spectrum was sliced into self-contained and isolated segments which shared little knowledge.

Self-managing work teams constitute cognitive blocks, i.e., clusters of activities that are organized around capabilities, intellectual assets, and knowledge processes in such a way as to maximize the ability of the organization to learn (Stewart 1997). Moreover, the organization, as a value-creating partner system, constructed for knowledge production, is much like an organism: "because of the tacit nature of knowledge, a firm is capable of doing things that it cannot easily describe" (Minkler 1993:583). Obviously, these different blocks of knowledge must be technically compatible, but what is most important is their capacity to "progress in concert" (Moati et Mouhoud 1994:59). In such a context, hyper-specialization generates rigidities and proves dysfunctional. The mastery of a block of knowledge requires *learning communities* or *com-munities of practice* that are bound by conventions, and are unlikely to be hyper-fragmented.

Interactivity connotes the complex form of dialectical relations among agents and segments, and their evolution through time. It harmonizes (1) organizations' different capabilities (technical, organizational, strategic, learning); (2) organizations' particular capacities (to solve problems, to absorb knowledge, to innovate and experiment, and to incorporate new knowledge in its functions); (3) the interactions with the environment and with other organizations; and (4) the degree of dynamic increasing returns for the organizations in learning by learning.

Interactivity entails some sort of cumulative process of learning built on externalities with much potential for irreversibility and inflex-ibilities of all sorts (Le Bas 1993: 13). But it mostly entails the genesis of institutions: a set of guideposts, the locus for the memorization and transmission of routines and tacit knowledge, through conventions, contracts and contraptions that form a cognitive framework that guides the learning process (Llerena 1997).

221

In the new cognitive division of labour, interactivity is the glue that brings forth social learning, but the institutions that underpin interactivity also constrain the nature of the exploration for, and the exploitation of new knowledge: they orient the future directions of learning.

The learning economy was already in embryonic form in many of the earlier Lamberton papers, but it was in his 1996 paper in all but name. This paper not only suggested a new cognitive division of labour, but also a new mode of production of knowledge that is akin to Gibbons' Mode 2. While Mode 1 production of knowledge was disciplinary, governed by the norms of the scientific method, carried out in stable hierarchical organizations, Mode 2 production of knowledge is transdisciplinary, heterogeneous, carried out in transient heterarchical contexts of applications, and more socially distributed and therefore socially accountable (Gibbons 1994; Gibbons et al. 1994). This new complementary mode of production of knowledge is seen as better adapted to a world where knowledge is *de facto* segregated, tacit, and distributed. However, it poses immense problems of coordination as the number of stakeholders, the number of perspectives, the numerous types of accountabilities, and the required trespassings are multiplied.

But having set the stage so nicely for developing his new vista – and acknowledged Foray and Lundvall's 1996 work on the learning economy (Lamberton 1997:75) – Lamberton then abandoned this gambit to return to a taxonomy of information as his preferred *stratégie de sortie de crise*.

Illuminating Lamberton's implicit *problématique*

It is a daunting task to piece together the tacit intellectual strategy of a prolific and eclectic writer like Don Lamberton , who has chosen not to burden himself with an explicit *problématique*. It is an effort to codify Lamberton's tacit knowledge, and this sort of endeavour may well introduce rigidities, inflexibilities, and biases that never existed in the original perspective.

To guard against that danger, I have tried to keep in mind four important characteristics of Don Lamberton's work.

First, Lamberton is a true representative of the Marshallian tradition who has been tantalized and, at times, mesmerized by the immense powers of integration of the neo-classical general equilibrium paradigm, but has remained persuaded during most of his intellectual life that it was ill-equipped to give knowledge and information its due place. Still, Lamberton has refused the radical option of abandoning the neo-classical paradigm altogether, even as it became progressively clearer that it might not be capable of meaningfully integrating these crucial dimensions. In that sense, Lamberton is a Shackle who continued to hope that some reconciliation of Marshall and Walras was possible.

Second, Lamberton's crusade to persuade mainstream economists to pay attention to knowledge and learning has been paralyzed by a certain fixation on the concept of information. Even in 1996, when he became most disenchanted with what the neo-classical paradigm has been able to generate, he fell back on a taxonomy of information as a strategy likely to guide him out of the wreckage. This insistent focus on information led him to all but exclude a number of promising paths he had himself explored only in the most general fashion, and to ignore a number of potential allies that might have been most helpful in his quest. In particular, the hesitation to pursue further some of his reflections on learning and cognition in the 1994 paper, and the neglect of the works of Hayek (1948) and Richardson (1960) have been most unfortunate.

Third, Lamberton's *problématique* has nonetheless evolved considerably over time, even though it has retained some of its basic original features. In particular, he has begun of late to shift his attention away from information *per se* toward knowledge, cognition, capabilities, and learning. Although this *outillage mental* has been used in a rather loose way, and not in the form of a technical model, the assemblage of these concepts in Lamberton's *problématique* constitutes an analytical framework with important heuristic power: "a set of relationships that do not lead to specific conclusions about the world of events... (but constitute) the mold out of which the specific types of theories are made" (Leibenstein 1976:17-18).

Fourth, the easiest way to illustrate the heuristic power of this implicit *problématique* is to show that it can serve as an apparatus to make sense of many new developments in the recent literature emanating from economics and management. Lamberton's framework (as it has been collated from the margins of his papers) is, we claim, an integrating scheme capable of serving as a synthetic tool, but also of guiding a most powerful search engine.

In order to do justice to this ambitious agenda within a few pages, I suggest the following shortcut: (1) to set the broad stage, Lamberton is first characterized as a reluctant or closet Austrian Marshallian, and it is argued that his implicit analytical framework is definable in large part by this lineage; (2) I then sketch what the learning economy à la Lamberton might look like in the light of some recent works flowing from the same inspiration; (3) finally, I argue that Lamberton is setting the stage for a new mode of knowledge (cognition) and knowledge acquisition (learning), and that his eclectic approach to these activities is an instance of Mode 2 production of knowledge.

i.   In a very perceptive essay about another student of John Hicks, G.B. Richardson, Nicolai Foss (1995) identifies Richardson as an "Austrian Marshallian". This is an epithet used by Foss to underline Richardson's eclectic, pragmatic, and non-mechanistic approach, à la Marshall, and his constant focus on the centrality of knowledge and coordination, à la Hayek. The same may be said about Lamberton, with the caveat that only in the latter stage of his intellectual journey has he been willing to explicitly acknowledge the central importance of Hayek.

There is, however, a significant difference between Richardson and Lamberton. Richardson has chosen to sketch starkly an alternative to the neo-classical paradigm. But his gambit has failed to attract support and his alternative paradigm has therefore attracted little interest until the recent past. Indeed, Richardson became so discouraged by the little attention paid to his work that he abandoned economics altogether. Lamberton chose rather to avoid any confrontational endeavour. As a *rassembleur*, he used and still uses his synthesis-building talents and powers in an effort to show that the mainstream or quasi-mainstream of the economics and management disciplines could incorporate with minimal adjustments many of the new developments in information economics suggested by the new realities, and to construct bridges between the canonical view, and a more cogent apprehension of these new realities.

Characteristically, Lamberton has made use of the least controversial new elements brought forth by cognitive economics and evolutionary economics to construct an ever evolving *problématique*, that now incorporates an explicit concern with the different types of knowledge (codified and tacit) à la Michael Polanyi, a capabilities view of the firm, à la Langlois and Robertson (1995), and some explicit reference to cognition and learning as processes.

ii.   In the learning economy that Lamberton has begun to probe, the exploration for and the exploitation of new knowledge are the driving forces. This requires organizational arrangements at the production level, but also at the corporate level, designed to do the job as well as possible. To deal with this challenge, Lamberton has put at the center of the stage the notion of organizational capital. This is a field of study already tilled by some economists and other specialists in organizational design: for them, what they call "structural" capital captures ways to better manage tacit knowledge and mobilize all the persons involved for learning (Langlois and Robertson 1995; Saint-Onge 1996). Lamberton's learning economy problématique is in this vein (Lamberton 1997).

Structural capital is defined as the capabilities of the organization, and capabilities are "forms of knowledge about how to carry out productive tasks" (Langlois and Robertson 1995: 16). The central point in Saint-Onge's argument is that much of this knowledge is tacit, i.e., unarticulated. For Saint-Onge, structural capital consists of four elements - *systems* (the way its processes and outputs proceed), *structure* (the arrangement of responsibilities and accountabilities among the members of the organization), *strategy* (the goals of the organization, and the ways it seeks to achieve them), and *culture* (the sum of individual opinions, shared mindsets, values and norms within the organization) (Saint-Onge 1996:13). And the major barrier to success is the lack of a fit or an alignment among these four elements.

The design or redesign of the organizational or structural capital amounts to the creation of new capabilities: a new organizational feature arises as an answer to a problem of coordination, a problem of alignment between systems, structure, strategy, and culture. While much work has been done on organizational design, such work does not suggest the conditions necessary for the required alignment referred to above. At all times, one is tempted to use one of the four components as a lever, and to simply adjust the other three to the ruling one. This has proved rather disastrous as a search for value-creation and value-added. For instance, the re-engineering of systems has been presented as a panacea, and has failed miserably (Ferrand et Paquet 1994). In the same manner, restructuring may capture a portion of the necessary adjustment, but is unlikely to suffice.

Saint-Onge suggests that even though tacit knowledge has an impact on all four components of structural capital, culture tends to be the most implicit, and the connections between strategy and culture are likely to be the most potent. But it is the goodness of fit among the four components (systems, structure, strategy, culture) that is central: the alignment and congruence of the tacit knowledge held by the human capital (assumptions, values and beliefs characterizing the mindset of individuals), the customer capital (the mindsets of customers that shape their perception of valued added) and the structural capital (the collective mindsets of the organization's members that shape its culture — i.e., its norms and standards —but also act as filters and form a mental grid that shapes systems, structure, and strategy) (Saint-Onge 1996).

One has no difficulty seeing that Lamberton is drifting in the same direction, when he attacks the extraordinary limitations of the concept of infrastructure as unduly focused on physical and material structures, at a time when in fact the organizational capital is becoming much more important and infinitely more central to the *explanans* in a learning economy (Lamberton 1996b).

The nexus of forces at the core of the structural capital almost naturally breeds misalignment. Whether one tackles the production or the organizational sides of the firm, the problem of the lack of goodness of fit among these four elements of structural capital (systems, structure, strategy, culture), very much like the lack of goodness of fit among the three components of intellectual capital (human, customer, structural), stands as the source of much of the firm's poor performance. These coordination failures continue to be misunderstood, denied or suppressed in the public discourse surrounding firms (de la Mothe and Paquet 1997).

Although much work has been done on the coordination failures in organizational learning, and on the way in which organizational learning proceeds *in situ*, our knowledge base remains very skimpy (Levinthal and March 1993; Bianchi 1995; Darr, Argote and Epple 1995; Nevis, DiBella, Gould 1995; Epple, Argote and Murphy 1996; Miller 1996; Howells 1996). This is especially clear when one tries to find studies that take into account the whole complement of the four elements of structural capital and the three components of intellectual capital. The land has been cleared, but the building Lamberton and others want to construct is not yet in sight. Indeed, from this capharnaum of efforts, it is still impossible to say what sort of edifice might emerge. It is therefore unrealistic to expect an integrative scheme to materialize in the very near future. One will have to deal with issues on a piecemeal basis for quite a while before one can expect an operationalization of the Lamberton perspective (Baldwin and Clark 1997).

iii.   Lamberton has not only sketched a general direction for exploration, he has also of late suggested not that the simplifying language of economics be abandoned, and that a complementary mode of production of knowledge be used. What Lamberton suggests is very close to what has become known as Mode 2 production of knowledge, which is said to operate "*in the context of application*". This means that knowledge is "always produced under an aspect of continuous negotiation, i.e., it will not be produced unless and until the interests of the various actors are included" (Gibbons 1994:263). Mode 2 production of knowledge is a "socially distributed knowledge production system", i.e., "this type of knowledge is both supplied by and distributed to individuals and groups across the social spectrum" (Gibbons 1994:268). This entails that current knowledge producing institutions must be *de-centered*, they must become more permeable to allow much broader participation in knowledge generation, and much more *capable of diffusing* this knowledge throughout society.

This means that the traditional distinction between science and professional practice has all but disappeared, that collaborative ventures are now the rule, that co-evolution by all those involved in this production ensues in the negotiating arena, where the new knowledge is produced and disseminated. Brokering this complex form of arrangements, at a time when the context of application is evolving rapidly, and when the continuous negotiation and interaction among the interested actors raises complex questions of 360-degree accountabilities, is quite a challenge. Much of the requisite co-evolution may be prevented by institutional rigidities, or the lack of the necessary framework rules in the existing institutional order.

Lamberton has not been very precise about the exact nature of the transdisciplinary framework he intends to construct, but it is clear that for him, as for Gibbons, in the beginning is the issue. The context of application and the nature of the problem generate a creative process: this is the world of Delta knowledge, knowledge as a result of reflection-in-action, not the application of already existing knowledge, but the development of learning by doing (Schon 1983; Gilles et Paquet 1991). In that sense, the framework is continually evolving in a way that is akin to the situation of the designer who tries to find some goodness of fit between two intangibles – a form that still does not exist, and an evolving context that cannot be fully described since it is constantly evolving (Alexander 1964).

To deal effectively with this challenge, the team must draw from many sources of knowledge, from many types of expertise, from a variety of persons and organizations that have different norms and standards, and different ways of benchmarking their work. Moreover, as the work proceeds, the membership in the team evolves, and the gauges by which the work is assessed are also evolving. This is bound to create much difficulty in mobilizing these transient groups while maintaining the coherence of the enterprise.

The problem becomes even more difficult when it is realized that the criteria to assess the quality of the work are bound to be as diverse as the nature of the stakeholders. Nothing as simple as peer review will suffice – we no longer know who the peers are at any given moment. The context of application, the different intellectual interests, the breadth of the social composition of the range of stakeholders make the notion of quality "more composite, multidimensional" (Gibbons 1994:267): it is an essentially contested and inherently paradoxical concept (Gallie 1964; Harmon 1995). This entails a much more complex process of evaluation by negotiation to ensure that the different perspectives are given their requisite valence.

Even though Lamberton would appear to be ready to search outside the world of economics for the *outillage mental* he needs to proceed further, he is most reluctant to abandon the old paradigm, and it is not clear that, despite his frustrations, he will ever be ready to scrap it. Like any true Marshallian, Lamberton is more likely to mix Mode 1 and Mode 2 production of knowledge, and to continue to hope that, in some way, in due time, a new synthesis keeping most of the old paradigm and incorporating much of the new perspective will evolve.

One cannot expect a radical reformulation of either Lamberton's perspective or his epistemological strategy. He will remain somewhat loyal to the old paradigm, and at best a modest user of the new perspective and the new epistemology, at least in the immediate future.

It is not difficult to understand why he remains unrepentantly so tolerant of and accommodative to the traditional economic perspective. Lamberton is first and foremost an economist, and in the parlance of Isaiah Berlin), a hedgehog. Archilochus has written "The fox knows many things, but the hedgehog knows one big thing". The economic vision is the one in terms of which Lamberton understands, thinks, and feels. He cannot be swayed by foxes who pursue many ends, often unrelated or contradictory, and connected if at all only in some *de facto* way, because he "knows" that "the fox, for all his cunning, is defeated by the hedgehog's one defence" (Berlin 1957:7).

Conclusion

It may appear irreverent to some to tease out of the work of an eminent and prolific economist a strand of thought that the principal has chosen not to present himself as his main hymn book.

The rationale for such a piece of work is that Lamberton has practiced the art of tact and civility in his academic work to a degree that may have been a disservice to his own insights. My contention is that there is more to Lamberton than meets the eye in the theoretical domain. If the case has been made persuasively, this may lead to a rereading of his work.

The Lamberton accommodating strategy of little steps, rooted in a single powerful unifying vision, may not have generated the alternative paradigm, but it has served Lamberton and the economics profession well, in ways that are not always easy to track down through the use of bibliometric techniques.

For one of the most important impacts of Lamberton as hedgehog has been that the repetition of his message over the years has significantly transformed the *weltanshauung* of a large number of economists who have not necessarily been swayed by his conciliatory approach, but have been forced by his intelligent defense of the possibilities of the neo-classical paradigm to refine and to considerably deepen their attacks on the ruling paradigm.

Personally, I have always found Lamberton's quiet leadership most stimulating, and on at least two occasions, in the 1970s and in the 1990s, his relentless probing has pressed me to explore, however ineffectively, a continent he had discovered but had decided not to explore himself (Paquet 1977, 1994). On those occasions, I have felt that Lamberton, though he may still be reluctant to set foot in the gardens of the promised land of cognitive and evolutionary economics, has been the one who has guided many of us there, and has strongly influenced our first forays into this *terra incognita*.

What more can a crusading hedgehog hope for?

References

C. Alexander, *Notes Toward a Synthesis of Form*. Cambridge: Harvard University Press, 1964.

C. Y. Baldwin and K. B. Clark, "Managing in an Age of Modularity" *Harvard Business Review,* 75(5), 1997, 84-93.

I. Berlin, *The Hedgehog and the Fox*. New York: Mentor, 1957.

M. Bianchi, "Markets and Firms – Transaction Costs versus Stategic Innovation" *Journal of Economic Behavior & Organization* 28, 1995, 183-202.

P. J. Boettke, "What Went Wrong with Economics?" *Critical Review*, 11 (1), 1997, 11-64.

E.D. Darr, L. Argote and D. Epple, "The Acquisition, Transfer and Depreciation of Knowledge in Service Organizations: Productivity in Franchises" *Management Science* 41(11), 1995, 1750-1761.

de la Mothe and G. Paquet (Eds) *Evolutionary Economics and the New International Political Economy*. London: Pinter, 1996.

J. de la Mothe and G .Paquet, "Coordination Failures in the Learning Economy" in J. de la Mothe and G. Paquet (Eds) *Challenges Unmet in the New Production of Knowledge*. Ottawa: PRIME , 1997, 3-26.

D. Epple, L. Argote, and K. Murphy, "An Empirical Investigation of the Microstructure of Knowledge Acquisition and Transfer Through Learning By Doing" *Operations Research 44* (1), 1996, 77-86.

D. Ferrand et G. Paquet, "Apprentissage organisationnel et ré-engineering" *Logistique et Management* 2(1), 1994, 45-58.

R. Florida, "The New Industrial Revolution" *Futures* 23 (6), 1991, 559-576.

R. Florida and M. Kenney, "Innovation-Mediated Production" *Futures* 25(5), 1993, 637-651.

D. Foray and B.A. Lundvall, "The Knowledge-Based Economy: From the Economics of Knowledge to the Learning Economy" in *Employment and Growth in the Knowledge-Based Economy*. Paris: OECD, 1996, 11-32.

N.J. Foss, "The Economic Thought of an Austrian Marshallian: George Barclay Richardson" *Journal of Economic Studies*, 22 (1), 1995, 23-44.

W. P. Gallie, *Philosophy and the Historical Understanding*. London: Chatto & Windus, 1994.

M. Gibbons. "Transfer Sciences: Management of Distributed Knowledge Production" *Empirica*, 21, 1994, 259-270.

M. Gibbons et al., *The New Production of Knowledge*. London: Sage Publications, 1994. `

W. Gilles et G. Paquet, "La connaissance de type Delta" in G. Paquet et O. Gélinier (Eds) *Le management en crise: pour une formation proche de l'action*. Paris: Economica , 1991, 19-36.

M.M. Harmon, *Responsibility as Paradox*. London: Sage Publications, 1995.

F.A. Hayek, *Individualism and Economic Order.* Chicago: University of Chicago Press, 1948.

J. Howells, "Tacit Knowledge, Innovation, and Technology Transfer" *Technology Analysis and Strategic Management* 8(2), 1996, 91-106.

A. Jacquemin, "Capitalism, Competition, Cooperation" *De Economist* 143 (1), 1995, 1-14.

K. Kelly, "New Rules for the Economy" *Wired* 5 (9), 1997, 140-197.

R.N. Langlois and P.L. Robertson, *Firms, Markets and Economic Change*. London: Routledge, 1995.

C. Le Bas, "La firme et la nature de l' apprentissage" *Economies et Sociétés* Série Dynamique technologique et organisation, 1 (5), 1993, 7-24.

A. Levinthal and J. G. March, "The Myopia of Learning" *Strategic Management Journal* 14, 1993, 95-112

D. Llerena, "Coopérations cognitives et modèles mentaux collectifs: outils de création et de diffusion des connaissances» in B. Guilhon et al. (Eds) *Economie de la connaissance et organisations*. Paris L'Harmattan, 1997, 356-382.

D.M. Lamberton, *The Theory of Profit*. Oxford: Blackwell, 1965.

D. M. Lamberton (Ed.) *Economics of Information and Knowledge*. Harmondsworth: Penguin Books, 1971, (Introduction, 7-17).

D. M. Lamberton, "Information and Profit" in C. F. Carter and J. L. Ford (Eds) *Uncertainty and Expectations in Economics*. Oxford: Basil Blackwell, 1972, 191-212.

D.M. Lamberton, "The Theoretical Implications of Measuring the Communication Sector" in M. Jussawalla and D.M. Lamberton (Eds) *Communication Economics and Development*. Oxford: Pergamon Press, 1982, 36-59.

D.M. Lamberton, "The Emergence of Information Economics" in M. Jussawalla and H. Ebenfield (Eds) *Communication and Information Economics: New Perspectives*. Amsterdam: North-Holland, 1984, 7-22.

D.M. Lamberton, "The Information Economy Revisited" in R.E. Babe (Ed.) *Information and Communication in Economics*. Boston: Kluwer Academic Publishers, 1994, 1-33.

D.M.Lamberton (Ed.) *The Economics of Communication and Information*. Cheltenham, U.K.: Edward Elgar Publishing, 1996, (Introduction: 'Threatened Wreckage' or New Paradigm? xiiixxviii.

D.M. Lamberton, "Infrastructure: A Nebulous and Overworked Concept" *International Journal of Technology Management*, 12 (5/6), 1996b, 696-703

D.M. Lamberton, "The Knowledge-based Economy: A Sisyphus Model" *Prometheus*, 15 (1), 1997, 73-81.

H. Leibenstein, *Beyond Economic Man*. Cambridge: Harvard University Press, 1976.

F. Machlup, *The Production and Distribution of Knowledge in the United States*. Princeton: Princeton University Press, 1962.

F. Malerba, "Learning by Firms and Incremental Technical Change" *Economic Journal* 102 (July), 1992, 845-859.

R.A. McCain, *A Framework for Cognitive Economics*. New York: Praeger, 1992.

D. Miller, "A Preliminary Typology of Organizational Learning: Synthesizing the Literature" *Journal of Management*, 22 (3), 1996, 485-505.

A.P. Minkler, "The Problem with Dispersed Knowledge: Firms in Theory and Practice" *Kyklos* 46 (4), 1993, 569-587.

P. Moati et E.M. Mouhoud, "Information et organisation de la production: vers une division cognitive du travail" *Economie appliquée* 46 (1), 1994, 47-73.

R.R. Nelson and S.G. Winter, *An Evolutionary Theory of Economic Change*. Cambridge: Harvard University Press, 1982.

E. C. Nevis, A. J. Dibella, J. M. Gould, "Understanding Organizations as Learning Systems" *Sloan Management Review*, Winter, 1995, 73-85.

G. Paquet, "L'économie non marchande dans l'économie de marchés: à la recherche d'un cadre de référence" *Revue d'économie politique*, 87, 4, 1977, 607-625.

G. Paquet, "From the Information Economy to Evolutionary Cognitive Economics" in R. E. Babe (Ed.) *Information and Communication in Economics*, Boston: Kluwer Academic Publishers, 1994, 34-40.

M.U. Porat, *The Information Economy*. Washington: U.S. Department of Commerce, 1977.

G.B. Richardson, *Information and Investment*. Oxford: Oxford University Press, 1960.

H. Saint-Onge, "Tacit Knowledge: The Key to the Strataegic Alignment of Intellectual Capital" *Strategy and Leadership*, March-April, 1996, 10-14.

D.A. Schön, *The Reflective Practitioner*. New York: Basic Books, 1983.
T.A. Stewart, *Intellectual Capital*. New York: Doubleday/Currency, 1997.

Chapter 10

Evolutionary Cognitive Economics

*"What is now needed is a far-from-equilibrium
information economics which allows for innovation,
evolution, and learning."*

−Max Boisot

Introduction

An economic system is a set of conversations, rationales, protocols, conventions, organizations, and institutions, providing the coordination and the orientation maps to ensure a viable process of production, allocation, and distribution of goods, services and information for a population. It can also be defined as the communication system that underpins this process of coordination of production and exchange.

It is one of the great merits of information economists to have generated a greater awareness (1) of the extent to which economic systems have been transformed, over the last few decades, from arrangements centered on the production, allocation, and distribution of material goods to arrangements with a focus on knowledge production; and (2) of the extraordinarily crude simplifications that the conventional neo-classical paradigm has imposed on its analyses of the economy as communication system. Machlup (1962), Porat (1977) and others have shown that there has been a dematerialization of economic activity; Hayek (1945), Shackle (1949), Simon (1955), Boulding (1956) and others have demonstrated in quite different ways how inadequate the neo-classical approach has been in its treatment of the knowledge base of modern economies.

233

Our objective in this note is to build on this second strand of argument, in order to show that whatever heuristic power the neo-classical paradigm may have had in other times, it has become inadequate to deal with contemporary realities. In the first section, we will indicate briefly why this is the case. In the following section, we outline the contours of a heuristically powerful alternative paradigm based on cognitive and evolutionary economics. We then proceed in section 3 to show how this alternative paradigm reveals new terrains and suggests new prescriptions. In conclusion, we bemoan the fact that it is unlikely that this paradigm will yield its full complement of insights in the near future: the neo-classical paradigm is a sacred cow, and putting it out to pasture may take a little while.

The limitations of the conventional paradigm

Perfect information has been a traditional assumption of neo-classical economics. Market economies have been presumed to be composed of autonomous mildly self-reflective individuals, optimizing their objective function subject to constraints, and these individuals have been assumed to know what they wanted, and to know their environment. Nobody bothered to inquire as to where that knowledge was coming from (Piore 1995:100). Numerous theorems were constructed on these foundations, showing that, in a perfectly competitive world, these omniscient agents would be induced to take action that would lead to a social optimum making the highest and best use of existing resources.

Many have been uneasy about this triplet of assumptions: (1) perfect information, (2) perfect competition, and (3) a focus on allocative efficiency within a fairly static Newtonian economic world (Boisot 1995:11). This condition has generated two sets of responses: one has been bent on exorcising some of the unreasonableness of the first two assumptions, without damaging the overall Newtonian economics edifice; while the other has been geared to constructing a viable alternative paradigm to the Newtonian edifice that allocative efficiency concerns have built.

In the first case, this has led to the blooming of frictional economics: a variety of scenarios to get around the pure and perfect competition assumption (from the transaction costs world of Coase (1937, 1960) and Williamson (1975, 1985) to the contestable markets of Baumol et al. (1982) but also to thirty years of exploration of a world where perfect information might not prevail (when information is costly, asymmetric, etc.), and therefore calling for slight amendments to the traditional analytical apparatus to accommodate the ensuing friction.

In the second case, this has led to a variety of alternative *weltanschauungen*: from Hayek (1945) and the numerous economists working in the Austrian tradition (see O'Driscoll and Rizzo 1985 for a good overview), and their emphasis on the role of knowledge and discovery, to the exploration of cognitive structures (Boulding 1956), to the abandonment of the Newtonian equilibrium models altogether in favor of the study of adaptive or Schumpeterian efficiency and chaotic evolutionary processes (Leydesdorff and van den Besselaar 1994).

Despite these responses, the neo-classical paradigm still reigns supreme in the economics profession. Even the recent attempts at building syncretic information economics perspectives, by the admission of their authors (McCain 1992; Lamberton 1994; Boisot 1995; Castells 1996), have not produced "the new viable paradigm" likely to be adopted as a new vision of the world by the economics profession.

This is ascribable to a variety of reasons.

First, the immense amount of intellectual capital invested in the traditional paradigm, and the most effective protective belt and "dynamic conservatism" generated by the very exclusive process of hiring, promotion and publication that exists within the economics profession (Katouzian 1980), have made it very difficult for anyone who is not a member of the tribe to achieve any position of authority in the most influential economics departments.

Second, there has been an unfortunate tendency, even among the very best information economists, to avoid confrontation with the traditional tribe, and to continue to regard information as "a commodity", albeit "only to a limited extent" (Lamberton 1994); this has been the case even though Lamberton and others recognized that "economic activity is a process, its participants having both histories and contexts", and that "progress lies in learning" (our emphasis). If this is the case, communication and information cannot simply be reduced to the level of physical inputs (Paquet 1994), and informational resources allocated like physical resources.

Third, there has been a fundamental misunderstanding generated by the focus on information processing, rather than on knowledge production, in the development of the alternative paradigm. This has sterilized much of the work in information economics, for attention has been focused exclusively on explicit information flows processed by rational actors, while much of cognition is buried in tacit knowledge. This has derailed information economics away from the problem of cognition (Baumard 1996).

Yet despite those blockages, three fundamental challenges have been mounted against the ruling paradigm, and would appear not to have been countered:

(1) there may not be a need to build our view of the world, as the neo-classical paradigm does, on autonomous individual rational decision-making: first, because there are numerous reasons to believe that this "irrational passion for rationality" is most unrealistic; and second, because the most simplistic irrational behavior might yield the traditional results through simple natural selection processes (Perlman 1990);

(2) the focus on the pursuit of static efficiency in the use of existing resources (that has prevailed in the neo-classical paradigm) is at odd with the central concern for social learning as a way to progressivity (i.e., the right evolving mix of exploration of new processes and exploitation of existing processes) that underpins modern economies (de la Mothe and Paquet 1996);

(3) the link between an actor's or a group's representation of the world and contextual reality may not be as unproblematic as is presumed by the neo-classical paradigm: all sort of rationales, cognitive structures, conventions, and institutions are mediating the relationships between agents and context in fundamental ways, and are in many ways more meaningful units of analysis than either agents, organizations, or context.

The evolutionary cognitive paradigm

These flaws in the traditional paradigm (an undue focus on individual instrumental rationality, an unduly static view of the world, and an unduly parsimonious characterization of the complex world of cognition) would appear to warrant our exploring other avenues.

The challenges that the new paradigm must face are

(1) to ensure that the centrality of cognition as a neural and social process is factored into the analysis, and that there is full appreciation that the process of cognition is neither unbounded nor costless, nor unbiased;

(2) to ensure that a realistic appreciation of the structures of the socio-economy organized around knowledge production replaces the antiquated industrial-age images of the socio-economy organized around energy and material resources; and

(3) to ensure that one can explicate the dynamic joint processes of exploration and exploitation in organizational learning and in the evolution of the institutional order.

In the next two sub-sections, we describe (i) the novel approach suggested by cognitive theory, and (ii) the new mechanisms unveiled by evolutionary theory. We then show in the third subsection how these might be combined into a new evolutionary cognitive economics paradigm.

i.   Even though we have covered this territory to a certain extent in the last chapter when describing the "promised land" to which Don Lamberton was taking the economics profession, it may be useful to repeat the core message of cognitive economics. It examines the process of extraction of information from the environment through perception, and the development of knowledge through communication. In this framework, information exists to the extent that it becomes embodied in the brain as a pattern or in an artifact (capital) designed to act as a surrogate for the brain. Instead of focusing on the allocation of existing informational resources, cognitive economics focuses on the production of new knowledge.

Cognitive economics focuses on cognition as the source of meaningful, i.e., behaviorally-relevant information, and aims at developing a higher ratio of meaningful information to noise through an improvement of the various information/communication enhancement mechanisms: more effective skills at extracting patterns, easier transformation of frames of reference, reduction of cognitive dissonance, etc.

But cognition is neither unbounded, nor costless, nor unbiased. Leibenstein and Simon have done much to show that human reasoning proceeds through selective search by applying rules of thumb, and that such a search stops when a satisfactory solution is found (Weiermair and Perlman 1990; Simon 1992). This sort of search builds on experience, and is therefore conditioned by the existence of frameworks that evolve over time both through interaction with the environment and with other agents. This family of readinesses or interpretative frames is a series of filters that stand between agents and their environment. These frames may either accelerate or decelerate a capacity for an individual to learn from experience (Ciborra 1990). Such frameworks may be culturally determined, but they are not invariant. They evolve as a result of experience and context, through selection and mutation.

Knowledge is not only objective and social. It is often subjective and idiosyncratic. There are forms of connoisseurship or tacit knowledge that may be non-communicable, but may allow one to develop a winning strategy (Baumard 1996). This sort of knowledge may be the result of implicit learning or the embodiment of much social practice. It takes the form of a sort of *flair* that one may not be able to explain, but that is nevertheless useable knowledge.

Cognition does not occur only at the individual level. Creative individuals can rarely reach their goals in isolation. They operate in the context of organizations embodying a communication network. Organizations also learn from experience. Experiences with real-world groups (Hutchins 1991) have shown that new circumstances or breakdown/loss of perceptual equipment, generate new stable work configurations that are not unlike a modified neuronal network.

There are also interactions between organizational learning and cognitive structures: framing a challenge as a puzzle means that it will be receiving some attention, while framing it as an anomaly may simply mean that it will be ignored and rationalized away. In the first case, learning is probable; in the second case, most unlikely (Kahneman and Tversky 1979).

ii.   Evolutionary economics is built on the assumption of limited cognitive capabilities, for both humans and organizations. This entails a continuous process of trial and error. And since the cost of thinking is not zero, once some appreciation of context has been arrived at, routines, conventions, and standard procedures are adopted that would appear to ensure survival or satisficing performance.

These routines, rooted in context and history, are embedded in a pattern of rationales, rules, conventions, and institutions that provide the process of decision-making and learning with unity and stability. In this world, the meaningful units of analysis are the parallel patterns of belief systems and mental representations and techno-organizational conventions and rules in which the process is vested.

At any time, these representations and rules may be more or less fitting, i.e., they may be more or less effective socio-technical armistices between the evolving physical environment, and the evolving values and plans of agents and groups. The degree of fitness is not invariant as circumstances change: it is rooted in the probability of survival and in the capacity to develop the requisite competences and capabilities to survive.

Given the always imperfect nature of the mental representations, and of the conventions and rules, and the mistake-ridden learning process, the modification of both representations and rules constitutes the way in which the socio-economy evolves, transforms and learns. This learning may be more or less effective, depending on the nature of the challenges generated by the environment, and the nature of the competences, readinesses, and reactive capacities of agents and organizations. For instance, the pattern of representations and rules may easily accommodate minor variations in the environment, and adapt quickly to these new circumstances. However, it may only be capable of limited learning within a narrow band of circumstances. In the face of radical changes in the environment that call for a dramatic reframing of representations, rules and conventions, it may mainly generate a great deal of cognitive dissonance and dynamic conservatism, and be incapable of learning (Ciborra 1990:210).

Indeed, as Nelson and Winter have shown (1982), organizations tend to stick to their usual routine as long as performance remains above certain target levels. It is only when performance indicators fall below such levels that the organization searches for better alternatives.

This balance between the exploitation of the available knowledge and the exploration and search for new knowledge and new possibilities (underlined by March (1991) is closely related to the mechanisms of selection and mutation: a procedure or routine that performs well being adopted by the system (i.e., a higher probability of survival being bestowed on it) in the case of selection, while some misfit between routines and the changing milieu may lead to a mutation in the routine or procedure (Dosi and Marengo 1994).

Evolution emerges from this process of mutual learning between agents and organizations, in the form of the parallel and interactive processes of selection and mutation. This learning may be faster or slower, depending on the nature of the organization. For instance, hierarchical organizations may be able to filter out new local events and prevent learning of certain sorts: the design of organizations most efficient for knowledge exploitation purposes may lead to learning disabilities in exploration, and to organizations that have lesser exploratory competences.

Toulmin has sorted change mechanisms into four categories (Toulmin 1981).

Calculative change is triggered by rational choice, as employed by mainstream economic theory; homeostatic change occurs in response to stimuli in accordance with fixed rules, as in single-loop learning in an organization (using new means); development change is typified by life-cycle theories and might correspond to instances of double-loop learning (learning new goals), i.e., to the restructuring of the selecting unit, its goals or mission; finally, populational change is triggered by changes in the environment and in the adoption of selective units (i.e., a change in its probability of being adopted and nurtured by the environment) – natural selection.

An adaptation-adoption model built entirely on the sole calculative and populational forces of change is somewhat simplistic. Individuals, more or less deliberately, create institutions and organizations that evolve, and inject homeostatic and development changes. The nature of organizations, and the modification of their rules of functioning, may dramatically affect the direction and speed of the learning process: new information may either feed or inhibit evolution, and the cognition process may accelerate or decelerate the process of change. Indeed, one may even have to unlearn in order to be able to progress. Evolution is not unbounded, but evolutionary epistemology is already a blossoming field, capable of clarifying these boundaries (Hahlweg and Hooker 1989).

iii.   The concerns raised by the neo-classical paradigm over the last century have generated a large number of efforts at constructing meaningful alternative paradigms. Many of these efforts have been carried out under the general flag of a *refurbished cognitive approach* (Piore 1992) and others under the label of an *evolutionary approach* (Witt 1993). However, most of those efforts, despite much imagination, have been unable to shake off more than a few of the shackles with which the neo-classical paradigm is burdened. A reasonable and workable alternative to the traditional paradigm might be what we call the evolutionary cognitive paradigm, (ECP), built on a more realistic appreciation of both cognition and the evolutionary processes.

In a summary way,

1. the ECP posits a complex and turbulent environment;
2. it also assumes bounded and selective rationality, and imperfect mental representations;
3. great importance is given to cognitive structures as filters in the cognition process;
4. the unit of analysis is the pattern or the net of relationships: the cognitive representations, technical arrangements, and organizational routines within which mistake-ridden individual and organizational learning occurs;
5. the governing relation is the fitness of pattern and milieu;
6. the dynamics stems from a mixture of milieu selection mechanisms adopting the most viable patterns, representations, rationales, rules and conventions on the one hand, and network mutation activities through which the rationales, rules and patterns adapt to the evolving milieu;
7. this sort of adaptation/adoption dynamics operates at many levels, and in different segments of the network space, and it is the resulting mix of specialization and integration that ensues transversally that distills the institutional order;
8. the institutional order is the set of orientation maps guiding the co-evolution of patterns, networks, absorptive capacity, capabilities,

and competences with the regimes in force in the contextual environment.

There is a degree of congruence between the neural net character of the cognitive structures and the neural net character of the learning organizational/institutional networks. In both cases, learning is akin to the transformation of the pattern. Both the neural network and the social networks are self-organizing information systems. Indeed, both the cognitive space and the organizational/institutional space are self-organizing neural net patterns of the kind to be found in a living brain, where the nodes are neurons or nerve cells, connected both locally, and over long distance, by fibrous dendrites and axons, and are organized in layer structures.

This connectionist model suggests that "a layered system of many signal-processing units, interconnected and interacting in parallel within and between layers, has some remarkable properties" (Ziman 1991:74). By allowing each node to respond to incoming signals, a neural net can learn pattern recognition. For neither the cognition nor the organizational/institutional process are passively receiving information: they are actively pattern searching. Our mind invents and imposes patterns where none existed previously. The same may be said about the organizational-institutional network: "parallel regions in the network search for similar patterns, some of which can be combined to demonstrate the presence or absence of higher order patterns" (Coward 1990: 59).

It is in the invention of those higher order patterns that creativity lies. Both in our cognitive and organizational spaces, different neural nets extract different patterns and combine them to produce and integrate recognizable wholes. The mind and the organization recreate the whole or invent a new whole: learning is about pattern extraction capability, and about the ways in which one can integrate in parallel (or in a cascading way) the diversity of patterns extracted by different regions of the brain or of the organization. Evolutionary development is no quantum leap: it is a smooth progression of developing complexity by adding connections and cascading patterns to the cognitive or organizational space (Coward 1990:76).

To build the ability to analyze and respond to radically different types of experience requires a transformation of the patterns, a creation of new regions the mobilization of unused neurons, and the development of new connection sensitivities (1) to support patterns-extraction experiences that are analogous to those the brain or organization has experienced, but reframed somewhat, and perceived in a slightly different way; and (2) to generate pattern cascades from previously disparate regions of experiences, and to make new cascade patterns (Coward 1990; Ziman 1991).

New terrains, new prescriptions

The evolutionary cognitive paradigm, based on individual and organizational learning in a world of bounded and selective rationality, pattern thinking, pattern causality, self-organization and evolutionary change, opens new vistas and forces the revision of many prescriptions. This is not the place for a comprehensive list of such new insights. But a few examples of new terrains open to investigation, and of new prescriptions, might help to fix ideas about the heuristic power of the new paradigm.

i.   Chief among the new terrains open to exploration by the new paradigm are three areas pregnant with new insights into the structure and functioning of modern economies.

First, one must single out the world of inert areas, selective rationality, cognitive filters and cognitive failures that has been probed and analyzed in the mildly heterodox literature over the last decades (Leibenstein 1976; Kahneman and Tversky 1979; Akerlof and Dickens 1982; Mc-Cain 1992). Their surprising results have been interpreted as a string of anomalies. Consequently, they were either ignored or rationalized away.

Yet those results have opened a new frontier in economics and in public policy. They invite an analysis of the power of mediating cognitive structures (Elster 1989; Frey 1990) and an inquiry into areas like the cognitive basis of entrepreneurship, the search for novelty, creativity, and impulse-filtering in organizations.

In all those areas that have been somewhat neglected by neo-classical economics, the evolution of belief systems and cognitive structures has become a subject of more attentive analyses. They have also become the focus of public policy in a way that had been anticipated by Simon and Leibenstein: cognitive economics has simply been intent on extending and radicalizing many of their ideas on cognition.

Second, the whole area of norms, conventions, routine patterns and other organizational features (the organizational equivalent of cognitive structures) has also become of central importance. The *pattern of relationships* is the new unit of analysis: this is the world of rationales, techno-organizational patterns, networks, and moral contracts. They are embodied in neural-network-type relationships that are very similar to those that embody knowledge in the brain: learning or the production of new knowledge takes the form of a new pattern of relationships, and social learning means embodiment in a new set of relationships (North 1996).

The reconfiguration of the net, either by the addition of one node or by the modification of its structure through a change in the valence of one node, or the connections with it, is the vehicle of change, and therefore of collective learning (Favereau 1994).

Third, the new centrality of patterns of relationships cannot but bring to the center of the stage the challenge of understanding the dynamics of evolutionary self-organized economic systems.

These issues have already caught the attention of even those most determined to work within the neo-classical paradigm (Schelling 1978; Leydesdorff and Van Den Besselaar 1994; Krugman 1996). While this new approach in terms of self-organization is nothing but another name for network learning, it suggests a new interest in network externalities, Myrdalian cumulative processes, dynamic increasing returns, cumulative technologies, and emergent properties of complex systems.

This constitutes a world quite different from the Newtonian world of neo-classical economics. It is a world full of non-linearities, where old-fashioned predictability is becoming much more difficult, if not completely impossible, and where emergent properties are the new rule. Moreover, the ECP provides for interesting ways to take into consideration biased representations and cognitive structures as major elements in the shaping of path-dependent long-run trends (North 1996).

ii   This new paradigm is bound to force much reformulation in our analyses and policy prescriptions.

First, the new paradigm focuses on rules of thumb, or routines or patterns that are rooted in belief systems and cognitive structures, and embedded in a social context. It is therefore impossible to presume that individuals accultured in certain ways, or whose circumstances are different, would elect the same strategies. Economics needs to address language and culture as filters, and the socio-cultural context as an important component in the emergence of certain rationales, conventions, and rules. This might help to gauge the impact of cultural and belief systems (noted by Hampden-Turner and Trompenaars 1993) and the social capital effects (noted by Putnam 1995) on the institutional order and on economic performance (North 1996).

In this search for an interpretation of belief systems and context, *technical rationality* is not as helpful a guide as positivists have suggested. It leads to a "dilemma of rigor and relevance": it fails to provide useable knowledge to practitioners as long as the analysts pretend to stay outside the concreteness of experience. The analysts are forced to track down pattern causality in their investigation of collective learning: they work like a plumber, tracing back "a leak to its source ... through a chain of possible causes ... at different locations in the system ... on the basis of a background knowledge of the system, which is commonplace and largely tacit" (Schon 1995:83).

Policy action in such a context has to deal directly with the cognitive structures and belief systems, with the cultural filters, with the perception of the diffuse pattern causality, and even with social capital, as a way of addressing the problem of economic performance, rather than counting exclusively on modifying the incentive reward system of monads (Tussman 1977).

Second, the requirement to shift the focus of analysis away from idealized individuals to patterns of action, routines, etc., is bound to shift much of the analyses toward a probing of the cognitive and learning styles of organizations, in an effort to understand and to influence the cumulative learning process that is at the source of good economic performance and progressivity.

Organizations, like individuals, have patterns of cognition and learning.

Case studies have documented their differential capacity to navigate the whole field of individual and collective, and explicit and tacit knowledge (represented as a 2x2 table): the particular type of knowledge management and learning strategy adopted (its capacity to make sequentially the highest and best use of the four types of knowledge – (individual/explicit, individual/tacit, collective/explicit and collective/tacit) explains the success or failure of an organization (Baumard 1996). There is no unique path through this 2x2 matrix any more than a set of rigid sequential rules for a surfer: much depends on the context and on the particular capabilities of the organization.

Baumard's case studies of the strategic management of knowledge by Indigo, Qantas, Pechiney and Indosuez have revealed that difficult and ambiguity-laden crises are resolved at the meso level, at the level of the community of practice, that actors develop attitudes calling for tacit alliances and informal relations, and that their actions use repertories of routines that are in good currency in the organization, and rely on local collective knowledge (Baumard 1996:195).

Third, the recognition of the immense importance of tacit knowledge in individual and social learning has led to much interest in the possibility of designing *loci of conversation and creativity* equipped to make the highest and best use of this reservoir of knowledge. In a rapidly evolving, surprise-generating context, organizations are the locus of ongoing conversations that will produce new knowledge and add value through networking and partnering. And these conversations are more fruitful at the level of the community of practice. That is the central message of Wikstrom and Normann (1994): the value-creating process is the result of coproduction through interlinkages and conversations among all partners. The main challenge is to determine what is the best way to organize knowledge production, if the objective is to generate an organization characterized by learning and innovation.

Corporate culture generally embodies unwritten principles meant to generate a relatively high level of coordination at low cost by bestowing identity and membership (Kreps 1990). This corporate culture is nested at the organization level in the central features of work practice: stories of flexible generality about events of practice that act as repositories of accumulated wisdom, the evolution of these stories constituting collective learning of an evolving way to interpret conflicting and confusing data, but also an ongoing social construction of a community of interpretation.

It is not easy to construct a robust corporate culture. It is fundamentally a matter of trust. Trust is at the core of the fabric of the communities of practice. Trust is a way to transform "laborers into members", to convert an employment contract into a membership covenant: "the concept of membership, when made real, would replace the sense of belonging to a place with a sense of belonging to a community" (Handy 1995). And belonging is one of the most powerful agents of mobilization. One may therefore expect a redefinition of work as conversation, as sharing stories, and as becoming a member of a community of practice as suggested in the writings of Peters (1994) and Handy (1995).

Conclusion

But no reform of economics should be expected overnight. "For the reformer has enemies in all those who profit by the old order, and only lukewarm defenders in all those who would profit by the new order, this lukewarmness arising partly from fear of their adversaries, who have the laws in their favour; and partly from the incredulity of mankind, who do not truly believe in anything new until they have had actual experience of it" (Machiavelli (orig. 1537) 1952:49-50)

It is only when economists have developed, on the one hand, a much greater awareness of the results generated by cognitive science over the last few decades, and, on the other hand, a much greater appreciation of the complexity of the socio-political nexus of organizations and institutions that one may hope that a new synthesis might emerge.

Some progress has already been made on the second front. There is some recognition of the need to enrich the neo-classical paradigm with a better appreciation of organizational and institutional issues (Langlois

1986, 2007). There are already journals and forums where these issues are debated. On the first front, little progress has been made up to now because of the mental block surrounding rational decision-making as an icon. But the McCain synthesis in 1992 and the Nobel lecture of Douglass North in 1993 indicated that the time for a breakthrough may be near (McCain 1992; North 1996).

Moreover, evolutionary economic models have explored a relatively large array of situations in which both cognitive and organizational issues have been explicitly taken into account. And they have begun to do so in a formalized manner in places like the *Journal of Evolutionary Economics*. This is not unimportant.

As the 2008 Nobel Laureate economist Paul Krugman noted, in the present context of the economics profession, "an academic idea flourishes best if it is expressed in a rather technical way, even if the technical difficulty is largely spurious" (Krugman 1996:16). So, given the taste for pyrotechnics in the economics profession, one may expect that some technical versions of the ECP may become widely disseminated within the economics profession over the next decade.

But the likely scenario is that the evolutionary cognitive paradigm will subsist in the underground until such time as one *cause célèbre* is found that demonstrates quite dramatically that the new paradigm generates dramatically different policy recommendations in a domain of acute public concern. It is only on the occasion of such crises that there may be a hope to see a "representational redescription" (as North might call it).

But this cautiously optimistic scenario may be unrealistic, for many such occasions have presented themselves and have been missed. Nelson and Winter's classic book did not have anything but a *succès d'estime* in 1982, even though it proposed new insights for the explanation of the productivity slowdown of the 1970s that had stumped the profession. One must therefore not underestimate the formidable resilience (another name for a capacity for dynamic conservatism) of some of those neo-classical ideas perpetrated by defunct economists.

References

Akerlof, G. A. and W. T. Dickens, The economic consequences of cognitive dissonance. *American Economic Review* 72 (3), 1982, 307-319.

Baumard, P. *Organisations déconcertées: la gestion stratégique de la connaissance.* (Masson, Paris) 1996.

Baumol, W., J. Panzar and R. Willig. *Contestable markets and the theory of industry structure* (Harcourt Brace Jovanovich, New York) 1982.

Boisot, M. *Information space* (Routledge, London) 1995

Boulding, K. E., *The image* (The University of Michigan Press, Ann Arbor) 1956

Castells, M. *The rise of the network society* (Blackwell, Oxford) 1996

Coborra, C.U., "X-efficiency, transaction costs, and organizational change". In: Weiermair, K. and M. Perlman (Eds) *Studies in economic rationality - X-efficiency examined and extolled: Essays written in the tradition of and to honor Harvey Leibenstein* (The University of Michigan Press, Ann Arbor), 1990, 205-222.

Coase, R., The nature of the firm, *Economica*, 4, 1937, 386-405.

Coase, R., The problem of social cost, *Journal of Law and Economics* 3 (1), 1960, 1-44.

Coward, L.A. *Pattern thinking* (Praeger, Westport, Conn.) 1990

de la Mothe, J. and G. Paquet (Eds) 1996, *Evolutionary economics and the new international political economy*, (Pinter, London) 1996

Dosi, G. and L. Marengo, 1994, Some elements of an evolutionary theory of organizational competences. In: England, R. W. (Ed) *Evolutionary concepts in contemporary economics* (The University of Michigan Press, Ann Arbor), 157-178.

Elster, J. *Nuts and bolts for the social sciences* (Cambridge University Press: Cambridge) 1989.

Favereau, O., Règle, organisation et apprentissage collectif: un paradigme non-standard pour trois théories hétérodoxes. In: Orléan, A., (Ed.) 1994, *Analyse économique des conventions* (Presses Universitaires de France, Paris), 113-137.

Frey, B. S. "Human behavior: ipsative and objective possibilities." In: Weiermair, K. and M. Perlman (Eds) *Studies in economic rationality - X-efficiency examined and extolled: Essays written in the tradition of and to honor Harvey Leibenstein* (The University of Michigan Press, Ann Arbor), 1990, 71-93.

Hahlweg, K. and C.A. Hooker (Eds), *Issues in evolutionary epistemology* (State University of New York Press, Albany) 1989.

Hampden-Turner, C. and A. Trompenaars *The seven cultures of capitalism* (Currency/Doubleday, New York) 1993

Handy, C. Trust and the virtual organization, *Harvard Business Review* 73 (3), 1995, 40-50.

Hayek, F.A, The use of knowledge in society, *American Economic Review* 35 (4), 1945 19-530.

Hutchins, E., Organizing work by adaptation, *Organization Science* 2 (1), 1991, 14-39.

Kahneman, D. and A. Tversky, Prospect theory: an analysis of decision under risk, *Econometrica* 47 (2), 1979, 263-291.

Katouzian, H., , *Ideology and method in economics*, (New York University Press: New York) 1980..

Kreps, D. M. Corporate culture and economic theory. In: Alt, J. E. and K. A. Shepsle (Eds) *Perspectives on Positive Political Economy*, (Cambridge University Press, Cambridge) 1990, 90- 143.

Krugman, P.R. *The self-organizing economy* (Blackwell: Oxford) 1996

Lamberton, D.M. The information economy revisited. In: Babe, R.E. (Ed.) *Information and communication in economics* (Kluwer Academic Publishers, Boston), 1994, 1-33.

Langlois, R.N. (Ed.), *Economics as process - Essays in the new institutional economics* (CambridgeUniversity Press, Cambridge) 1986

Langlois, R.N. *The Dynamics of Industrial Capitalism – The Graz Schumpeter Lectures* (Routledge, London) 2007

Leibenstein, H. *Beyond economic man* (Harvard University Press, Cambridge) 1976.

Leydesdorff, L. and P. van den Besselaar (Eds) *Evolutionary economics and chaos theory* (Pinter: London) 1994.

Machiavelli, N. *The Prince* (Mentor Book, New York) 1952 (orig. 1537)

Machlup, F, *The production and distribution of knowledge in the United States*, (Princeton University Press, Princeton) 1962.

March, J. G. Exploration and Exploitation in Organizational Learning, *Organization Science* 2 (1), 1991, 71-87.

McCain, R. A., *A framework for cognitive economics* (Praeger, Westport, Conn.) 1992

Nelson, R. R. and S. G. Winter, *An evolutionary theory of economic change* (Harvard University Press, Cambridge) 1982

North, D.C., Economic performance through time. In:. Alston, L. J. Eggertsson, T. and North, D.C. (Eds) *Empirical studies in institutional change* (Cambridge University Pres: Cambridge) 1996, 342-355.

O'Driscoll, G. P. and M. J. Rizzo (Eds) *The economics of time and ignorance*, (Blackwell, Oxford) 1985.

Paquet, G., From the information economy to evolutionary cognitive economics. In: Babe, R. E. (Ed.) *Information and communication in economics* (Kluwer Academic Publishers, Boston), 1994, 34-40

Perlman, M. The evolution of X-efficiency theory. In: Weiermair, K. and M. Perlman (Eds) *Studies in economic rationality - X-efficiency examined and extolled: Essays written in the tradition of and to honor Harvey Leibenstein* (The University of Michigan Press, Ann Arbor), 1990, 7- 25.

Peters, T. 1994, *Crazy times call for crazy organizations* (Vintage, New York).

Piore, M.J. Fragments of a cognitive theory of technological change and organizational structure. In: Nohria, N. and R.G. Eccles (Eds), *Networks and organizations* (Harvard Business School Press, Boston), 1992, 430-444.

Piore, M.J. *Beyond individualism* (Harvard University Press, Cambridge) 1995

Porat, M.U., *The information economy* (U.S. Government Printing Office, Washington) 1977

Putnam, R.D. Bowling alone: America's declining social capital, *Journal of Democracy* 6 (1), 1995, 65-78.

Schelling, T, *Micromotives and macrobehavior* (Norton, New York) 1978.

Schon, D.A., Causality and causal Inference in the study of organizations. In: Goodman, R.F. and W.R. Fisher (Eds) *Rethinking knowledge* (State University of New York, Albany) 1995, 69- 101.

Shackle, G.L.S., *Expectations in economics* (The University Press, Cambridge) 1949

Simon, H.A., A behavioral model of rational choice, *Quarterly Journal of Economics*, 59, 1955, 99-118.

Simon, H.A., et al., *Economics, bounded rationality and the cognitive revolution* (Edward Elgar, Aldershot) 1992

Toulmin, S. Human adaptation. In: Jensen, U. and R. Harre (Eds) *The philosophy of evolution* (St Martin's Press, New York) 1981

Tussman, J., 1977, *Government and the mind* (Oxford University Press, New York)

Wikstrom, S. and R. Normann *Knowledge and Value* (Routledge, London) 1994.

Williamson, O. E. *Markets and hierarchies* (The Free Press, New York) 1975

Williamson, O. E. *The economic institutions of capitalism* (The Free Press, New York) 1985

Witt, U. (Ed.) *Evolutionary economics* (Edward Elgar, Aldershot) 1993

Ziman, J. A neural net model of innovation *Science and Public Policy* 18 (1), 1991, 65-75.

Conclusion

Guideposts on the road to collaborative governance

"...de nouvelles subversions sont possibles..."

–Marc Guillaume

Introduction

This conclusion (in the manner of the Handover Note submitted by the Head of Mission for his successor when an ambassador leaves his post) can only give a sketchy personal appreciation of what remains to be done. It is bound not to be comprehensive, and to be somewhat idiosyncratic.

First, it underlines the centrality of the concern for cognition, knowledge production, and learning as the key levers, and says a few words about the task at hand: transforming the neural net of patterns and cascades of cognition, conversation, and organization that underpin and make up the institutional order, so as to promote a broader and richer multilogue both at the national level and in the different issue domains.

Second, it indicates what public intellectuals should regard as their burden of office in the efforts to nudge the cognition, organizational and institutional orders toward a more effective collaborative governance: in a world where no one is in charge, the public intellectuals must accept their roles as catalysts, connectors, reframers.

Third, it points to the even more important role of the citizenry in the construction of the required collaborative governance regime: for active citizens must of necessity get involved as producers of governance, and must be provided with the means to do their governing work.

Fourth, it draws attention to the ethical corridor that must be kept

251

in mind in this ongoing tinkering. Collaborative governance will entail the forging of a multitude of conventions, moral contracts, norms and rules that will have to meet certain standards to be regarded as ethically sound, as within the bounds that define legitimacy and propriety.

Finally, it draws attention to the centrality of the notion of contingent moral contracts and reflexivity in the generation of the new arrays of flexible patterns, cascades, and mechanisms necessary for collaborative governance to be nudged into existence.

The connectionist perspective

As explained in the last chapter, but also as illustrated in the different design sketches of Part III, the governing relation is the fitness of pattern and milieu: the challenge is to add connections and cascading patterns to the cognitive and organizational/institutional space. The new unit of analysis is the pattern of relationships, and the challenge is not to redesign the whole texture and conversational substance of the net of relationships by decree, but to partake in the reconfiguration of the net by the addition of nodes, by some tinkering with the valence of certain nodes, by modifying the messages and connections ever so slightly so as to trigger evolutionary self-organization, novelty, and creativity – i.e., collective learning.

For at the core of this view of the world is self-organization – a nexus of forces that social scientists have largely ignored. Such forces (both cognitive and organizational) have been shown in both spatial and temporal contexts to be able to generate dynamics where somewhat unstable (or not completely stable) arrangements, in the face of random perturbations, tend to get reconfigured as a result of slight changes in the underpinnings of either the cognitive or the organizational space through self-organization.

Schelling (1978) has shown that introducing mild preference about the culture of your neighbour, quite consistent with maintaining an integrated residential pattern, typically lead to a high degree of segregation: local short-range interactivity creating large-scale organizational change. In the same spirit, Krugman (1996) has speculated on the synchronization forces that bring socio-economies like the USA and the EU (trading with each other a very small portion of their output, and therefore with limited interdependence) to see their levels of economic activities suffering from phase locking.

In all such self-organizing worlds, there always are some critical thresholds at which, after gradual change that left the system unmoved, an additional minute change sets the system adrift in search of a new equilibrium. The whole management literature on tipping points is based on the recognition that a better understanding of the cognitive and organizational space reveals where the system might afford the possibility of effective intervention (Shapiro 2003).

Such interventions need not (and often cannot) be orchestrated from above. Indeed, the complexity of the neural net cognition and organization space is such that it poses wicked problems to potential interveners. On the one hand, unintended consequences, network externalities and cumulative causation at critical points – part of the dynamics of self-organization – often swamp the original intervention and neutralize or distort its impact; on the other hand, these forces may, if one has a fair strategic understanding of the interface between cognition and organization, and of the dynamics of self-organization, amplify and enrich the impact of an anonymous intervention in an open-source context.

The burden of office of a public intellectual

The public intellectual is a person or concern that "expresses himself in a way that is accessible to the public, and the focus of his expression is on matters of general public concern". Richard Posner adds that the intellectual often has an ideological or political cast, but he need not be ideological (Posner 2001:35).

This definition underlines three broad features: the public intellectual expresses himself in the vernacular; he focuses his attention on matters of general public concern; and his discourse often has a political angle, i.e., is committed to promoting transformation and improvement in the polis, the community, and is presented not as a defence of any orthodoxy, but as the echo of "an incorrigibly independent soul answering to no one" (Jacoby 1987: 235).

To illustrate what such a creature might look like, Posner has suggested a list of genres of public intellectuals who have flourished in modern times, have acquired some legitimacy, and have proved value-adding to a certain extent. A few examples: those known for having worked at the popularization of their own research results (Amartya Sen), those who have built their public persona on own-field policy proposing (Milton Friedman), real-time commentators (George Orwell and Aldous Huxley), those generating prophetic commentaries (Alvin Toffler), jeremiahs (Christopher Lasch), public philosopher involved in social criticism (Richard Rorty), etc. If one were to put a Canadian flavour into this sort of list, the names of Marshall McLuhan, George Grant, and Charles Taylor come to mind, and, in the younger generation, those of Mark Kingwell, Joseph Heath, to name a few.

There was once a time when one could get the whole range of these characters between the covers of the same book (Ross 1954). This is no longer likely.

The decline of the public intellectual

It has been argued that there has been a decline of the public intellectual over the last while (Jacoby 1987). As college campuses became the new "home" of intellectuals, and academics became more and more specialized, and less and less interested in speaking to the general public, the vernacular was surrendered. Deans and colleagues were more interested in "how one fit in than in how one stood out", so in academe the monograph and lecture, and the grant application (not the essay) prospered (15, 31), so the public intellectual faded away. Indeed, even more so, as academe became captured by academic snobbery and ideologies in good currency, and paralyzed by the fear of being politically incorrect.

But the true meaning of the decline is not really a matter of numbers. In fact, there has been a multiplication, and a diversification of opinions, commentaries and essays on issues of public concern by an ever larger number of academic and non-academic babblers, using an ever larger number of channels of diffusion. Blogging is the latest generation of channels, allowing almost anyone with a modicum of means to send messages worldwide. The question is rather a problem of quality: as Jean-Jacques Simard would put, it "on n'a plus les intellectuels qu'on avait ... on n'a plus les grands intellectuels publics qu'on avait" (Simard 2003).

"C'est la légitimité d'un certain modèle de l'intellectuel qui est en déclin : ce personnage qui ayant établi son autorité dans un domaine éthéré de la culture seconde (arts, lettres, sciences) fait irruption sur la place publique, se "mêle de ce qui ne le regarde pas", s'engage dans les affaires générales, prend position, se fait conscience critique de la cité commune, pourfendeur du mensonge et de l'injustice, porteur de transcendance, allumeur d'avenir et défenseur d'éternité" (Simard 2003). "Allumeur d'avenir" ...what a nice and illuminating expression!

The public intellectual has two strikes against him: greater complexity of the context and polycentric collaborative governance. As the world has become more complex and the very notion of power has been transformed, public intellectuals came to be (1) not only criticized for their amateurism, but also (2) more and more unable to use their intellectual powers to influence the course of events, as governance came to be polycentric in a world where nobody is in charge (Cleveland 2002).

Is this gap worth filling?

These constraining features have not eliminated the role of the public intellectual. There is a value-adding function for persons or mechanisms that are capable of developing broader perspectives, of cutting through the jargon to get at the core issues, of adding to common knowledge, and of clarifying the matters of public concern thereby revealed, in a manner that is both accessible to the public, politically incorrect if necessary, but ensuring that the public policy consequences are fully explored and widely communicated.

Posner diagnosed the central challenge: "the market for public intellectuals is failing to deliver a product of high average quality" (388). The output of public intellectuals is a classic "credence good" -- a good that the consumer must take on faith because he cannot easily inspect it and determine its quality.

Under lax market discipline (poor information for consumers, no warranty for product quality, low exit costs for sellers detected selling poor quality products, etc.), the only protection the public has "against the high variance and low average quality of public intellectual work… (is)…*not taking it seriously*"(388).

The cost of this market failure is high, and modern universities (with their encouragement of professionalization and specialization of knowledge, but most importantly because of their profound conservatism) would appear congenitally incapable of taking on this task: crippled epistemologies are too deeply entrenched, and the taste for experimentation and prototyping has been extinguished. Yet there is a gap to be filled, and an opportunity to seize.

Can this gap be filled?

The answer is yes, but only if some prerequisites are fostered, and if the work of the public intellectual in catalyzing emergent publics is facilitated.

i.   basic prerequisites

The prerequisites for any one person or organization with ambitions to act as a public intellectual are well known: the shedding of pomposity, the courage to tackle taboo topics, and a capacity for meaning-making. These are not meant to be all inclusive, but indicative of certain basic elements that would appear to be essential if such an effort is to succeed.

Pomposity is a standard feature of persons or groups who claim to know. Since they are experts, they cannot learn: if they could learn, it would mean that they were not experts to begin with. Many want-to-be intellectuals are not immune to this illness. They may be either personally so arrogant or so immersed in technical jargon as to become incapable of engaging anyone's interest, or so much under the influence of an ideology as to make all their arguments highly predictable. Intellectuals have to develop an engaging public persona, whatever their personal character, if they wish to communicate and have any influence.

Tackling taboo topics is not everyone's cup of tea. The reason is that such topics, despite their importance, usually lead to some strong reactions both from those whose interests depend on the status quo, and from those who have a profound dislike for robust public debates – the congenital consensus-at-all-cost-through-no-confrontation-please types, those suffering from the collegiality disease. The latest incarnation of this refusal to debate is political correctness: a new form of despotism (Delsol 2005) that Alexis de Tocqueville had already anticipated when he foresaw that, in republican democracies, one would not be bodily mauled for holding different ideas, one would simply be ostracized. As Judge Sopinka used to say, political correctness is the most important restriction on the freedom of speech, and consequently on the freedom of thinking. Democracy feeds on robust debates; but such debates entail great personal cost when political correctness becomes "un nouveau et indolore despotisme".

Finally, the public intellectual must be in the business of making sense: the need for public intellectuals is rooted in "une fringale de sens". People want to understand. They want clarification of thorny issues; they want help in making sense of these issues. Meaning-making is the public intellectual's burden of office! If "meaning can be thought of as naming, interpreting, and making commitments to action, to other people, and to values, then meaning-making is the process of creating names, interpretations and commitments" (Drath and Palus 1994: 9). The public intellectual creates meaning and ways of understanding the world through words, plots, characters, metaphors, and stories, and suggests a framework within which to act.

ii. The dynamics of emergent publics

Of all these prerequisites, the most difficult to acquire is the capacity for meaning-making. The public intellectual is showing the limits of ideas in good currency, he is a critical thinker, an ironist. But word-smithing and story-telling do not suffice; there must be a new frame, making sense of the mess out there. There must be entrepreneurship in social change.

Public intellectuals are very much like entrepreneurs. Sometimes they are *gap-fillers*, persons who see that there is a missing link and forge it Sometimes they are *reframers* who provide an entirely new *manière de voir*, and thereby reveal an alternative reality that people were not aware they were missing. In general, they pose new questions: why is this gap not filled? why don't you see that this picture shows a young woman not an old one, a rabbit not a duck? When they describe, they evoke, they wish to create a social movement. Indeed, public intellectuals do not wish to preach in the desert, but wish to get an emergent public to come to life.

It starts with a diagnosis: calling attention to problems of social importance, and engaging persons in discussion and debates. In so doing, public intellectuals create new forums, bring new actors onto the scene, and "make questionable what has previously not been questioned and thereby open up larger areas of social life to public discussion, decision, and action" (Angus 2001:65). Often the most revolutionary diagnoses come from bringing to light an assumption the group was not aware it was making. The debates that ensue expand the range of options discussed within the public sphere (Mesthene 1970: 49ff).

Putting new questions on the table opens up new possibilities, but it also leads to identifying those who are in denial vis-à-vis such questions and possibilities. In so doing, a new "social imaginary" evolves: what Charles Taylor calls "ways people imagine their social existence, how they fit together with others, how things go on between them and their fellows, the expectations that are normally met, and the deeper normative notions and images that underlie these expectations" (Taylor 2004:23). This imaginary in turn shapes the identity of communities and their actions, but also the identity of their enemies.

In that sense, "the intellectual is the eternal irritant: the grit in the oyster" (Fuller 2005: 163). He sharpens the tensions underlying the texture of society; he is a trouble-maker. "Conflict is central to the intellectual mode of intellectual life, criticism. Criticism involves the formation of a judgment towards something that the critic believes could – and typically should – have been otherwise." (Fuller 2005:149).

Despite strong impressions to the contrary, such tensions and conflicts are the fount of social cohesion. This Gauchet-Dubiel thesis, elegantly defended by Albert Hirschman (1995: 235ff), suggests that a society with freedom of speech and association that produces "a steady diet of conflicts that need to be addressed and that the society learns to manage" acquires vitality, and a capacity to renew itself. It underlines the important role of the intellectual as conflict-generator, and as the indirect source of social cohesion through the conflicts he stimulates. There is no place for such behaviour in the ivory tower!

A major role of the public intellectual involves cleansing the communication systems of scorias: crippling epistemologies, ideological filters, cognitive dissonance, political correctness and the like, that prevent the information and communication system from functioning well, and that therefore generate institutional and organizational pathologies, and governance failures.

This calls for critical thinking's being reinstated as a dominant value in lieu of the prevalent conformism. This is an invitation to subversion.

The citizen's burden of office

A much more important task, falling on the shoulders of the citizenry at large as its burden of office, is to shake-off the indolence generated by fifty years of welfare statism and *servitude volontaire*, and to generate the basic conditions that will lead the citizen to engage actively in experimentalism, prototyping, and serious play with the existing information and communication systems. Tinkering and *bricolage* are *de rigueur*, but also sabotage when what is going on is unacceptable. This requires citizens to mind their own business, but really mind it.

The rationale for getting involved is that neither complete abdication nor waiting for a saviour will do. As Ernst Jünger put it: "c'est l'une des marotte de notre temps que de confier des scènes importantes à des acteurs quelconques…des figures telles qu'il s'en trouverait … dans d'obscurs caravansérails" (Jünger 1957 : 31). This is why the citizen has come to refuse to be imposed upon by unworthy authorities, and yet has not yet decided to take matters into his own hands even though dissent and self-empowerment are both socially and politically useful, and probably the only way to generate social change (Sunstein 2003).

The call to action for the citizen is a gamble on mass collaboration without the need for a potentate. It is a gamble on democracy being strong enough to allow one to get rid of the last bit of scaffolding pretending to hold it together – the State. This does not mean neglecting the necessary upkeep of the required state structure, but simply abandoning the false assumption that the scaffold is more important than the building.

Emergence

What is this collaborative work trying to achieve? It is the construction of a collaborative governance regime.

As we mentioned in chapter 5, in the case of the stylized idealized contexts like a free market, price becomes the focal point, and the price system the governance regime. In the case of total panic, the crowd movement becomes the focal point, the governing force. In both cases, coordination of a sort ensues, without any need for a personalized governing agent (Dupuy 1992).

In more complex situations, the reconciliation of the different frames of reference of the different potential partners does not necessarily emerge spontaneously. It is a result of some action by a variety of agents, much interaction, substantial unintended consequences, and an ensemble of social armistices and balancing acts, embodied in various mechanisms making up the governance regime: an amalgam of mechanisms (formal and informal) – always in the process of being reshaped – that define a set of norms, principles, rules and protocols underpinning the decision process, and the process of implementation of these decisions (Paquet 2005a:76-78; 2005b: ch. VIII).

The governance regime is the locus of discernment and the source of the mental map of the organization, of its environment, of its mission, of its projects. Its task is sense-making, grappling and grasping, and reflective and reflexive learning that generates transformation, innovation, renewal. The appropriate mechanisms for an effective collaborative governance are multilogues, much experimentation and learning, and the construction of what is nothing less than a "community of sense", some form of collective intelligence.

The technocracy and the managerial class in the private, social and public sectors have until recently done their utmost to insist that their technical expertise should prevail. We have referred to such efforts in chapter 6 as an *epistemological coup d'état*. The citizenry has been made to feel like a nuisance. As a result, confrontation and litigation have become a way of life, with collaboration being seen in this context as the strategy of choice only for suckers in a nasty zero-sum game. Persuading the citizenry to get involved anew will be as difficult as persuading the technocrats that they need the information and suggestions of the citizens if they wish to do their job at all well in our turbulent and heterogeneous world.

It is fair to say that the technocrats, as a result of many recent well-publicized governance failures, have come to be alerted to the cost of the non-collaboration of the citizenry, and yet the scepticism of the citizenry has continued to grow. It shows up in the ever greater degree of disengagement and cynicism that has been displayed in recent years. The citizenry has become passive-aggressive in some ways: passive, disengaged, falling into learned helplessness and voluntary servitude, and yet full of suppressed resentment, quickly able to become obstructionist, and even capable of reacting extremely strongly and violently to minor provocations.

Persuading the citizenry that it should engage in the process of collaboration and contribute creatively to the governance multilogue will require much persuading, and a demonstration, up front, of the feasibility and likelihood of quick success of these sorts of relationships. Otherwise, they are unlikely to succeed.

How to work at it

A promising way to develop the requisite organizational platforms for collaboration is
(1) to allow it to emerge after a period of discussion so that some relevant prototypes can be ascertained as of common interest, and some non-negotiable constraints, well understood; and
(2) to work at developing these platforms only in restricted issue domains where the relevant stakeholders have some common knowledge and where both common interest and non-negotiable constraints are well known and likely to be quickly ascertainable.

By partitioning the overall terrain into issues domains, corresponding to communities of meaning or communities of fate (i.e., assemblages of people united in their common concern for shared problems or a shared passion for a topic or set of issues), it is possible to identify a number of sub-games that each requires specific treatment. Each issue-domain (health, education, environment, etc.) is multifaceted, and must be dealt with on an ad hoc basis with a view to allowing the design of its own stewardship to emerge.

However, it is not sufficient to ensure open access to the people who have a substantial stake in the issue; one must also ensure that the appropriate motivations are nurtured, so that all citizens are willing and able to engage in "serious play" (i.e., become truly producers of governance, through tinkering with the governance apparatus within certain limits). This in turn requires taking communities of meaning seriously: very different arrangements from place to place, and the importance of regarding any such arrangement as essentially temporary – since the ground is in motion and diversity is likely to acquire new faces, patterns of organization design may have to evolve through time.

Consequently, collaborative governance would not only rely on a much more flexible toolbox, but would require that any formal or binding arrangement be revisited, played with, and adjusted to take into account the evolving diversity of circumstances. It would open the door to the design of more complex and innovative arrangements likely to deal more effectively with deep diversity (Michael 1993; Sabel 2001, 2004).

Prototyping would appear to be the main activity underpinning serious play:

- identifying some top requirements as quickly as possible,
- putting in place a quick-and-dirty provisional medium of co-development,
- allowing as many interested parties to get involved as partners in improving the arrangement,
- encouraging iterative prototyping, and
- thereby encouraging all, through playing with prototypes, to get a better understanding of the problems, of their priorities, and of themselves (Schrage 2000: 199ff).

The purpose of the exercise is to create a dialogue (creative interaction) between people and prototypes. This may be more important than creating dialogue between people alone. It is predicated on a culture of active participation that would need to be nurtured.

The ethical corridor

As governing is becoming an ongoing conversation within and among these issue domains games without a master, the new basic unit of analysis is the relation (Laurent et Paquet 1998). These relations take the form of contracts or conventions that can be more or less formal (Paquet 1991-2, 1997; Enjolras 2006) and define roughly the legitimate expectations of the partners, and therefore the foundations of both accountability (what is the expected performance) and ethics (what is regarded as acceptable performance).

In order to develop the sort of apparatus or sextant likely to be of use in guiding behavior and choice in such a world, one must be able to build on three components: (a) a good appreciation of context; (b) a sense of the extent to which the organization allows more or less latitude in redefining and re-framing issues, in order to ensure goodness of fit with the whole range of potentially contradictory expectations of the partners; and (c) a broad set of reference points that might serve as generic guideposts in defining "good" behavior.

It is in the triangulation of these guideposts that one may find ways to navigate safely. It should be explained that safety in ethics amounts to ensuring that decisions are made and action taken in such a manner that (1) all moral contracts are honored, and conventions respected; and (2) all decisions and actions that might violate these norms can be explained in a language that all would find acceptable.

Critical description is not entirely a matter of individual perception. The cultural environment shapes what one is allowed to perceive. Indeed, the sociality of the organization defines the way in which issues are framed, and constitutes a set of lenses imposed on the individual as a result of his having been somewhat programmed by the social framework within which he is embedded.

In no organization can it be said that all assumptions can be questioned, and all members can allow themselves to tinker with mechanisms, structures, and values. Indeed, this is generally the other way around. Most organizations have an "appreciative system", and those who do not share it are deviant, outsiders. Moreover, as Warren Bennis put it, "most organizations would rather risk obsolescence than make room for the non-conformist in their midst" (Bennis 1976: 40). Indeed, most institutions are more or less neurotic.

Finally, given a good appreciation of the context and of the sociality (i.e., the constraints and the degrees of freedom that the organization avails to its members in developing strategies within a certain corridor, and the support or non-support for efforts to extend the width of the corridor of acceptable behavior), it remains but to add the sort of minimal basic references in relationship to which acceptable behavior might be defined.

Margaret Somerville defines her "ethical canary" as based on two focal points: respect for life, and protection of the human spirit ("the intangible, invisible, immeasurable reality that we need to find meaning in life and to make life worth living" (Somerville 2000). Another benchmark that might serve as a reference is the balancing of the imperatives of the four cardinal virtues: (I) temperantia – an awareness and sense of limits; (II) fortitudo – a capacity to take into account context and long term; (III) justitia – a sense of what is good, and an inclination to search for it; and (IV) prudentia – a sense of what is practical and reasonable.

Taking this secular source of wisdom as a guide may not appear to be much help to navigation. Indeed, it leaves a lot to moral imagination and so it should. What is involved is a minimal number of reference points to keep in mind as one is trying to determine where the lines in the sand are, the boundaries one should or should not ignore separating the zones of moral comfort and discomfort.

Contingent moral contracts and reflexive governance

The ethical concerns raised above must constrain the sort of arrangements that will emerge from the process of engagement, collaboration, prototyping, serious play, etc., that may be generated by the efforts to develop a collaborative governance regime.

The efforts of public intellectuals to reframe the debates and to kickstart discussions and the contribution of the different groups of citizens (if appropriate channels of communication and loci of discussion are in place) are likely to generate many suggestions. Not all suggestions emerging from the citizenry or from the different partners when power, resources, and information are widely distributed (and therefore nobody fully in charge) are equally acceptable, legitimate, and reasonable. What is expected is that these suggestions are likely to be vetted with the view of ascertaining which ones will improve the governance regime by improving the degree and quality of the cognition, knowledge production, and conversation – i.e., the degree and quality of collaboration.

Since the different parties have different representations of the world, and different frames of reference, the arrangements likely to be negotiated may be regarded as social armistices or moral contracts, arrived at by negotiations (explicit or tacit), and purported to be acceptable to most if not all parties. They are bound to be flexible and loose enough to be consonant with the different norms and standards of the different groups, and capable of meeting various stringent tests of acceptability before being adopted: reasonableness, fairness, ethical acceptability, legitimacy, efficiency, etc.

The best way to understand how this process can be operationalized is to recognize that it is the result of two intertwined sub-processes: the emergence of contingent moral contracts as a way to make less intangible the relationships involved in collaborative governance, and the learning-by-doing and doing-by-learning through which these moral contracts are continually modified as problem handling and reflection on the whole social learning process reveal the need to do so.

Contingent moral contracts

As Christopher Wilson (2007) has suggested, collaboration is always contingent: it is built on the tentative premise "I will if you will", and it does not crystallize instantaneously – it develops in stages. After a period of frustration when it becomes obvious that one cannot do whatever has to be done alone, and when potential somewhat-trusted partners are identified, a period of experimentation driven by costs-benefits considerations becomes possible. In this second stage, building relations and close monitoring are the order of the day; joint action is tentatively experimented with, and trust is strengthened. In the third stage, increased confidence prevails, organizational memory is built, and the possibility of extending the scope of collaboration is envisaged.

A most important way to make tangible and verifiable the process of deepening of trust and confidence, and yet of not killing the budding confidence by demanding very formal contractual arrangements, is the development of loose, flexible, and non-enforceable instruments in the nature of memoranda of understanding. Whether these take the form of moral contracts or loose conventions, these instruments provide a certain degree of tangibility in a world that remains very elusive.

These modifiable moral contracts serve two major purposes. First they embody some mechanism of coordination, some basis for defining agreed-upon representations, some ground for justification, and some elements to help shape interpretation when some is needed. Second, they serve as a way to anchor, ever so loosely, the basis for monitoring and sanctioning as a foundation for social learning.

On the first front, it should be clear that collaboration cannot be reduced to mechanical coordination devices. Such devices serve well at a first level, but if collaboration is going to be evolving smoothly, it must entail the development of some agreement on methods of evaluation and justification for action, and even provide help in interpreting whatever agreement has been arrived at, if and when it becomes necessary.

A whole literature on the economics of convention has emerged over the last 20 years, and it has shown how such conventions or contingent moral contracts are crucially important in collaboration (Revue économique 1989; Orléan 1994; Batifoulier 2001; Eymard-Duvernay 2006; Enjolras 2007). This is a new frontier in the development of collaborative governance, for it provides the raw material and the intellectual vocabulary necessary to discuss critically the emergence and the design of the network of relationships underpinning successful collaboration.

On the second front, these loose moral contracts provide sufficient precision to allow monitoring and sanctioning to be meaningful. As Howard Rheingold would put it, such monitoring and sanctioning is crucial to social learning, and "serve the important function of providing information about others' actions and levels of commitment" (Rheingold 2002:176 - cited by Wilson 2007) – a matter of crucial importance when it is understood that all collaboration is contingent.

Reflexive governance

However useful moral contracts and conventions might be, they are deliberately elusive and flexible because they will need to serve as guideposts as long as certain circumstances prevail, but may need to evolve as circumstances change. This calls for reflexive governance – governance that has a propensity to self-subversion (as Albert Hirschman would put it), that constantly calls into question its own foundations (i.e., its concepts, practices, moral contracts, and conventions), envisions alternatives, and reinvents and reshapes these foundations in the light of changing circumstances and unintended consequences (Voβ and Kemp 2006: 4).

This calls not only for double-looped learning à la Argyris and Schön (i.e., revising not only the means as learning proceeds, but also revising the goals pursued) but for second-order governance – the emergence of an approach reflecting the interdependencies, understanding the effects of specialized concepts and strategies, and reflecting on the very working of collaborative governance (Voβ and Kemp 2006: 6-7).

Reflexive governance underlines the process of continuous social learning at its core, but requires that the continuous feedback not be restricted to means and ends within a given problem definition, but that reflexivity also triggers problem redefinition as experience is accumulated, and even a reconfiguration of the very approach to governance.

This is a second important new frontier for work on collaborative governance. For it suggests the need for a meta-governance in order to be able to ascertain and manage the rules by which governance regimes are defined and implemented, the rules to change the rules of governance. This level of analysis has an autopoïetic quality. It does not pertain only to the process of self-steering, self-regulation, or self-organization, but it aims at disclosing the process of continual self-renewal and self creation (Paquet 2005b: ch.V). This general level of analysis would aim at producing a grammar of collaborative governance regimes, in the same way as Elinor Ostrom (2005: ch V) has been trying to develop a grammar of institutions.

While exploring those new frontiers would appear to be presenting a Himalayan challenge, it should be clear that it is no different than dealing with constitutional issues: the constitution is the law that regulates the changes in laws. It may be a bit more abstract, but it is so consequential that it would appear to be inevitable that governance studies drift in this direction in the near future.

In governance textbooks, the topic of meta-governance is already lightly but importantly broached (Kjaer 2004).

Conclusion

Whether this invitation to subversion, and to mass collaboration through open-source and prototyping, will resonate with the readers, and whether scheming virtuously to get there will turn out to be appealing for public intellectuals and citizens, remains to be seen. Whether the economics of conventions and meta-governance will appeal to governance experts also remains to be seen.

What is clear, however, is that the alternatives (wallowing in voluntary servitude and zooming in exclusively on state administration) is not very appealing.

The central mental prison is the difficulty in accepting that nobody is in charge. Once this new reality is fully understood and accepted, and once the unease or panic such realization generates has subsided, the challenge of collaborative governance appears as an imperative. How is one to try to contribute to the evolution of the social learning apparatus capable of ensuring effective coordination, in a world where power, resources, and information are widely distributed? And such a challenge should be exhilarating for citizens, public intellectuals, and governance experts.

Recreating fictional potentates will no longer appear satisfactory. Working collaboratively at putting in place an informational and communication system likely to do the job is a promising alternative. It may be a job best tackled *par morceaux*, at the levels of sub-systems. It may also be one where satisficing might have to be good enough: the best may be enemy of the good. Finally, one may even have to be satisfied with preventing harm – and this may mean being able to do nothing more than sabotaging a mechanism that generates harm.

These very prudent conclusions may however be temporary.

To the extent that the program of research around the cognition, knowledge production, and organization space hinted at in this volume can be expected to progress over the next little while, and that the parallel paths followed by the followers of Hayek, Hurwicz, North, etc. (however divergent they originally were), converge somewhat, another progress report in a decade or so may have a more upbeat message to convey (Atkinson 2004).

References

I. Angus, *Emergent Publics*. Winnipeg: Arbeiter Ring Publishing, 2001.

G. Atkinson, "Common ground for institutional economics and system dynamics modeling" *System Dynamics Review*, 20 (4), 2004, 275-286.

P. Batifoulier (ed) , *Théorie des conventions*, Paris: Economica, 2001.

W. Bennis *The Unconscious Conspiracy*. New York: AMACOM. 1976.

R.P. Chait et al, *Governance as Leadership*, Hoboken, N.J.: Wiley, 2005.

H. Cleveland, *Nobody in Charge*. San Francisco: Jossey-Bass, 2002.

C. Delsol, "Le nouveau despotisme" *Géopolitique*, no. 89, 2005, 25-28.

W. H. Drath, C. J. Palus, *Making Common Sense*. Greenboro, N.C.: Center for Creative Leadership, 1994.

J.P.Dupuy, *Introduction aux sciences sociales – Logique des phénomènes collectifs*, Ellipses/Ecole Polytechnique, 1992.

B. Enjolras, *Conventions et institutions*, Paris : L'Harmattan, 2006.

F. Eymard-Duvernay, *L'économie des conventions, Tomes I et II*, Paris : La Découverte, 2006.

S. Fuller, *The Intellectual*. Cambridge: iconbooks, 2005.

A. O. Hirschman, *A Propensity to Self-Subversion*. Cambridge: Harvard University Press, 1995.

R. Jacoby, *The Last Intellectuals: American Culture in the Age of Academe*. New York: Basic Books, 1987.

Ernst Jünger, *Traité du rebelle*. Monaco: Editions du Rocher, 1957.

A.M. Kjaer, *Governance*, Cambridge: Polity Press, 2004.

P. Krugman, *The Self-Organizing Economy*. Oxford: Blackwell 1996.

P. Laurent, G. Paquet. *Epistémologie et économie de la relation*. Paris/Lyon : Vrin, 1998

Emmanuel G. Mesthene, *Technological Change*. New York: Mentor, 1970.

D.N. Michael "Governing by Learning: Boundaries, Myths and Metaphors" *Futures*, 25(1), 1993, 81-89.

A. Orléan, *Analyse économique des conventions*, Paris: Presses Universitaires de France, 1994.

E. Ostrom, *Understanding Institutional Diversity*, Princeton: Princeton University Press, 2005.

G. Paquet "Betting on Moral Contracts" *Optimum* 22(3), 1991, 45-53.

G. Paquet "The Burden of Office, Ethics and Connoisseurship" *Canadian Public Administration* 40(1), 1997, 45-71.

G. Paquet, *The New Geo-Governance – A Baroque Approach*, The University of Ottawa Press, 2005a.

G. Paquet, *Gouvernance: une invitation à la subversion*, Montréal: Editions Liber, 2005b.

R.A. Posner, *Public Intellectuals: A Study of Decline*. Cambridge: Harvard University Press, 2001.

Revue économique, Special issue on the economics of conventions 40 (2) 1989.

H. Rheingold, *Smart Mobs*, Cambridge: Perseus, 2002.

M. Ross (ed), *Our Sense of Identity: A Book of Canadian Essays*. Toronto: The Ryerson Press, 1954.

C. F. Sabel, "A Quiet Revolution of Democratic Governance: Towards Democratic Experimentalism" in *Governance in the 21st Century*, Paris: OECD, 121-148, 2001.

C. F. Sabel, "Beyond Principal-Agent Governance: Experimentalist Organizations, Learning and Accountability" in E. Engelen and M. Sie Dhian Ho (eds) *De Staat van de Democratie. Democratie Voorbij de Staat*. WRR Verkenning 3. Amsterdam: Amsterdam University Press, 173-195, 2004.

T. Schelling, *Micromotives and Macrobehavior*, New York: Norton, 1978.

M. Schrage, *Serious Play*. Boston: Harvard Business School Press, 2000

A. Shapiro, *Creating Contagious Commitment – Applying the Tipping Point to Organizational Change*, Hillsborough, N.C.: Strategy Perspective, 2003.

J.J. Simard, "Désarroi chez les intellectuels" *Le Devoir* 15-16 mars 2003.

C.R. Sunstein, *Why Societies Need Dissent*. Cambridge: Harvard University Press, 2003.

D. Tapscott, A.D. Williams, *Wikinomics*, New York: Porfolio, 2007.

Charles Taylor, *Modern Social Imaginaries*. Durham: Duke University Press, 2004.

J.P. Voβ et al.(ed) *Reflexive Governance for Sustainable Development*, Cheltenham: Edward Elgar, 2006.

C. Wilson, "Facilitating Contingent Cooperation" www.optimumonline.ca 37(1) 2007, 1-8.

Acknowledgements

Although they have been modified substantially a number of times, segments of several chapters have been drawn from previously published papers:

Paquet, G., 1971
"Social Science Research as an Evaluative Instrument for Social Policy", in *Social Science and Social Policy*, Nettler, G.E., Krotki, K. (Eds.), Human Resources Research Council, 49-66.

Paquet, G., 1980
"A Political Economy Perspective of the Early 1980s", in *Key Economic and Social Issues of the Early 1980s*, Barrett, C.A. (Ed.), Conference Board of Canada, Ottawa, 71-81.

Paquet, G. 2007
"Letting the cat out of Gow's bag" www.optimumonline.ca 37 (4), 45-49.

Hubbard, R., Paquet, G., 2007
"The Governance of Solidarity Organizations: An Exploratory Essay" www.optimumonline.ca 37 (4), 2-22.

Paquet, G. 2008
"Governance as Stewardship" www.optimumonline.ca 38 (4) 14-27

Paquet, G., 1977
"Notes on Federalism as Social Technology", *Options*. Conference on the Future of the Canadian Federation, John Evans (Ed.), The University of Toronto Press, Toronto, ON, 281-302.

Paquet, G., 1978
"The Regulatory Process and Economic Performance", in *The Regulatory Process in Canada*, Doern G.B. (Ed.), Collier MacMillan, Toronto, 34-67

Paquet, G., 1985
"An Agenda for Change in the Federal Public Service", *Canadian Public Administration*, 28(3): 455-461.

Paquet, G., Pigeon, L., 2000
"In Search of a New Covenant", in *Government Restructuring and the Future of Career Public Service in Canada*, Lindquist, E. (Ed.), Institute of Public Administration of Canada, Toronto, 475-498

Paquet, G., 1999
"Lamberton's Road to Cognitive Economics", in *Information and Organization: A Tribute to the Work of Don Lamberton*, Macdonald, S., Nightingale, J. (Eds.), North Holland, Amsterdam, 63-79.

Paquet, G., 1998
"Evolutionary Cognitive Economics", *Information Economics and Policy*, 10(3): 343-357.

Paquet, G. 2005
"The RSC as Public Intellectual" www.optimumonline.ca 35(4), 3-40.
Lecours, P., Paquet, G., 2006
"Communication and Ethics: How to Scheme Virtuously"
Optimumonline, 36(2), 12-26.

Index

Invenire Books, an imprint of Invenire

Other books in the series:

Invenire Books   **Robin Higham**
Who do we think we are: *Canada's reasonable (and less reasonable) accommodation debates,*

is a readable and entertaining short-course for ordinary citizens, non-experts who want to participate in the national conversations about the challenges and opportunities generated by the arrival in Canada of so many newcomers. The characters in these twelve contrived discussions discover a uniquely Canadian modus-vivendi that keeps us negotiating and accommodating rather than deciding and excluding. They propose an updating of the model in order to keep the file on the identity question open and active and to ensure continued debate about who we think we are. Can we hold it all together while they talk about it?

Quality paperback 2009, 6x9" 144pp, ISBN 978-0-88970-132-8

Invenire Books   **Ruth Hubbard**
Profession: Public Servant

offers glimpses into the federal government's corridors of power during a decade of profound change and underscores the importance of learning for individuals, groups, and organizations in today's fast-paced world. It sets out a former deputy minister's take on the "burden of office" of the role and on the difficulties of staying out of one ditch – excessive concern with safeguarding a few key principles – without sliding into another – being too anxious to please or too tempted to put personal interests first. The story emphasizes the constructive contribution of experience and imagination, especially when it is enriched by on-the-job reflection.

Quality paperback 2009, 6x9" 136pp, ISBN 978-0-88970-130-4

sample chapters and further information at www.invenire.ca/books

Invenire *is an Ottawa-based "idea factory" specializing in collaborative governance and stewardship. Invenire and its authors offer creative and practical responses to the challenges and opportunities faced by today's complex organizations.*

For more about Invenire: www.invenire.ca